HUNTINGTON LIBRARY PUBLICATIONS

"I am always writing bad prose, or worse verses, either of rage or raillery, whereof some few escape to give offence, or mirth, and the rest are burnt."

—SWIFT TO BOLINGBROKE, MARCH 21, 1729/30

RAGE OR RAILLERY

THE SWIFT MANUSCRIPTS AT
THE HUNTINGTON LIBRARY

BY GEORGE P. MAYHEW

WITH A FOREWORD BY

HERBERT DAVIS

The Huntington Library

SAN MARINO, CALIFORNIA

MCMLXVII

For Joan

Foreword

IN 1943 I went to the Huntington Library to spend a few weeks looking through the collection of Swift manuscripts, which I knew I should need to use for my edition of Swift's *Prose Writings*, that I had then been engaged upon for some time. I had occasion to talk about the collection at an exhibition at the Grolier Club in New York on November 15, 1945, arranged to commemorate the bicentenary of Swift's death, when I spoke about "Some Swift Manuscripts in the United States." When this talk was, in part, reprinted by Louis Landa and James Tobin with their . . . *Jonathan Swift, a List of Critical Studies Published from 1895 to 1945*, I hoped that it would prompt someone to prepare a full, detailed description of all the manuscripts in these important collections.

I am therefore very happy to welcome this volume in which George Mayhew gives so full an account of the Swift manuscripts in the Huntington Library: their contents, their significance, and their provenance. For some years now we have become accustomed to the careful and valuable studies of this material, which he has published in the *Huntington Library Quarterly*; and I have myself been particularly fortunate in having so good a correspondent and so generous a collaborator always ready to help in the difficult matter of transcription and interpretation of these texts, which he has studied so carefully. No one knows more about these manuscripts than he does; no one has become so familiar with every scrap of them. The autographs carry their own stamps of authenticity; but the genuineness of other pieces in the hands of Swift's friends and the reliability of unique contemporary copies of passages from his verse too dangerous to print at the time depend upon the establishment of the provenance of this whole Theophilus Swift collection, which can be traced back to Mrs. Whiteway and Deane Swift, of Goodrich in Hereford—much of it, after being broken up in the nineteenth century, now safely brought together here.

But this volume contains much more than a list and detailed description of the manuscripts such as I had in mind. Some of them provide valuable evidence, which has prompted a further study of certain biographical matters of great interest. The manuscript notes for a part of the *History of the Four Last Years* are turned to account to give us further glimpses of Swift as he worked over the materials he had collected for the writing of that history. A little fresh information is added to what we knew about the circumstances of the very young lady to whom Swift addressed that delightful letter on the occasion of her marriage, which strangely enough continues to disturb and annoy even his sophisticated readers today. Additional variants are also shown for some of the dangerous passages in *An Epistle to a Lady* and *On Poetry: A Rapsody*, taken from another contemporary transcription which is now bound up in an original subscriber's copy of the first four volumes of Faulkner's edition of Swift's works. Finally there is a study of some of the fragments in Anglo-Latin by one who has made himself something of an expert in these games in which Swift and Sheridan seem to have found considerable amusement.

I can only hope that this volume will be followed by further studies of all the autograph manuscripts of Swift which have been preserved both in the United States and in Great Britain and Ireland.

HERBERT DAVIS

Contents

ILLUSTRATIONS

(*between pages 38 and 39*)

A LEAF FROM SWIFT'S "Letter to a Young Lady" (1723).

A DRAFT OF JONATHAN SWIFT'S FIRST WILL (1727).

AN EARLY DRAFT OF SWIFT'S AUTOBIOGRAPHICAL POEM "*On His Own* DEAFNESS" (1734).

A FRAGMENT OF SWIFT'S *Polite Conversation* IN MANUSCRIPT (1734-35).

Introduction

THESE ESSAYS on the Swift manuscripts at the Huntington Library are the result of more than twelve years of study. Chapter VI, on the manuscript version of Swift's poem *"On His Own* Deafness*,"* was begun while I was a graduate student at Harvard at work under the direction of the late Professor George Sherburn upon my doctoral dissertation, "Jonathan Swift's Games with Language." It was characteristic of Professor Sherburn's great generosity toward young scholars that he one day showed me photostats of some Swift manuscripts at the Huntington Library, San Marino, California, where he had recently been visiting. Among them were several pages of those Anglo-Latin games with language which Jonathan Swift and his Irish friend Dr. Thomas Sheridan exchanged about 1734-1736. The material was precisely the kind I wanted to treat in my dissertation, as Professor Sherburn well knew, and he therefore good-humoredly allowed me to borrow the photostats for as long as I needed. Examining them later, I recognized among the Anglo-Latin jottings, tucked away on one page of manuscript, a first draft in his own hand of Swift's moving autobiographical poem of 1734 on his deafness. I also realized that hitherto the poem had been incorrectly printed, since this autograph version was then completely unknown. With the kind of excitement only a graduate student in literature can understand, I called upon Professor Sherburn in Widener Library early the next morning to report what I had found. His response was typical of the man: he shared in my excitement; asked me several shrewd questions to make sure that I knew what I was doing; and then concluded by saying, "You must now write all this up properly and send it off to be published. I suggest that you try the *Huntington Library Quarterly*."

I did as I was directed, and in this way began what has been for me a happy and friendly relationship, not only with the *Quarterly*, where four of the following seven essays were first published, somewhat altered, but with the Huntington Library itself, which did me the honor of choosing me a fellow for 1962-1963. Chapter I, in fact, was given as a talk in connection with that fellowship. It has not been published previously, nor have the two essays that constitute Chapter III on Swift's "Letter to a Young Lady," completed only recently under the influence of Herbert Davis of Oxford, and Chapter VI on Swift's deafness, expanded from my first Note in the *Quarterly*

(XVIII [1954], 85-87). The Huntington's fair copy of the "Letter to a Young Lady" of 1723 is in Swift's hand, and it has never before been published. As Dr. Davis surmised, this manuscript is the very copy which Swift sent to the young lady concerned, kept by her until her death, and thereafter by members of her husband's family in Ireland. About the middle of the last century it was sold by a later owner, then on the point of emigrating to the United States, where the manuscript itself subsequently arrived by a quite different and more circuitous route.

I can never be sure how much Herbert Davis and I agree or disagree in our respective readings of Swift's attitude toward women and of theirs toward him, a most important question in Swift's life and art. I shall also be forever in doubt whether Professor Sherburn knew that an autograph version of Swift's poem on his deafness was buried among the Anglo-Latin jottings he lent me and merely wished to see if I would recognize the poem when I came upon it. But to have known as friends and masters in the study of Swift two such men as Professor Sherburn and Dr. Davis is a privilege of which I am daily more proud.

The seven chapters and appendix of this work draw upon manuscripts at the Huntington Library and are primarily bibliographical, biographical, or critical in nature. The first chapter, mainly bibliographical, supplies the content and provenance of the Swift manuscripts and is supplemented by the appendix, a short but complete *catalogue raisonné*. The second chapter (*HLQ*, XXIV [1961], 311-322) studies Swift at work as a historian, and, more particularly, as a Tory historian attempting to write accurately and impartially about contemporary events which ultimately resulted in far-reaching and unfortunate consequences for his Tory friends, Oxford, Bolingbroke, and Ormonde. Swift was throughout his life a historian *manqué*; in this respect he resembles his beloved master Sir William Temple. Had he been appointed to the position of Historiographer Royal to which he aspired in 1713, we should now have a presumably accurate and interesting account of the transfer of political power from the world of Queen Anne, the last of the Stuart monarchs, to that of George I, the first Hanoverian. But then, had Swift remained in Whig England as a Tory historian, we might not have the *Drapier's Letters* nor even *Gulliver*.

Chapter III and Chapter VII (*HLQ*, XVII [1954], 133-159) concentrate upon Swift's prose art as exemplified by other Swift manuscripts at the Huntington. His "Letter to a Young Lady on Her Marriage" was finished in February 1723, and it is, for the first time, here printed from Swift's fair copy with Chapter III, which presents new facts about the young lady addressed and discusses the nature of her marriage. The "Letter" has a bearing upon the counterclaims of Esther Johnson, Swift's "Stella," and Esther Vanhomrigh, "Vanessa," for Swift's affections during this same period of 1723, a few months before Vanessa's death. The "Letter" is also a brilliant example of Swift's familiar essay style at a period when he was more than halfway through the composition of *Gulliver's Travels* and not long before he began the composition of the first of the *Drapier's Letters* of 1724. The seventh chapter deals with what may be the only extant manuscript fragment of the last of Swift's major prose works to be published in his lifetime, the *Polite Conversation* of 1738. It also examines critically the clever and often amusing Anglo-Latin dialects which Swift and Dr. Thomas Sheridan exchanged in 1734-1736, witty displays of verbal ingenuity at which Swift grew so adept that to write in one or another of the Anglo-Latin "languages" in both prose and verse became, as he said, almost second nature.

Chapter V (*HLQ*, XXIII [1960], 159-180) and Chapter VI concern themselves with Swift's poetry from the period of 1732 to 1734 and more particularly with what may be considered, after "The Legion Club" of 1736, two of Swift's longest and most brilliant late satires in verse, his *Epistle to a Lady* and *On Poetry: A Rapsody.* Strictly speaking, the material in Chapter V is not in Swift's hand, although it is from his pen. It is a contemporary manuscript transcription in the hand of an anonymous scribe of these two highly treasonous, libelous, and offensive (to Walpole and Queen Caroline) verse satires. But the versions discussed here contain unique readings; and as a complementary pair they neatly illustrate Swift's exquisite mastery of two highly demanding forms of irony: *raillery* and *mock panegyric.* The autobiographical poem of 1734 on his recurrent deafness, by contrast, begins upon what is for Swift a most rare note of self-pity, but with its concluding parallel stanzas in Latin and English it more characteristically resolves into tones of mockery and detachment. It was also characteristic of Swift to jot down carelessly in the midst of Anglo-Latin *jeux d'esprit* and to give without a thought to a servant who begged it this moving poem, and to allow it to be published immediately in several Dublin and London newspapers in an altered or even an incorrect form.

The central chapter, IV (*HLQ*, XXI [1958], 295-322), presents what may be, biographically speaking, the single most important manuscript among the Swift papers at the Huntington Library—a draft of Swift's first will made and then revoked in anger in 1727 when he was almost sixty. It devised a generous gift of twelve hundred pounds to establish a "Swift's Fellow" at Trinity College, Dublin, his alma mater. This benefaction was intended to help worthy young Irish-trained scholars and divines of his old university at a time when almost all important civil and ecclesiastical posts, as a principle of deliberate policy, were given only to compliant Englishmen and loyal Whigs. As is only too well remembered, Swift eventually left his modest fortune to found a hospital at Dublin for fools and madmen. Whether this was done out of a satiric bitterness and from misanthropic motives, as is commonly assumed, or whether it was done more in that spirit of compassion and concern for the welfare of Ireland with which his first will was made, may now be better determined. For Swift's first will illustrates the charitable and unostentatious form in which his pity and compassion expressed themselves, as always, in practical terms. When the Anglo-Irish Dublin Parliament subserviently gave away its powers to the English in 1720, Swift once more reluctantly resumed political action in defense of Irish liberty. His reasons for canceling his will in righteous anger illustrate the hopelessness and despair with which Irish-born and Anglo-Irish-trained talent faced exploitive Whig policy after the Drapier controversy of 1724. So temporary was the victory of the Drapier and so successful, after 1724, was the Whig exploitation of Ireland, that by 1729-1730 the only possible response for someone like Swift was the shocking and savage manner of *A Modest Proposal* —that or total silence. Swift's cancellation in June or July 1727 of his generous bequest may mark the dashing of his last hope that things would be better under King George II, with whose reign began the growing misanthropy and settled gloom of the Tory satirists.

More than most scholars, who are privileged at best to work for only a year or two at the Huntington Library, I am heavily indebted to the director, Dr. John Pomfret, and to the librarian, Mr. Robert O. Dougan, for their constant help, and to the obliging members of their staff whose devoted efforts for so many years have assisted me in my study of the Swift manuscripts. I should like to mention with gratitude the names of Dr. French Fogle, now of Claremont Graduate School, Dr. Robert Wark, Curator of the Huntington Art Gallery, and Dr. John M. Steadman, successive editors of the *Quarterly*; Mrs. Nancy C. Moll, Mrs. Winifred Freese, and Mrs. Kathleen Beyloos, of the Publications staff; Mr. Herbert Schulz, Curator of the Manuscript Department, and Miss Phyllis Rigney; Miss Constance Lodge, Head of Preparations; Mr. Lyle H. Wright, Head Reference Librarian; Miss Mary Isabel Fry, Reference Librarian and Registrar; Miss Anne Hyder, Rare Book Reading Room; Mr. Erwin Morkisch, Photographic Reproductions; and many other members of the Rare Book, Manuscript, Preparations, and Reference departments who have helped over the years. In addition, I wish to thank Mr. J. S. Ritchie, Deputy Assistant Keeper of Manuscripts, and the National Library of Scotland for the use of manuscripts in their keeping.

I am also very much indebted to Professor Hallett Smith, Chairman of the Division of Humanities and Social Sciences, and to the President and the Trustees of the California Institute of Technology, for allowing me to take a year off in order to accept a Huntington Library fellowship in 1962-1963. I wish to thank my colleagues, Dr. Robert Huttenback and Dr. David Smith, and my fellow scholars at the Huntington, Dr. Paul Zall of California State College at Los Angeles and Dr. Gilbert McEwen of Whittier College, for their personal encouragement and for the interest they have shown in my work. To Hanna, Scotty, and Sam, who have long had to live with their father's single-minded interest in Jonathan Swift, my great thanks for generous forbearance and intelligent understanding. My greatest debt is to my wife, the person for whom, all along, this book was really written, and to whom it is most lovingly dedicated.

Pasadena, California
November 30, 1964

WORKS MOST FREQUENTLY CITED

Ball, *Corresp.*
The Correspondence of Jonathan Swift, D.D., ed. Francis Elrington Ball, 6 vols. (London, 1910-14).

Boulter, *Letters*
Letters Written by His Excellency Hugh Boulter . . . to Several Ministers of State in England, 2 vols. (Oxford, 1769-70).

Burtchaell
Alumni Dublinenses, comp. George Dames Burtchaell and Thomas Ulick Sadleir (London, 1924).

Forster Nos. 504-589
The John Forster Collection of Swift Manuscripts, Victoria and Albert Museum, South Kensington, England.

Journal to Stella
Jonathan Swift: "Journal to Stella," ed. Harold Williams, 2 vols. (Oxford, 1948).

Nichols, *Illustrations*
John Nichols, *Illustrations of the Literary History of the Eighteenth Century*, 8 vols. (London, 1817-58).

Orrery's *Remarks*
John Boyle, 5th Earl of Cork and Orrery, *Remarks on the Life and Writings of Dr. Jonathan Swift* (London, 1752).

Pilkington, *Memoirs*
Memoirs of Mrs Letitia Pilkington, ed. J. Isaacs (New York, 1928).

Poems
The Poems of Jonathan Swift, ed. Harold Williams, 2nd ed., 3 vols. (Oxford, 1958).

Prose Writings
The Prose Writings of Jonathan Swift, ed. Herbert Davis, 14 vols. (Oxford, 1939-66).

T. Scott, *Prose Works*
The Prose Works of Jonathan Swift, ed. Temple Scott, 12 vols. (London, 1897-1908).

Sheridan, *Life*
Thomas Sheridan, *The Life of the Rev. Dr. Jonathan Swift, Dean of St. Patrick's, Dublin* (London, 1784).

Stubbs, *History*
John Stubbs, *The History of the University of Dublin* (Dublin, 1889).

Swift's *Works* (1735)
The Works of J.S., D.D., D.S.P.D., 4 vols. (Dublin: George Faulkner, 1734-35).

Swift's *Works* (1824)
The Works of Jonathan Swift, ed. Walter Scott, 2nd ed., 19 vols. (Edinburgh and London, 1824).

Wilde, *Closing Years*
William R. Wilde, *The Closing Years of Dean Swift's Life*, 2nd ed. (Dublin, 1849).

Williams, *Corresp.* (or) *Corresp.*
The Correspondence of Jonathan Swift, ed. Harold Williams, 5 vols. (Oxford, 1963, 1965).

NOTE

In manuscript transcriptions <*angular brackets*> enclose words canceled but still legible, [*square brackets*] editorial insertions; 2-em and 3-em dashes show deterioration of paper or ink; superior letters are brought to the line.

RAGE OR RAILLERY

Chapter One

THE SWIFT MANUSCRIPTS AT
THE HUNTINGTON LIBRARY

I

THERE ARE MANY QUESTIONS still to be answered about what, precisely, are the Jonathan Swift manuscripts at the Huntington Library, where they came from, what they contain, and how they arrived there—questions I should like to discuss in the present chapter. In subsequent chapters, by interpretations of several particular manuscripts, I should like to show something of their usefulness toward gaining a better understanding of the life and art of Jonathan Swift. A number of reasons, including, perhaps, the failure to make better known the extent of the collection, account for the comparatively little use which has been made of these documents until recently. Not until Sir Harold Williams and Herbert Davis in the 1930's began the task of editing for our times the works of Swift, were the manuscripts at the Huntington again scrutinized as they had been, more than a hundred years before, by Sir Walter Scott, when he had them at his disposal for his nineteenth-century editions of Swift's works. For instance, an important essay on the major manuscript collections at the Huntington Library appeared in the first number of the *Huntington Library Bulletin* for May 1931.[1] For reasons of space it had, of necessity, to be limited and arbitrary about the Huntington Library collections. But the fact is that it nowhere mentions the name of Swift. Later, I shall mention one or two circumstances that help to explain why the Swift manuscripts at the Huntington Library, until recently, were less well known than they deserve to be.

For the collection of Swift manuscripts at the Huntington is a considerable one, possibly the third or fourth largest of its kind in the

[1][George Sherburn and staff members of the Huntington Library], "Huntington Library Collections," pp. 54-55.

world. Since March 1939 these manuscripts have been preserved in seventy separate folders numbered HM 14326-14390 and HM 24016-24018.[2] Another of the Huntington manuscripts, a fair copy in the hand of Swift of his "A Letter to a Young Lady on Her Marriage" (1723), was simply but elegantly bound in russet morocco early in the nineteenth century, and it is therefor numbered out of series as HM 1599. In order to explain here what later may appear to be a discrepancy in the numbering, it should be noticed that several of the folders at present contain two or more related manuscripts that earlier were separately numbered.

Sixty or more of these manuscripts were in the possession of Theophilus Swift, Jonathan's distant kin, at the time of his death in September 1815. Theophilus Swift had inherited all of them in 1783 upon the death of his father, Deane Swift of Goodrich, Hereford, Jonathan Swift's cousin, editor, and biographer. Some of the manuscripts had originally belonged to Mrs. Martha Harrison Whiteway, née Swift, the Dean of St. Patrick's cousin, a daughter of his uncle, Adam Swift, and Swift's friend and counselor at Dublin in his last years before his death there in October 1745. In 1739 Mary or "Molly" Harrison, Mrs. Whiteway's daughter by her first marriage, married Mr. Deane Swift. Thus she became the mother of Theophilus Swift, who was born in 1746. Thus also it was that the manuscripts from both sides of his family came finally to fall into the hands of Theophilus Swift upon the death of his father.

In 1761 the Swift family left Dublin for England; they settled at Worcester, where Mrs. Whiteway died in 1768, and where Mr. Deane Swift died in 1783.[3] At the time of Jonathan Swift's death in 1745 Mrs. Whiteway and Deane Swift, as his two closest relatives, appear to have inherited about half of such Swift manuscripts as then remained, George Faulkner, Swift's Dublin printer, and Dr. John Lyon, Swift's keeper in old age, evidently getting the bulk of the remainder. The manuscripts which came into the possession of Mr.

[2]FAC 456, a photostatic reproduction of a letter of May 8, 1766, from Deane Swift writing from Worcester, the gift of Herbert Davis, and HM 22660, half a letter from Swift to Sheridan from Dublin, June 15-16, 1735, are also numbered out of series. Since this book was written, the Huntington Library has acquired another Swift manuscript (HM 27943), a list of bishoprics (1713), which is not mentioned in the text but is briefly described in the Appendix.

[3]See John Nichols, *Illustrations*, V, 383, for a letter to Nichols from Deane Swift, Worcester, June 7, 1778: "She [Mrs. Whiteway] came over with her daughter and me to England, seventeen years ago, and died in our house at Worcester, in the year 1768."

Deane Swift and Mrs. Whiteway included most of those now in the Huntington collection, which they removed out of Ireland to England, presumably at their departure in 1761. Sometime after his father's death in 1783, Theophilus Swift carried some, at least, of these same manuscripts back to Ireland. Of all the manuscripts that were once in his possession, however, and mostly through his own carelessness, only sixty or so, fifty-six of which constitute the backbone of the Huntington collection, now remain. These have a romantic and confused later history, about which more will be said presently. It is enough here to say that these sixty manuscripts—or most of them[4]—can be traced back directly to the Dean of St. Patrick's through their successive owners, Swift's cousins, and that their authenticity is beyond question.

Sometime after the death of Theophilus Swift in September 1815, but sometime before April 1820, James Smith, Esquire, a generous-hearted merchant of London and Bideford, Devon, rescued these manuscripts from destruction and oblivion, a matter to which we shall return. They were next purchased at a Sotheby, Wilkinson & Hodge sale in July 1877 by Frederick Locker (after 1885, Locker-Lampson) for his famous Rowfant Library in Sussex. In the *Catalogue* (1886) of his Rowfant Library, Locker-Lampson provided a fairly complete listing, together with some brief personal annotations, of the Swift manuscripts then in his possession.[5] The accompanying commentary was evidently taken from the penciled notations made by Locker-Lampson in the two finely tooled volumes into which he had the manuscripts bound sometime after he had purchased them. They were still in these bindings when Mr. Hun-

---

[4]Nine manuscripts from the papers of Deane Swift and Theophilus Swift have little or nothing to do with Jonathan Swift:

(1) HM 14352: "An Elegiac poem on ye Death of ye Rt honble Mary Ponsonby late Countess of Drogheda. By Mr. [Moore] Booker."
(2) HM 14353: "A Tale," "Verses by Mr [Moore] Booker."
(3) HM 14358: John Calder's annotations upon Swift's "Character of Lord Wharton" from Nichols' ed. of *The Tatler* (1786).
(4) HM 14365: A note from ___ Garbet to Mr. and Mrs. [Deane?] Swift.
(5) HM 14367: "[To] Lucy Young, Countess of Rochford."
(6) HM 14371: "English Blunders" in hand of Deane Swift.
(7) HM 14375: "From W: T: to C: W: the Second Part to ye same tune."
(8) HM 14377: A Song, "Not half so charming seem'd the Queen of Love."
(9) HM 14379: "Sir x x x Speech upon the Sea."

[5]*The Rowfant Library. A Catalogue of the Printed Books, Manuscripts, Autograph Letters, Drawings and Pictures, Collected by Frederick Locker-Lampson* (London: Bernard Quaritch, 1886). Hereafter referred to as *The Rowfant Library*. See pp. 216-217.

tington acquired them, and the two volumes once bore the Huntington numbers HM 2590 and HM 2591. Although the manuscripts
were removed to separate folders in 1939, as has been said, the bindings have been preserved. In what was HM 2590, Locker-Lampson
noted in pencil on the flyleaf:

I bought these MSS at Messr. Sotheby's in July 1877. a list of them may
be found at the end of the Volume, as well as of some others, which, being larger, in form, & not quite so interesting, are bound up separately in a
folio Volume. and there is an MS., apparently in Dr. Sheridan's hand,
which makes a third (4to) Vol:—

From what was HM 2591 came these notes:

These MSS were sold at Sotheby Wilkinson Co. Wellington St. Strand. in
July 1877. with other even more interesting MSS connected with the
Dean of St. Patrick's. I have had the others bound separately. one in 4to
the most interesting: the other ½ bound also 4to which is only an MS of
Dr. Sheridan (Swift's friend)* There is a leaf at the end of this Volume
which gives more information as to the nature of the rest of the MSS./FL

At some time Locker-Lampson added the asterisk above and the following correction below: "*No! This is a Goldsmith MSS!" The
two bindings also bear the numbers 1043 and 1044, possibly their lot
numbers at a later sale, perhaps when purchased by E. Dwight
Church, for example, or by W. K. Bixby, two subsequent American
owners of these two volumes.

After the death of Locker-Lampson in 1895 his Rowfant Library
was purchased by the American collector, Elihu Dwight Church, of
Brooklyn, New York, who, as early as 1905, evidently, removed it
to the United States and began selling some of the manuscripts, as
well as many of the printed books, to other interested American col-
lectors. The way in which Mr. Church distributed portions of the
library so that they became, in time, valuable additions to many great
American collections is still not altogether clear, at least to me.
What is clear, however, is that soon after the breakup began to be
known, leading British bookmen began agonizing and making re-
proving noises. Alfred W. Pollard, who had helped Locker-Lampson to compile *The Rowfant Library* catalogue, in an essay entitled
"The Rowfant Books," which appeared in the *Library* for June
1905,[6] deplored the fact that a library so carefully assembled as

[6]VI, 309-314.

Locker-Lampson's was being dispersed and sold piecemeal at that very moment by E. Dwight Church, its new owner. Pollard was more concerned with the printed books than with the manuscripts, but he did say indignantly that "the manuscripts are finding their ways to various American collections" (p. 311). In his admirable essay on Locker-Lampson, Madison C. Bates[7] has recently mentioned that it was "about 1908" when Paul Warburg acquired from Dodd, Mead & Company, who handled the sale of parts of the Rowfant Library for Mr. Church and his heirs, Locker-Lampson's "Great Album" containing three Swift manuscripts now on deposit at the Houghton Library of Harvard University. As late as 1916, Mr. Church sold to Mr. Huntington Lot No. 1130 from the Huntington-Bixby-Church sale of March 31, held at the Anderson Galleries, New York City, the first of the many Swift manuscripts that he was thereafter to acquire—HM 22660.

HM 22660 is the first part of a letter from Swift to Dr. Sheridan of 1735. Locker-Lampson had purchased it at Puttick's sales rooms on May 24, 1871, as Lot No. 961, according to a cutting from the sales catalog still attached to the manuscript at the present time. Among some uncataloged material in the Forster Collection at the Victoria and Albert Museum, South Kensington (Box F. E. 8), a note of John Forster indicates that it came from the "Sale of Mr. William Green's Library." Forster, who owned the second part of the letter, transcribed the first part at that time, a transcription (not altogether accurate) which F. Elrington Ball used in his edition of Swift's correspondence.[8] The most important fact here is, however, not so much that this was Mr. Huntington's first Swift autograph, as it is that as late as 1916 (and as early as 1905, or at least by 1908) Mr. Church was selling off Swift manuscripts, including the Theophilus Swift collection, from the Rowfant Library, having been in possession of them for about a decade.

Probably in this same period (about 1905 to 1908), William K. Bixby of St. Louis, Missouri, purchased the bulk of the Theophilus Swift manuscripts—with two exceptions[9]—after they had come to

---

[7] "'That Delightful Man': A Study of Frederick Locker, Pt. II," *Harvard Library Bulletin*, XIII (Spring 1959), 282.

[8] V, 191-194; Williams, *Corresp.*, IV, 349-352.

[9] The two exceptions are the "Great Album," containing Swift's "Penitential Letter" to Sir William Temple of Oct. 6, 1694, an undated note to Pope of about 1726-27, and a letter of July 23, 1736, to Marcus A. Morgan, at the Houghton Library; and HM 22660, the half of a letter of June 15-16, 1735, to Dr. Thomas Sheridan.

the United States and had for some time been in the possession of Mr. Church. They did not come to Bixby directly from the heirs of Frederick Locker-Lampson as suggested by the laconic phrasing in the first *Huntington Library Bulletin*, "assembled from the Locker-Lampson sales." Whenever or however he may have bought the Swift manuscripts, Mr. Bixby, sometime in 1918, most likely in August, sold them in turn to Mr. Huntington for what now seems an absurdly low price of $3,000 in a private sale arranged by that remarkable New York City dealer, George D. Smith.[10] Having crossed the Atlantic and, next, half the continent as far as St. Louis, the Swift manuscripts completed the journey to the West Coast of the United States. When the new Huntington Library was opened at San Marino, California, in 1920, they were then removed to their present location. Thus, some two hundred or more years after leaving Ireland, and after many vicissitudes, they are, what is left of them, housed safely half a world away from Dublin.

Mention should also be made here of a copy of *A Tale of a Tub* (1704) with a MS recipe in Swift's hand for making leavened bread pasted onto the flyleaf. It is dated March 26, 1730. This volume was once a part of Locker-Lampson's library (*The Rowfant Library*, p. 176); his "Jester" bookplate faces the bookplate of E. Dwight Church, from whom it was purchased. It is now cataloged as one of Huntington's rare books, Accession No. 106600, although the recipe, given below, is actually a two-page MS in Swift's hand.

[p. 1]   Leaven bread

Sift the flower twice; first through a course Sieve, the second time through a Silk one. Get some leaven to leaven it with. Steep the leaven well in luke-warm water a whole night, next morning heat it. Get some luke-warm water, make use of it in proportion to the flower,—according to the quantity of bread you propose to make. Put in a proper quantity of Salt; that is; to each half bushell of bread 4 handfulls. Beat well the dough; and, when you find it will easily separate from the hand—then you judge it to be sufficiently kneaded. After kneading cut the dough into three or four parts, roll them out in the trough, strewing thereon some fresh flower: place them on one Side of the trough, carefully piling one part of them on the other, after which cover them well with a linnen cloth. <which> If you knead/ [p. 2] at five in the morning, let the dough lye in the trough two hours, to have time to leaven: and take care it be not too much leavened; for then it will sour. Having found (by tasting) the dough to be as it ought, put it into the oven and leave it there from two hours and a half to three hours.

March. 26th 1730.

I got this from Monsieur de Ponchart lately come from Paris. [P. 3 is blank. P. 4 is endorsed:] Mar: 26th 1730 Monsr Ponchart's receit to make leaven Bread. [Signed below in ink:] Frederick Locker

[10]A record of the purchase is to be found buried in a long typewritten list kept among the Huntington records and headed on the first page merely "1918." *HLB*, I, 55, says the sale was made "in August, 1918." On fol. 17r of the typescript is listed: "Swift, Jonathan——MS. in writing of Dean Swift, Pope, etc., 2 vol. from collection of F L Locker——3000."

II

BETWEEN 1923 and 1925, Mr. Huntington added to the collection fourteen other Swift manuscripts, including a valuable series of eleven letters from Jonathan Swift to Alderman John Barber, in 1732-1733 the first printer ever to be chosen Lord Mayor of London.[11] Sometime after 1784 these letters and a few more fell into the hands of John Nichols, another printer and the chief London editor of Swift's works at the end of the eighteenth century.[12] Presumably they came from the estate of Alderman Barber, who had died in 1741, and they were first published by Nichols separately in 1789.[13] In August 1925 Mr. Huntington also purchased from Charles Sessler of Philadelphia the unpublished fair copy of Swift's "A Letter to a Young Lady on Her Marriage" (HM 1599). Herbert Davis believes that this fair copy may well have been the very copy presented by Swift to the young lady to whom it is addressed, Deborah Rochfort, née Staunton, to be consulted frequently, as Swift had urged her to do in the course of his advice.[14] It was preserved, after the untimely death of the young woman in 1737, among the papers of the Rochfort family of County Westmeath until 1849. Still other unpublished letters, including five to and from Sir Walter Scott (HM 14331-34,

[11]Late in 1923 Mr. Huntington bought from Maggs Bros! Catalogue No. 445 (1923), Lot No. 2909, a letter from Swift to Alderman Barber of March 30, 1737 (HM 24017), but he missed Lot No. 2910, another letter to Barber dated Oct. 27, 1735. In April and Aug. 1925, as I have been informed in a letter from Miss Mabel Zahn, Mr. Huntington bought from Charles Sessler of Philadelphia the ten letters to Barber (HM 14381-90); the fair copy of "A Letter to a Young Lady" (HM 1599); Swift's letter of Oct. 26, 1725, to Edward Harley (HM 24016); and a forgery, a supposed letter from Swift at Moor Park of March 7, 1697/8 (HM 24018). Miss Zahn, who kindly wrote on my behalf, reports that Maggs, from whom Charles Sessler bought the MSS, no longer has any record of the provenance of these MSS.

[12]Fourteen letters from Swift to Alderman Barber came into the hands of John Nichols too late to be included in his ed. of Swift's works which he and Thomas Sheridan put out in 1784. They must therefore have come into his possession after 1784 and before 1789 when he published them separately.

[13]*Miscellaneous Pieces, in Prose and Verse. By the Rev. Dr. Jonathan Swift, Dean of St. Patrick's, Dublin. Not Inserted in Mr. Sheridan's Edition of the Dean's Works. London: Printed for C. Dilly, in the Poultry. MDCCLXXXIX.* See pp. 91-120. All eleven letters from Swift to Barber now at the Huntington were here published for the first time. Three others that were then published are now missing from the series: the letter of Sept. 11, 1732 (pp. 93-94); one from 1733 (pp. 97-99); and one dated Dec. 8, 1736 (pp. 105-106). For some reason the letter of Oct. 27, 1735, offered for sale by Maggs in 1923 but not purchased by Mr. Huntington, was also not among those published by Nichols in 1789. For information about John Nichols' part in printing these letters see the Preface and his *Illustrations*, V, 392.

[14]*Prose Writings*, IX, xxvii, and Chap. III, below.

14337) and one from Sir Henry Craik (HM 14327), concern the use of the Theophilus Swift papers by these two nineteenth-century editors and biographers of Swift.

Thus, from the time when James Smith, Esq., rescued what remained of the Theophilus Swift papers until the present moment, every owner or user of the manuscripts, except one, has added something of value to what is now the present considerable collection.

Twenty-seven of the Huntington manuscripts are in the hand of Swift. About half as many more are endorsed, annotated by, or addressed to him. The holographs include unique versions of four of Swift's poems composed by him in Ireland between 1719 and 1734. They were used as the basis of his text by Sir Harold Williams in his monumental Clarendon Press edition of Swift's poems in 1937, or in his second edition of 1958. The four poems are: HM 14336, an ingenious reply in verse, with thirty-three or more similar rhymes that echo the word "Wine," to Dr. Thomas Sheridan's rhymed invitation of December 15, 1719, to a wine-bottling party, the kind of entertainment with which Swift and his circle amused themselves about this time (*Poems*, III, 1016-18); HM 14335, "The Beau's reply to the five Ladyes answer" (1728), probably composed within a month of Stella's death, a taunting exchange in verse by Swift on one side, posing as "the Little Beau," a well-known Dublin rake, and Sheridan, four unidentified ladies, and Esther Johnson, Swift's "Stella" on the other side (*Poems*, II, 427-428); HM 14339, "An Answer to a Late Scandalous Poem, Wherein the Author Most Audaciously Presumes to Compare a Cloud to a Woman" (1732), an amusing reply in 180 lines of verse to a poem by Sheridan calumniating women in general (*Poems*, II, 616-622); and, finally, HM 14338, fol. 12b, a most moving autobiographical poem "*On His Own Deafness*" composed by Swift in September 1734, just as he was beginning another lengthy attack of the deafness and giddiness that afflicted him for most of his adult life (*Poems*, II, 672-674). As I shall mention in Chapter VI, the first draft of this poem (all that remains of it in manuscript) is to be found sandwiched in between specimens of Anglo-Latin writings that Swift and Sheridan exchanged from 1734 to 1736.

At this point it should probably also be noted that there are in the Huntington collection two copies, in contemporary hands that are not Swift's, of his poem of 1728 (HM 14340), "An Answer to the

Ballyspellin Ballad" (*Poems*, II, 440-443), possibly in the hand of the Reverend John Worrall, Swift's Vicar at St. Patrick's; and HM 14345 in the hand of Deane Swift, Jonathan Swift's lengthy verse satire of 1734-1735, "On Bishop Rundle" (*Poems*, III, 819-821). The Huntington also owns a unique copy, in the hand of a scribe, of extensive passages omitted from Swift's two major satires in verse of 1733 (see Chapter V), *An Epistle to a Lady* and *On Poetry: A Rapsody* (*Poems*, II, 628-659). At the time of publication and for some years after, these offensive passages were considered to be both libelous and treasonous. They are to be found tipped in the handsomely bound second volume on large paper of the Huntington's four-volume Dublin octavo edition of Swift's works printed by George Faulkner in 1735 and cataloged now as a rare book, Acc. No. 81494. It is a great pity that Sir Harold Williams was unable to incorporate these Huntington copies in his second edition of Swift's poems.

Ten of the autograph manuscripts are in prose: chiefly the fair copy of "A Letter to a Young Lady" mentioned above; some notes (HM 14380), written possibly in May 1713 and intended for emendation of Swift's *The History of the Four Last Years of the Queen*, a work that was finally published posthumously in 1758, but one on which Swift set great store and upon which he worked conscientiously until his death (see Chapter II); two drafts (HM 14342-3) of an entertaining dialogue, composed, as one draft has it, "in Hybernian Stile," that satirizes Irish "bulls," brogue, and Irishisms, what Swift called, in the heading of the other draft, "Irish Eloquence";[15] an outline from 1727 of heads of discourse for an essay (HM 14346) apparently to be entitled "Proposal for Virtue," a quality that Swift had succinctly defined elsewhere as "publick Spirit."[16] On the verso of the same manuscript is a draft of Swift's first will (discussed in Chapter IV), made and then canceled in anger in 1727; and there is also the codicil and attendant directions from a second will, also later canceled, from April 1737 (HM 14347).[17] Finally, there are twenty-eight pages written in the various Anglo-Latin languages that Swift and Sheridan exchanged about 1734-1736 (HM 14338, 14341; see Chapter VII). Tucked in among these last is a page

[15]*Prose Writings*, IV, 277-279.

[16]*A Letter to the Right Honourable the Lord Viscount Molesworth. By M. B. Drapier* (Dublin, 1724), i.e., the fifth Drapier's letter; *Prose Writings*, X, 91.

[17]*Prose Writings*, XIII, 198-200.

(HM 14341, fol. 2b) in English of clichés, platitudes, and trite sayings, probably all that remains in manuscript of Swift's last major work in prose to be published in his lifetime, his *Polite Conversation* of 1738.

In addition to the series of eleven letters from 1732 to 1739 to Alderman Barber, Swift's correspondence is represented in the Huntington collection by his letter (HM 24016) of October 26, 1725, from Dublin, to Edward Harley, second Earl of Oxford, upon his recent marriage, and the one half of a letter (HM 22660) from Swift in Dublin dated June 15-16, 1735, to Dr. Thomas Sheridan at his newly opened school at Cavan in the country near Dublin. The other half of the letter, as I mentioned earlier, is preserved now in the Forster Collection at the Victoria and Albert Museum, South Kensington, as Forster No. 552. The first half of the letter, most of which was written on June 15, is at the Huntington; the Victoria and Albert owns the second part, all of which was written on June 16.

The Huntington collection also includes an interesting series of poems and letters from Swift's English and Irish friends, many of them addressed to Swift and some of them annotated by him. There are, for instance, poems from such Dublin friends as George Rochfort, brother-in-law of Deborah Staunton (the young lady of Swift's essay) and an M.P. for County Westmeath in two Irish Parliaments (HM 14368; *Poems*, III, 965-966); HM 14362, a poem from Dr. Patrick Delany, Swift's future biographer and the future Dean of Down (*Poems*, III, 1049-50); three poems (HM 14335, 14336, 14369) from Dr. Thomas Sheridan, at that time the foremost classical scholar and the most famous schoolmaster in Ireland (*Poems*, II, 424-426; III, 1016, 1039-41); two poems (HM 14363, 14364) from the Reverend William Dunkin, a fellow of Trinity College and a leading Dublin wit (*Poems*, III, 831*n*); and a poem (HM 14354) from John Boyle, fifth Earl of Cork and Orrery, to Alexander Pope, on Pope's epitaph on John Gay. There is also a copy (HM 14328), in an unidentified hand, of Stella's poem to Swift on his birthday, 1721 (*Poems*, II, 736-738), as well as a transcript made for Sir Walter Scott in the early nineteenth century by the Dublin recorder of the will of 1723 of Esther Vanhomrigh, Swift's Vanessa (HM 14348). The will was dated May 1, 1723, about a month before Vanessa's death, and it is notable for *not* mentioning Swift's name, either as executor or as a legatee.

Among the correspondence addressed to Swift there is also a curious letter (HM 14330) from a passionate young lady who signed herself "Sacharisa." Since it refers to a reply to be inserted in George Faulkner's *Dublin Journal*, it must, therefore, have been written after that newspaper began publication in 1726. Possibly it is part of some kind of a practical joke played upon Swift by someone like Sheridan, the point of which is now lost. There are letters also to or about Swift (some of them addressed to Mrs. Whiteway, when Swift became too ill to write) from such English and Irish friends as Alexander Pope (HM 14326); a joint letter with Lord Orrery; one from Orrery himself (HM 14355) and two from his wife Margaret, née Hamilton (HM 14356, 14357); one from Dr. William King, principal of St. Mary's Hall, Oxford (HM 14329); and, finally a note dated November 8, 1733, to Swift and endorsed by him "Dr. Ratcliffs Receit for Deafness. Sent by My Lady Montcashel." This last, from Swift's old friend, Catherine Davys, Viscountess Mountcashell, the tragic mistress of the estate of St. Catherine's, Leixlip, just outside of Dublin, was first published by Scott. It will serve to illustrate the fantastic spelling of Lady Mountcashell and the extent to which both she and Swift were willing to go to shake off the deafness and dizziness that plagued them both.

HM 14360

Docter Ratliffs prescripction for a noisse in the head & deffness proseeding from a cold moyst humor in the head
Take a pint of sack whay made very clear halfe sack & halfe watter, boyle in it sum plain read sage, & asprige of Rossmery, take it gowing to rest wth thirty or forty drops of spirit of harts horn, continue it as long as you find beniffit by it expectly [especially ?] the wintor seson, he may swetn it or not with sirop of Cowsleps
    he orderd allsoe aspice capp: to be made of Cloves Masse [Mace?] & Nutymegs finely [?] pounded & put be twen two silkes & quelted to wear next the head, & for aman to be sewdd wth inside his wigg,

It seems to me very likely that Lady Mountcashell had forgotten, or possibly never knew, that in the middle of his *Discourse Concerning the Mechanical Operation of the Spirit*, appended to *A Tale of a Tub*[18] and published with it in 1704, Swift had ironically praised the homely remedy of wearing *"quilted Caps"* like this spice "capp." Swift said that it was "an Institution of great Sagacity and Use," and he gravely recommended it for preventing the evaporation of the

---

[18]Ed. A. C. Guthkelch and D. Nichol Smith, 2nd ed. (Oxford, 1958), pp. 276-277.

spirit upward anyway but through the mouth, "even as a skilful Housewife, that covers her Still with a wet Clout."

III

THUS, in possessing representative and typical examples of Swift's poetry, his prose, and his correspondence from 1719 to 1739, his last creative period in Dublin, the Huntington Library collection of Swift manuscripts both in quality and in quantity, in my estimation, compares very favorably with, for instance, the six poetical manuscripts from 1699 to 1723, the four prose manuscripts from 1707 to 1716, and the forty letters, to and from Swift, of 1709 to 1738 that make up the fifty items of the Swift collection in the Pierpont Morgan Library of New York City,[19] the only other American collection that can in any way be compared with the Huntington's Swift manuscripts. It seems to me that only the British Museum's extensive collection of Swift manuscripts, for the most part his correspondence as donated by Swift's various eighteenth-century editors, and the eighty-odd Swift manuscripts assembled in the first half of the nineteenth century by John Forster for use in his unfinished *Life of Jonathan Swift* (London, 1875) and preserved now at the Victoria and Albert Museum, South Kensington,[20] surpass in number and in importance the Swift manuscripts in the Huntington Library. In my opinion the Swift manuscripts in the Huntington Library rank third among the four major public collections of his manuscripts in the world for quality as well as quantity, and the collection is, I think, the finest, as well as the largest, outside London and the British Isles.

The basis of the Morgan Library collection is the so-called "Fountaine Manuscripts" discovered by John Forster in the nineteenth century at Narford Hall, Norfolk, the estate of Swift's early friend in England, Sir Andrew Fountaine.[21] After the death of Queen Anne in 1714 and because of political differences, Swift and Fountaine had little to do with each other except for an occasional letter. The Fountaine Manuscripts now at the Morgan Library thus represent Swift's early career in England to 1714, as the Theophilus Swift papers at the

[19]George K. Boyce, "Modern Literary Manuscripts in the Morgan Library," *PMLA*, LXVII (1952), 22.

[20]. . . *Forster Collection. A Catalogue of the Paintings, Manuscripts, Autograph Letters, Pamphlets, etc. Bequeathed by John Forster, Esq., LL. D.* (London, 1893), pp. 50-53. I do not here consider the extensive private collection of Lord Victor Rothschild.

[21]Forster, *Life*, pp. viii, 228, 235, 261.

Huntington Library represent the latter half of Swift's career in Ireland to 1739. Both American collections therefore complement each other most conveniently. By a striking coincidence, it even appears from a priced and marked catalog preserved at the Huntington of a Sotheby sale held in 1902[22] that the younger collector, Mr. Henry Huntington, may have been bidding—unsuccessfully, as it turned out —against his more experienced fellow countryman, Mr. J. P. Morgan, for the Fountaine Manuscripts when they were offered for sale.

If the Huntington collection of Swift manuscripts is as extensive and as important as I have maintained, why has it not been more widely known and used? Some answers may be found when one recalls the characters of previous owners of these manuscripts, the uses they made of them, and the inopportune moments at which the collection left Ireland for England, England for the United States, and the East Coast of the United States for the West Coast. The nature of the collection itself, concentrated as it is upon the latter part of Swift's life in Ireland, rather than upon his earlier life in England, may also have influenced its usefulness. Soon after Swift's death Mrs. Whiteway and to a certain extent Mr. Deane Swift were under considerable pressure from such powerful friends of Swift as the Earl of Orrery and Alexander Pope to produce for publication manuscripts and letters.[23] George Faulkner, Swift's Dublin publisher, was also eager to get his hands on some of these manuscripts.[24] Between the two of them, however, Mrs. Whiteway and Mr. Deane Swift seem to have resisted successfully most of these attempts and to have carried with them to England a considerable number of unpublished pieces by Swift.

Enough of importance remained in their hands, at any rate, to warrant Deane Swift's (and after him, Theophilus Swift's) contemplating an entirely new edition of Swift's works based in large part upon the many unpublished manuscripts then in their possession.[25] Mr. Deane Swift appears to have cultivated an almost obsessive suspicion

[22]Sotheby, Wilkinson & Hodge, No. 13 Wellington Street, Strand, W.C. [London]. *Catalogue of a Selection of Valuable Books & Manuscripts from the Library of Sir Andrew Fountaine, of Narford Hall, Norfolk . . . 11th day of June [-14 June], 1902.* Lot No. 824, consisting of twenty-four MS items, some in the hand of Swift, was sold to the dealer Perry for £400.

[23]*The Correspondence of Alexander Pope*, ed. George Sherburn, 5 vols. (Oxford, 1956), hereafter referred to as *Pope Correspondence.* See Vol. IV, passim; letters to and from Lord Orrery, Mrs. Whiteway, Deane Swift.

[24]Ibid., letters to and from George Faulkner.

[25]*Illustrations*, V, 375.

of most people and a fanatical hatred of Dr. Patrick Delany. Delany's *Observations upon Lord Orrery's Remarks on the Life and Times of Dr. Jonathan Swift* (1754) was answered by Deane Swift, employing some of the manuscripts then in his possession, in his *Essay upon the Life of Swift* (1755). He also made good use of additional manuscripts, until then unpublished, in the volumes he edited in 1765 and 1768 for Hawkesworth's continuing quarto and octavo editions of Swift's works printed at London.[26] But neither he nor his son Theophilus believed that they had by any means exhausted the materials in their hands. In 1780, three years before his death, Mr. Deane Swift, overcoming his suspicious nature, offered John Nichols, the London printer, a chance to go into partnership with him on an entirely new edition of Swift's works, and in 1784, a year after his father's death, Theophilus made Nichols a similar offer.[27] Possibly because the Swifts were such touchy or turbulent characters, possibly because his own plans were then well advanced, Nichols refused and instead combined for his edition with Thomas Sheridan the younger, son of Swift's great Irish friend and the Dean's own godson. These manuscripts had also been twice offered to Dr. Samuel Johnson for use in his "Swift" in *The Lives of the English Poets*, but Johnson refused the offers.[28]

When the great "Magician of the North" Sir Walter Scott descended upon Swift's works early in the nineteenth century, he made great public play with the Theophilus Swift papers, some (but not all) of which were offered to Scott for this, his first edition of Swift's works[29] in 1814. In actual practice, as John Nichols ruefully noted,[30]

[26]Vols. XV, XVI, and XXI, XXII, XXIII in octavo; Vols. VIII, XII, XIII in quarto.

[27]*Illustrations*, V, 387, 389-390.

[28]Swift's *Works* (1824), I, 492: "When employed in writing the Dean's life, Dr. Johnson received two invitations from Deane Swift, Esq. to spend some time at his house in Worcestershire, one of which was conveyed by Mr Theophilus Swift, his son, to whom I owe this information. The purpose was to make every communication in his power, that might throw light on the history of his great and beloved relative. But Dr Johnson declined the invitation, and even refused to receive the information offered, or to communicate with Mr Deane Swift upon the subject."

[29]"Advertisement" to Scott's first ed. of Swift's *Works* (1814): "The present edition of this incomparable English Classic, is offered to the public with the advantage of possessing considerably upwards of a hundred original Letters, Essays, and Poems, by Dean Swift, which have not hitherto been printed with his works. These have been recovered from the following authentic sources:—*First*, The most liberal communications have been made by Theophilus Swift, Esq., Dublin, the son of the learned Deane Swift, the near kinsman and biographer of the celebrated Dean of St. Patrick's. . . ."

[30]*Illustrations*, V, 396-397.

what Scott did, with the help of his bibulous amanuensis, Henry Weber, was to cut and paste up Nichols' latest (1808) octavo edition of Swift's works, insert such new material as was then offered by Theophilus Swift and by the heir of Dr. Lyon in Ireland, write some witty and pertinent notes and a brilliant prefatory Memoir of Swift, meanwhile leaving to the sometimes careless Weber the tedious task of copying out the best of the new material. Evidence of this is, happily, still at hand at the Huntington, where a couple of Nichols' mutilated and annotated volumes from the edition of 1808 are now preserved.[31] As we shall see in a moment, all of Theophilus Swift's manuscripts that survived after his death in 1815 were in 1820 again offered to Sir Walter Scott for use in his second edition (1824) of Swift's works in nineteen volumes. Once more Scott seems to have left much of the work to a scribe, or at least to someone who could not read Swift's hand easily,[32] or who was only too willing to see in almost any eighteenth-century document evidence of what Scott called Swift's "disguised" hand.[33] For better or for worse, however, Scott's editions of Swift's works, especially his second edition of 1824, became the standard for Swift scholarship throughout the nineteenth century, just as Thackeray's chiaroscuro portrait of Swift as blackguard and apostate priest became the standard for the nineteenth century of Swift's character and personality.

John Forster and Sir Henry Craik, at the end of the century, began the necessary revaluation of Swift's life and art, and both had—or would have had—access to the manuscripts then owned by Frederick

[31]Huntington No. 141696, Vols. I and II. See also the British Museum copies (C. 28. h. 5.) of Vols. XI and XII of Nichols' octavo ed. "with copious MS. notes by Sir Walter Scott."

[32]Compare, for instance, the transcriptions made for Swift's *Works* (1824), VII, 154-157, of HM 14342 ("Irish Eloquence") and of HM 14343 ("A Dialogue in Hybernian Stile between A and B"), with the transcriptions in *Prose Writings*, IV, 277-279. See also Scott's thanks to Matthew Weld Hartstonge in a letter from Ashestiel, Selkirk, May 1, 1811, for "transcribing the whole" of the Theophilus Swift material that was loaned for the ed. of 1814 (J. Alexander Symington, *Some Unpublished Letters of Sir Walter Scott* [Oxford, 1932], p. 45). In the same letter Scott mentions that "My eccentric friend Miss White sent me the transcript of the MS notes on Clarendon" from a volume preserved in Marsh's Library, Dublin. Evidently Scott never saw many of the MSS he was allowed to use from among the papers in the Theophilus Swift collection for his first ed. of 1814. It was quite a different matter with the 1824 ed.; by that time the number of Swift MSS remaining extant was less than half of what it had been earlier.

[33]See, for instance, HM 14371, "English Blunders," in the hand of Deane Swift. A clear ref. in the next-to-last entry to "*Gloucester Journal* Octr 20 1761" should have ruled out Scott's attribution of the MS to Jonathan Swift or to Dr. Thomas Sheridan (Swift's *Works* [1824], VII, 158).

Locker-Lampson.[34] In 1876, however, Forster died after completing the first only of the three-volume *Life* he planned to write. Quite properly, since he was, in his first volume, dealing only with Swift's early life, Forster had concentrated most upon the Fountaine Manuscripts. Sir Henry Craik wrote to Frederick Locker-Lampson in June 1881 for permission, which was gladly given, to use the Swift manuscripts then at the Rowfant Library for his *Life* of Swift, which first appeared in 1882.[35] Craik's letter is chronologically the last item in the Huntington collection (HM 14327). To judge from Sir Henry's rather inaccurate transcription of Swift's "Proposal for Virtue" (HM 14346) and his unwarranted asumption that this was a draft of an essay for the *Craftsman*,[36] we may reason that Craik, like Scott, did not read Swift's hand easily, or that the copying out was left to someone else. In any case we may wonder why Sir Henry Craik and Sir Walter Scott, both of whom must have handled with some attention this very paper that contains "Proposal for Virtue," should have ignored Swift's first will of 1727, a draft of which is on the verso of the same folded sheet. So with the notes for Swift's *History of the Four Last Years of the Queen*, the draft of an autobiographical poem of 1734, and many pages of Anglo-Latin writings. Unfortunately for Swift scholarship, the Theophilus Swift manuscripts left England for the United States sometime after Locker-Lampson's death in 1895, just before the appearance of Temple Scott's valuable edition of Swift's prose works (1897-1908) and before the publication of the still more valuable edition of Swift's correspondence brought out by F. Elrington Ball (1910-1914). Both scholars therefore had to rely on transcripts made by John Forster, Sir Henry Craik, and others, or on Scott's second edition of 1824.

In fact, the Huntington manuscripts were not widely known or consulted until the publication of Sir Harold Williams' 1937 edition of Swift's poems and the appearance of the first volumes of Herbert Davis' edition of Swift's prose writings, begun in 1938, but then delayed by the war. As late as 1934 Sir Shane Leslie, lecturing in Philadelphia as a Rosenbach fellow, speaking of "The Script of Jonathan Swift," talked at length about the Fountaine Manuscripts at the Morgan Library and appealed in his conclusion for news of other Swift

[34]Frederick Locker-Lampson, *Patchwork* (London, 1879), p. 79.

[35]A second ed. appeared in 1894.

[36]Craik, *Life of Swift* (1894), II, 166*n*. Cf. T. Scott, *Prose Works*, VII, 375-376.

manuscripts in the United States "rather than leave some remote pebble unturned in California or Texas."[37] Sir Shane Leslie's instincts were right. Because of their removal at an untimely moment to the remote United States, and eventually their removal to an even more remote Southern California, and because of the late period in Swift's life that they cover, the Huntington manuscripts were relatively little known and less consulted by nearly all previous editors, who probably felt that they had been reproduced accurately enough.

IV

As I HAVE SAID, the core of the Huntington collection was the group of sixty papers that were rescued after the death of Theophilus Swift in September 1815 by James Smith, Esq. This is the important date to remember. Before that time the manuscripts were double or more the present number; after that date and for a period that may have been as long as several months or even several years, they were being dispersed gradually or destroyed outright as waste paper, until only the sixty remaining were saved by the generosity of James Smith, Esq. This is to assume (what possibly is not a valid assumption) that, between the dates of his father's death in 1783 and his own death in 1815, Theophilus Swift did not part with any of the manuscripts so piously preserved by his father and by his grandmother Mrs. Whiteway. For Theophilus Swift appears to have been something of an eccentric, hot-tempered, highly imaginative person. Although he was not educated, as was his father and his son, at Trinity College, Dublin, he seems successfully to have antagonized some of his learned friends there by libeling them. For this action he was for a while imprisoned at Dublin. In July 1789 he fought a duel with Colonel Lennox, afterward the Duke of Richmond, and was wounded. The quarrel was about another duel that Colonel Lennox had earlier fought with the Duke of York.[38]

The exact circumstances surrounding the death of Theophilus Swift need to be further examined. Such accounts as I can find show that Theophilus Swift died in Dublin, or at least in Ireland, about

[37] *The Script of Jonathan Swift and Other Essays* (Philadelphia, 1935), p. 20. See also what Sir Shane Leslie wrote in his essay of 1954 describing "The Swift Manuscripts in the Morgan Library," *Studies in Art and Literature for Belle Da Costa Greene*, ed. Dorothy Miner (Princeton, 1954), pp. 446, 448: "No American student need cross the Atlantic for assistance in deciphering or estimating an autograph of Swift."

[38] *Illustrations*, V, 387-391, and *DNB*.

September 30, 1815.[39] According to Sir Walter Scott, however, in his "Advertisement" to the second edition of Swift's works in 1824, Theophilus Swift died most romantically in London, in what begins to sound like a genteel and deodorized, nineteenth-century version of an actual eighteenth-century garret:

These valuable documents were in possession of the late Theophilus Swift, Esq., who, dying in furnished lodgings in London, his papers appear to have fallen into the hands of persons totally incapable of estimating their value. Many, indeed by far the greater part, were treated as ordinary waste paper, and the rest were saved from the same fate by Mr. Smith, a gentleman of taste and liberality, who was much grieved and surprised at the condition in which he discovered the correspondence of Swift, and of Pope, and several of the miscellaneous Poems of the former.[40]

Since Sir Walter Scott had earlier been permitted by Theophilus Swift, then "of Dublin," to use some parts of the manuscript collection for the 1814 edition of Swift's works, we may accept Sir Walter's word when he says "the greater part" of the collection was lost through ignorance and neglect. Since, however, there were not any letters from Swift and only a part of one from Alexander Pope among the Theophilus Swift papers (the correspondence with Alderman Barber was added in the 1920's by Mr. Huntington from another source), and since Theophilus Swift's death may have occurred in Dublin, possibly in more comfortable but perhaps less romantic circumstances than in London "in furnished lodgings," as described by Sir Walter, we may legitimately wonder whether the author of *Waverley*, a great romancer, was not unconsciously dressing up a bit the account he had received from James Smith, Esq., of the recovery of the remaining Swift manuscripts. Scott's editions were great money-makers. John Nichols ruefully estimated that Sir Walter Scott made thirty times more profit from his first edition of 1814 than Nichols had made from all three of his editions of Swift's works.[41] Although Scott good-naturedly admitted in his "Advertisement" that the Theophilus Swift papers "do not contain much that has not been already published," he still made the most of the romantic

[39]*Gentleman's Magazine*, LXXXV, Pt. II (1815), 380, under the heading "*Sept.* 30," records his death but does not say where it took place. *Illustrations*, V, 388, says that Theophilus Swift "died in Ireland, in the Summer [of 1815]"; *DNB* says merely that he died "in Dublin."

[40]Pp. viii-ix.

[41]*Illustrations*, V, 396-397.

recovery of these papers as the chief reason for producing a new edition.[42]

There is no question, however, about the fact that James Smith, Esq., of London and Bideford, Devon, did recover the Theophilus Swift papers after the latter's death, wherever it occurred. All but one or two of the letters exchanged by Sir Walter Scott and Mr. Smith between 1820 and 1825 concerning the loan of the collection for Scott's edition of 1824 are extant. Five of the letters are in the Huntington collection; two others are in the National Library of Scotland. Unfortunately, the very first letter to Scott from Mr. Smith is missing. In that crucial letter Mr. Smith would have offered Sir Walter Scott the use of the collection and explained to him the circumstances by which he recovered the manuscripts. In reply Sir Walter appears to have accepted the courteous loan of the Swift manuscripts and to have recommended wisely, for the protection of both, that Mr. Smith number the manuscripts from 1 to 60 before parting with them. Mr. Smith seems at first to have been reluctant to employ so businesslike and so ungentlemanly a method as numbering the documents to be loaned. On April 5, 1820, however, he sent Sir Walter Scott the package of Swift manuscripts and with it the formal, third-person covering note that is now preserved as HM 14337:

Mr. Smith presents Compts to Sir Walter Scot, with the accompanying Parcel (*numberd as he desired*) When Sir Walter has perused them (quite at his leisure) Mr. S. requests he will have the goodness to Transmit them from Scotland, to the Care of Mr. Joseph Hume <his friend, who is> Chymist No. 108 Longacre, who will take charge of them until Mr. S's return from the Continent. The Papers sent are 60 in Number.

Sir Walter Scott replied at once on the same date, writing from 96 Piccadilly and employing the same formal manner (HM 14331):

Sir Walter Scott with best compliments and thanks to Mr Smith has received a packet containing Sixty letters and papers being original documents concerning Dean Swift which Mr Smith has been so good as to allow Mr. Scott to retain and examine at leisure. Mr Scott will transmit them in safety to Mr. Joseph Hume Chymist Longacre agreeably to Mr Smiths desire.

Sir Walter Scott is greatly obliged by Mr Smiths liberal communication and wishes him and his family an agreeable tour on the Continent.

[42]Swift's *Works* (1824), I, viii-ix.

As an afterthought Scott added a postscript:

Mr Hume will receive in the course of a fortnight a set of Mr Scotts works for Mr Smiths acceptance

Also on April 5, 1820, but in more informal and much less starchy tones, Scott wrote to Archibald Constable, his publisher:[43]

I have had a very odd communication from a Mr. Smith concerning Swift. A quantity of original letters and papers, formerly the property of Theophilus Swift, the Dean's grand-nephew, were left in a lodging-house where he had died in miserable circumstances, and—wonderful judgment for some of the Dean's compositions—were found in the w.-c.-Mr. Smith secured them, and is to put them into my hands for the new edition. As far as I can judge, they contain some novelty, and deserve to be carefully examined.

When Scott's second edition appeared in July 1824, James Smith, Esq., appears to have begun to look proudly upon his Swift manuscripts as heirlooms to be passed down in his family, since Sir Walter Scott had made so much of them. He also became a little worried about Scott's failure to return them promptly. At any rate, in what is now HM 14333 (A and B), Smith noted down and quoted Scott's acknowledgements as they appeared at the end of Volume III of *Red Gauntlet* and in the "Advertisement" to the second edition of 1824. Then he added: "The papers alluded to within belong to me and I entrusted the use of them to Sir Walter Scot should he publish a 2d. Edition of Swifts Works & to be returnd to me when I require them & for which I have his acknowledgement & Receit. /J:S:/ I wrote this at Bideford 2d. Septr. 1824." On September 10, 1824, Mr. Smith was enough concerned to write to Sir Walter Scott requesting the return of his manuscripts.[44] On September 13, 1824, Sir Walter replied as follows (HM 14332):

Dear Sir

I am favour'd with your obliging letter and am much pleased with your expressing yourself satisfied with the use I have made of your curious manuscripts and the acknowledge (not less sincere than merited) which I have made of the favour. I will not fail to return them in the manner you direct so soon as I return to my researches in Edinburgh where they are safe in my private cabinet. This will not be untill the middle of No-

[43]H. J. C. Grierson et al., *The Letters of Sir Walter Scott* (London, 1934), VI, 171-172.

[44]The National Library of Scotland, Edinburgh, MS No. 3899, fols. 110-111.

vember however unless some unusual circumstances should call me to Edinburgh during the vacation when I will not fail to seek some safe <opport> mode of forwarding them in the way you direct   I only write at present to say that they are safe and to prevent your feeling any uneasiness at their not being instantly return'd

I am Dear Sir Very much your obliged humble

Servant

Walter Scott

Abbotsford Melrose

13 September

Despite his good resolves and his reassurances to the now very much worried Mr. Smith in Bideford, Devon, the matter *did* slip Scott's mind, as he very honestly admitted in his final letter to James Smith from Edinburgh, February 8, 1825, what is now HM 14334:

Dear Sir

I sent off by Thursdays post the Swift papers *Sixty* in number to A. Murry Angelo Esq Newman Street No 74 under Mr Frelings cover and with a letter to Mr Angelo begging him to acknowledge the receipt The truth is the matter had escaped my recollection in the course of various matters of consequence previous to my eldest sons marriage which took place on the third. I have taken the liberty to add to the collection an extract of Vanessas will from the Irish registry which I think may not be [an?] uninteresting addition to your collection

I am with many thanks for the loan of the papers very much

your obliged servant

Walter Scott

Edin. 8 feby 1825

With his usual generosity Sir Walter Scott thus began a tradition continued by most of the later owners of the manuscripts, that of adding something to the collection. Scott's gift to Mr. Smith of the copy of Vanessa's will made in the Dublin Registry Office is now even more valuable than in 1825, for in 1922 the original will was destroyed along with many other valuable records as a result of action connected with the Irish civil war. And alas for James Smith, Esq's proud dream of passing down to his descendants some Swift manuscripts that had been used by Sir Walter Scott. In July 1877 the lot—totaling now sixty-seven items and including the letters of Scott, the copy of Vanessa's will, a letter from the Countess of Orrery dated 1747, and something described as "Short A.L. s of Dean Swift to Mr. Simson"—was purchased at Sotheby, Wilkinson &

Hodge's sales room by Mr. Frederick Locker-Lampson.[45] Mr. Locker-Lampson added to the collection four Swift items that he had previously purchased at Puttick's on May 24, 1871,[46] and had the total collection bound by Roger DeCoverly in fine olive morocco bindings, two of which, together with Locker-Lampson's penciled notes, are still preserved by the Huntington, where the collection was in March 1939 once more disbound.[47]

It will be recalled that James Smith, Esq., upon the businesslike advice of Sir Walter Scott, had somewhat reluctantly numbered the manuscripts from 1 to 60. When Sir Walter finally returned them, he emphasized the fact that he was returning *sixty*. Mr. Smith's numbering, which he did apparently at random and in no very logical fashion, is still clearly visible on all but one manuscript. That one (HM 14361) is an epilogue to a school play, "A Farewell to the Audience, Written by Masr Dawncy (or Danncy)," and it may have come from Dr. Sheridan's new school at Cavan about 1735 or 1736. It has recently been remounted and in the process pasted down, so that the number on the back cannot be read. In all probability it would show on its verso one of the five numbers now missing from the collection when Mr. Smith's numberings are used to reconstruct the list of the sixty original manuscripts recovered by him. The missing numbers are 19, 24, 50, 58, and 60. Three other items which were once in Locker-Lampson's Rowfant Library after 1877[48] and which were originally among the Theophilus Swift papers were sold by W. K. Bixby on March 30, 1916, in the Huntington-Bixby-Church sale held at the Anderson Galleries on March 29-31, 1916.[49] The

---

[45]The portion of a page from the catalog, identified by an accompanying note in the hand of Locker-Lampson, is preserved now together with the two handsome Rowfant bindings that once held the Theophilus Swift papers. The purchase was Lot No. 973, which consisted of fifteen groups of MSS. The headnote reads as follows: "973. Swift (Jonathan) Dean of St. Patrick. An interesting and valuable Collection of Manuscripts, formerly in his possession, many of them in his autograph, rescued by Mr. James Smith from being treated as waste paper among the effects of Theophilus Swift, and lent by Mr. Smith to Sir Walter Scott, who used them in his second edition of the Works of Dean Swift, and duly acknowledged the loan." So far I have been unable to trace the exact date of the sale or the name of the owner of these MSS.

[46]The three letters now on deposit at the Houghton Library and the portion of a letter to Sheridan of June 1735 (HM 22660).

[47]Formerly HM 2590, 2591.

[48]*The Rowfant Library*, pp. 216-217.

[49]*Beautiful Bindings Rare and Fine Books Autograph Letters Valuable Manuscripts Being Duplicates and Selections from the Famous Libraries of Mr. Henry E. Huntington of New York and Mr. William K. Bixby of St. Louis with an Important Consignment of Rare Books on Early English Literature from the Estate of Mr. E. Dwight*

three lots were described in the catalog as consisting of Swift's note to "Mr. Simson" mentioned above; a document connected with St. Patrick's Cathedral dated February 7, 1715, and signed by Swift and Ludovic Moore; and three pages of a Latin poem and thirty-eight or more pages of notes explaining the diction therein, which Locker-Lampson first believed to be by Dr. Thomas Sheridan and later came to believe were by Goldsmith. I have been unable to trace the purchaser of these three items, but in all likelihood they hide now in some American library. These three and the school epilogue would thus account for four of the five missing manuscripts that were originally among the Theophilus Swift papers, and it would suggest that the collection, while being added to by Sir Walter Scott, by James Smith, Esq., by Frederick Locker-Lampson, and, most notably, by Mr. Huntington himself in 1923 and 1925, has lost only one item since the dispersal or destruction of those manuscripts that presumably occurred at the time of Theophilus Swift's death in September 1815.

The fortunes of the Swift manuscripts now at the Huntington are as remarkable for the great names in Swift scholarship that are not associated with a use of the collection as for those which are. Lord Orrery may have had some glimpse of it, but it was surely denied to Dr. Delany. Deane Swift used it extensively, but according to his son, it was twice offered to Dr. Samuel Johnson, when he was composing his account of "Swift" for *Lives of the Poets*, and twice refused or ignored.[50] Although it was tentatively offered to the tireless John Nichols, it twice eluded his grasp, as it had that of George Faulkner, Swift's careful Dublin editor. In the nineteenth century Sir Walter Scott had two chances to use material from the collection, and although John Forster did not live long enough to make use of the collection, it was consulted by Sir Henry Craik. On the other hand, it was unavailable to Temple Scott and F. Elrington Ball. Only in the twentieth century with the editions of Sir Harold Williams and Herbert Davis has the collection come to be scrutinized in the scholarly fashion it deserves. What is also impressive is the number of items that throw some new light on Swift's life and art that seem to have been overlooked by earlier editors and biographers.

Church Formerly of Brooklyn, To Be Sold March 29, 30, and 31, 1916 (New York: The Anderson Galleries, [1916]). See p. 132 (Lots Nos. 874-876).

[50]Swift's *Works* (1824), I, 492, and *Illustrations*, V, 388.

Chapter Two

NOTES FOR *THE HISTORY OF THE*

FOUR LAST YEARS, BOOK IV

I

HUNTINGTON MANUSCRIPT HM 14380 is a seemingly neglected and unpublished series of six entries in the hand of Jonathan Swift, notes intended for his posthumously published *The History of the Four Last Years of the Queen* (1758). From the time of its composition in 1712-1713 until 1737 Swift worked intermittently upon his *History* and set great store by the work as a historically accurate justification to posterity of the honorable actions of the Tory ministry in achieving the Peace of Utrecht. Yet, from the start, the *History* caused Swift much trouble in composition because of the lack of cooperation from some of his Tory friends. And later, in publication, Tory disapproval continued for parts of that work. From the time of its eventual publication, when Dr. Samuel Johnson first opened the question, until our own day, when Sir Harold Williams disposed of it once and for all,[1] the *History* has frequently been believed not to be by Swift at all.

In a small way these manuscript notes in the Huntington Library may reinforce what, by now, must be universally accepted: that the *History* is indeed by Swift, since he is here noting down in his own hand points that are later incorporated into that very *History* when published. In another direction the notes demonstrate how exactly and painstakingly Swift as Tory historian worked to gather precise data for the fourth book of his *History*, that section of his whole work which apparently caused him the most trouble. Before examining the Huntington Library notes, however, it seems to me best

---

[1]"Jonathan Swift and the *Four Last Years of the Queen*," in *Library*, 4th Ser., XVI (1935), 61-90; *Prose Writings*, VII, ix-xxviii.

to review briefly the history of the composition of Swift's *History of the Four Last Years* in order to fit these notes into place and to summarize the Duke of Ormonde's campaign of 1712 in Flanders, a subject which is treated at length in Book IV of Swift's work and with which these notes are exclusively concerned.

Swift composed his *History of the Four Last Years of the Queen* between September 1712 and May 1713; except for the last portion of Book IV the work was substantially completed by January 1712/3. From time to time during the 1720's and 1730's Swift reviewed his *History*, making revisions and corrections still with a view to publication. Of course the notes now in the Huntington Library may have been made at any of these times. But all of them have to do with recent military actions of the Duke of Ormonde, and are written down in a manner suggesting haste, which, coupled with the fact that sources of detailed information for such motives and actions as are here noted were subsequently made unavailable, leads me to believe that the notes were most likely jotted down by Swift sometime between September 1712 and May 1713, when he was busy with the original composition and corrections for his *History*.

On August 7, 1712, Swift first referred in his *Journal to Stella* to his *History* as "an Affair I am upon . . ." (II, 552). By October 28 the bulk of the work was done, and he had only thirty pages ("which will be sixty in print") left to write; however, he continued, "It is the most troublesome part of all . . ." (II, 569). Yet it is somewhat surprising to find that a month and a half later, on December 12, 1712, he had made little or no progress: "I have written 130 Pages in folio to be printed, & must write 30 more, which will make a large Book of 4s . . ." (II, 578). A month later, on January 12, 1712/3, despite having in the meantime seen and talked often with his friend the Duke of Ormonde, the recently returned commander of British forces in Flanders, Swift complained that "I can't finish my Work, these Ministers will not find time to do what I would have them" (II, 601). By January 18 he recorded that his *History* now stood "stock still" and added that "some think it too dangerous to publish . . ." (II, 604). Perhaps this was the true reason why "The Ministry," by which Swift seems to mean the uncooperative Bolingbroke, chief mover in international affairs, was not more forthcoming with the material Swift felt he needed to finish the fourth and last book.

Soon after the arrival in London of another Tory friend, Sir Thomas Hanmer, on February 4, 1712/3, Swift seems to have renewed his interest in finishing his *History*.[2] On February 22, Swift saw Hanmer in the company of the Duke of Ormonde at Lord Orkney's and wrote in his *Journal to Stella*, "I intend in a day or two to have an Hours talk with him on Affairs" (II, 625). On February 26 he dined at Hanmer's with Ormonde and Oxford and at that time probably gave his host one manuscript of his *History*, for he remarked in his *Journal* of the next day, February 27, "Sr T. Hanmer has my Papers now" (II, 628-629). By May 16, 1713, Swift could speak of his *History* as being "just finisht . . . & [I] must be ten days correcting it" (II, 669). Three days later, on May 19, Sir Thomas Hanmer sent Swift a note saying, "I keep only the last book which I shall have gone through before night. . . . I read with the same strictness & ill-nature as in the former part."[3] If Hanmer was as good as his word, Swift would have had time to incorporate any "observations" made by his friend on the fourth book in the remaining days of the ten he had allotted himself.[4]

Herbert Davis' recent edition of the *History* runs to 167 pages in print and is taken from the Windsor manuscript (a scribe's copy with annotations by Swift) containing 137 folio leaves or 273 numbered pages.[5] When Swift, in his *Journal* of December 12, 1712, said that he had written 130 folio pages and had thirty still to write, it is clear that he visualized a completed manuscript of 160 folio pages. In other words Swift, when he wrote in December, had probably reached page 136 in Davis' printed version and had just begun his presentation of the Duke of Ormonde's campaign of 1712 in Flanders, first mention of which occurs on page 122 of the modern edition. Swift admitted that those thirty pages left to write were "The most troublesome part of all," an apt enough description of the politico-military events in Flanders just coming to an end as he was writing. In broader terms, the Duke of Ormonde's campaign takes up the middle third of Swift's fourth and last book of his *History*, and it is just at this point in his composition that Swift seemed for so long to be stuck because of difficulties he anticipated and then actu-

---

[2]*Political State of Great Britain*, ed. Abel Boyer, 60 vols. (London, 1712-40); hereafter referred to as *Political State*. See V, 154.

[3]Williams, *Corresp.*, I, 351-352.

[4]As Sir Harold Williams has suggested, Swift may have retained and "finisht" a second MS, which he then revised and corrected (*Library*, XVI, 65, n. 6); *Prose Writings*, VII, xi, n. 2.

[5]*Prose Writings*, VII, xxii.

ally encountered. It is to this very portion of the last book of Swift's *History* that the notes in the Huntington Library apply.

From a military point of view the campaign of 1712 in Flanders was a strange one.[6] A force of 18,000 British troops (accompanied by a few battalions of loyal mercenaries) under the command of the Duke of Ormonde maneuvered so as to avoid any action with their enemies, the French, under the command of Marshal de Villars but in such a way as to appear as actively hostile to their allies, the confederated Dutch and imperial forces under the command of Prince Eugene of Savoy. Although the deception and menacing of his allies and the collaboration and collusion with his enemies were necessary for political reasons, they were none the less personally distasteful actions to the Duke of Ormonde, who was a military leader, and not a politician. For the Secretary of State, Henry St. John, Viscount Bolingbroke, these actions, from the point of view of international diplomacy, were a necessary prelude to Britain's achieving alone (or with her allies, if they agreed, as at first they did not) the peace with France that was finally concluded at Utrecht in 1713. As Swift when he was composing his *History* seemed to sense, Bolingbroke's orders and Ormonde's actions in the campaign of 1712 were not above suspicion and needed justification, or at least explanation. In fact, in 1715 they supplied some of the charges for the articles of impeachment and bills of attainder by which the vindictive Whigs punished the exiled Bolingbroke and Ormonde for their part in making the peace with France.

The Duke of Ormonde was appointed Captain General and Commander in Chief of her Majesty's forces in place of the disgraced Duke of Marlborough on April 7, 1712 (O.S.).[7] Ormonde left London two days later accompanied by his close friend Sir Thomas Hanmer and arrived at The Hague on April 23 (N.S.). There he conferred with the deputies of the States-General, made an inspection tour of Ghent, a supply-and-communication center for the English, and then joined Prince Eugene and the allied forces in the field at

---

[6]A convenient large-scale map of the area may be found in George M. Trevelyan, *England under Queen Anne: The Peace and the Protestant Succession* (London, 1934), III, Map No. 5, "The Netherlands: Campaigns of 1709-12."

[7]Information in the four following paragraphs is digested from two sources: Anonymous, *The Conduct of His Grace the Duke of Ormonde in the Campagne of 1712* (London, 1715); *Political State*, III, 339-340, 409-418; IV, 1-39, 80-106, 163-172. Dates in England are Old Style; those on the Continent are New Style.

Tournai on the fifth or sixth of May, 1712. By May 21 Ormonde had moved his headquarters forward to Marchiennes, and, in compliance with his orders from the Queen, had agreed with Prince Eugene to march in five days' time upon an aggressive invasion of northern France, after besieging such French outposts as Quesnoy (the modern La Quesnoy) and Landrecies. The lines of communication and supply of the allies were based on Bruges, Ghent, and Brussels, ran through Lille and Tournai, and channeled into the forward supply base and bottleneck of Marchiennes. The Earl of Albemarle with a sufficient force was detached southward across the river Scheldt to Denain to protect Marchiennes and the lengthening supply lines of the allies.[8] On May 24, 1712, two days before he was to march, Ormonde received Bolingbroke's notorious "Restraining Orders," dated from London on May 10.

To Ormonde these secret orders were an embarrassing surprise; they prohibited his besieging or engaging with his enemies the French. They also enjoined him from revealing his orders to his allies despite the fact that his chief opponent, Villars, was notified about them and had received similar orders, and that his allies soon got wind of his secret orders and asked Ormonde pointed questions that he could neither affirm nor deny. About all that the Duke could do was to agree to cover (but not to engage directly in) the proposed siege of Quesnoy and to await further orders from England about the occupation of Dunkirk as a cautionary measure preliminary to a suspension of arms with the French.

Somehow Ormonde managed to stall successfully for a month. On June 25, 1712, at the start of what was to be the most decisive and crucial period of the campaign, Ormonde finally received notice from the French that arrangements for occupying Dunkirk were now acceptable; on the same day he received orders from Bolingbroke to disengage and to send an occupation detachment to Dunkirk. But too much time had been wasted. Although Ormonde immediately alerted troops in British pay for a movement and proposed to his allies that the suspension of arms be made general, he was told after a few day's delay that his allies intended to go on fighting, that the Dutch would deny his troops passage through towns held by

[8]In view of what Swift was to make of Ormonde's subsequent warnings and Albemarle's later defeat at Denain, followed by the capture of Marchiennes, it is here worth noting that Ormonde maintained headquarters at Marchiennes for some time and knew the ground between it and Denain quite well.

them, and that mercenary troops in the pay of the British (as Ormonde had long suspected) had been tampered with and intended to join Prince Eugene's forces. On the same date (June 29) Ormonde heard from Villars that the cessation of arms must become general between armies (and not merely with the British forces) before Dunkirk would be turned over for occupation. From Bolingbroke he learned that—because of the special difficulties arising—Dunkirk would be occupied by forces sent from England. For the next two weeks affairs stood so perplexed.

On July 16, 1712, Prince Eugene and all but a few loyal battalions of the troops formerly in British pay separated from Ormonde's forces and marched south. The next day, July 17, Ormonde with his forces now reduced by about a half marched out of his headquarters at Cateau Cambrésis (the modern Le Cateau) in the general direction of Dunkirk. At sunset that same day by agreement with Villars, he formally declared a suspension of arms at his camp near Avesne-le-Secque (the modern Avesne). The following day, as he resumed his march, he learned that some of his officers of the advance guard had been denied passage through the allied-held towns of Douai, Bouchain, and Lille. At this point Ormonde determined to execute the most daring and only independent command decision he was permitted to make during the entire campaign. He wheeled his small force northward, and—despite the belated apologies and insincere reassurances of the Dutch and Prince Eugene—was very soon encamped around the city of Ghent which he occupied on July 27. By August 4, 1712, his forces had also occupied Bruges, and troops and supplies were on their way to Dunkirk, earlier occupied from England by a small force under Brigadier General Hill. Meanwhile Ormonde received news of the total defeat of Albemarle's forces at Denain at the hands of the French on July 24, 1712.

Thus, by early August 1712 British troops held an important Channel port of the enemy as a guarantee of a separate peace as well as two towns sitting astride the lines of supply of their wavering former allies. The successful French, however, pressing their attack upon the overextended and unprotected flank of the allies, took the supply bottleneck at Marchiennes. Before very long it appeared that Ormonde by occupying Ghent and Bruges had only forestalled the advancing French. By November 1, 1712, all the armies were in winter quarters; all sides (including the reluctant confederates) were preparing for a peace, and Ormonde was permitted to return to

England on that date. On November 4 he was received with gracious approbation by the Queen at Windsor.

II

HUNTINGTON MANUSCRIPT 14380 was written hastily by Swift in pen on one side only. Along the left-hand margin the six entries are set off from each other by a page number or by a dash. The first entry shows that the page numbers are all from Liber IV ("L. 4."). From the contents it is at once clear that they refer to pages 21-29 of a separately paged manuscript of the fourth book of Swift's *History of the Four Last Years*. Such pagination implies that the notes refer to a manuscript already in being and one that was completed, at least as far as the twenty-ninth page of the fourth book, at the time that the notes were made. They were therefore more likely to have been made between February and May 1713, when Swift resumed work on his *History*, than between October and December 1712, when Swift was stuck in composing this portion of his work.

The fifth entry, "Say a little more of te Approbation [?] & applaudig [sic] te dukes Conduct," is the kind of brief memorandum to ourselves that we make when something is fresh in mind, yet needing adjustment. As the notes go down the page, they are more careless or more hurried and harder to decipher; therefore a few difficult words are queried near the end. The ampersands, "te" for "the," "g" for "given," the abbreviations and misspellings are the kind of shorthand Swift used in writing other such notes to himself. The relevant parallel passages incorporating these notes are cited below from Davis' recent edition.

HM 14380

1 L. 4. P. 21. D. Ormd positively told by te Dutch, that they would not let his Troops pass—&c
—Ibid. D. Ormd could not send th Detachmt; because he had not te Fr Kings
orders, & Fr. chicaned because te Cessation could not be Generll-this wise
5 in te Duke.

P. 25. Lisle & douay, here; & satisfd Order was genrll—
—25. G which te dutch Army might Starve &c
—Say a little more of te Approbation [?] & applaudig te dukes Conduct

29. Abermarle at Denin to secure their Convoy from Marchiennes, too far

---

10 from their main Army, expln [?] their Conduct then

Lines 1-2   *Prose Writings*, VII, 138:

And he had sufficient Reasons to apprehend that the *Dutch* would either not permitt such a Detachment to pass through their Towns (as themselves had more than hinted to him) or would seize them as they passed.

Lines 3-5   Ibid., 138:

He thought it not prudent to expose them [Ormonde's troops] to march through the Enemy's Country with whom there was yet neither Peace nor Truce; ... At which the Marêchal [Villars] appeared extremely disappointed; Said, the King his Master reckoned, that all the Troops under His Grace's Command should yield to the Cessation. ... In short, the Opinion of Mons. *Villars* was, That this Difficulty cancelled the Promise of surrendring *Dunkirk;* which he therefore opposed as much as possible in the Letters he writt to his Court.

Line 6   Ibid., 141:

When he came as far as *Flines*, he was told by some of his Officers, that the Commandants of *Bouchain, Douay, Lisle* and *Tournay* had refused them Passage through those Towns, or even Liberty of Entrance; and said it was by Order of their Masters. The Duke immediatly recollected, that when the Deputies first heard of his Resolution to withdraw his Troops, they told him They hoped He did not intend to march through any of their Towns: This made him conclude that the Orders must be general, and that his Army would certainly meet with the same Treatment, which his Officers had done. ...

Line 7   Ibid., 142:

He knew very well, that while *Gand* was in the Queen's hands, no Provisions could pass the *Scheld* or the *Lis* without her Permission, by which He had it in his Power to starve their Army.

Line 8   Ibid., 142:

So that no Service could be more seasonable or useful in the present Juncture than this; which the Queen highly approved, and left the Duke a discretionary Power to act as he thought fit upon any future Emergency.

Lines 9-10   Ibid., 146-147:

For in a very few Days, after the Desertion of the Allies, happened the Earl of *Albemarle*'s Disgrace at *Denain*, by a Feint of the Marêchal's and a manifest Failure somewhere or other both of Courage and Conduct on the side of the Confederates, the Blame of which was equally shared between Prince *Eugene* and the Earl: although it is certain, that the Duke of *Ormonde* gave the latter timely warning of his Danger, observing he was neither entrenched as he ought, nor provided with Bridges sufficient for the Situation he was in, and at such a Distance from the main Army.

Several facts are at once apparent about these notes made by Swift. For example, all are concerned with the Duke of Ormonde's military campaign in Flanders in 1712; the Duke himself is mentioned by name in three of the entries. More particularly, they are concentrated upon the decisive events of the most crucial month of that campaign, the period between June 25 and July 24, 1712, and they all tend to magnify, or at least to justify, the difficult part played by Ormonde. All of them concern military actions with which Swift would be relatively unfamiliar and in which he might welcome the help of some knowledgeable person, although these same events grew out of international politics which Swift understood well enough, if he were given the facts.

Next, it should be remarked that Swift's notes are concerned with very *recent* foreign events, actions that (like the fall of Denain in July 1712) had taken place only a few months before Swift began his *History* and which were less than a year old when he finished in May 1713. They were events which, because of the necessary secrecy of international diplomacy and the confusion of a foreign war, as well as their proximity in time, might not be readily comprehensible to a contemporary English audience nor to a political historian, no matter how well informed.

Finally, and perhaps of most importance, is the fact that all the notes apply to that portion of Book IV of Swift's *History* which he told Stella was the "most troublesome" to write, and upon which he seems to have been stuck for so long. They come from that middle part of Book IV where Swift was to treat of Ormonde's recent campaign. This point in his composition he appears to have reached on October 29, 1712, only a day or so before Ormonde's arrival in England. But it is also where he still seemed to be stuck as late as December 12, 1712, despite the fact that in the meanwhile he had plenty of time to consult his friend of the "Brothers' Club," Ormonde, the chief actor in these events.

One can, of course, only speculate about the origin of the new information contained in these notes and incorporated in such a finished manuscript as that now at Windsor if the notes did not come from the Duke himself, the most logical source. At the conclusion of his "character" of Ormonde in *An Enquiry into the Behavior of the Queen's Last Ministry*,[9] Swift noted significantly that the Duke was "under some Disadvantage by an invincible Modesty," and these notes tend to glorify the part he played in the campaign of 1712. Again, Ormonde, a soldier, could not have been entirely proud of his actions in that campaign. He, like Bolingbroke, may also have been numbered among those Tories who, in January 1712/3 and later, for reasons other than those vital to the international negotiations in progress, opposed publication of Swift's *History* as "too dangerous."[10] So enlightened a historian as Trevelyan, for instance, entitles his appendix covering these events "The Military Betrayal of the Allies," citing Bolingbroke's giveaway of the "Restraining Orders" to the French, and Ormonde's warnings to Villars, relayed through Bolingbroke, of an impending confederate attack upon Nieuport or Flunes (the modern Furnes) as examples of the betrayal—actions which were later made the foundations for charges of high treason and causes for attainting by the Whigs of 1715.[11] For these reasons Ormonde (and probably Bolingbroke) cannot surely be taken (as logic would seem to demand) as the main source for the notes now in the Huntington Library. Yet, if Ormonde could not or would not supply the information for these notes, what were his reasons? And if not from Ormonde, then, from whom did Swift get his information? Without straining the facts, I believe that Sir Thomas Hanmer may be identified as that person. As Ormonde's close friend and one who accompanied him over to his new command as well as a person who held a position in Flanders equivalent almost to ambassador-at-large,[12] Hanmer appears to have been in close touch with Ormonde during the crucial days of June and July 1712 and was present at the occupation of Ghent.[13] Most certainly his cloak-and-dagger work behind the

[9]Irvin Ehrenpreis, ed. (Bloomington, 1957), p. 6.

[10]One of Bolingbroke's attempts about this time to keep something secret from Swift is recorded in *Journal to Stella* for Dec. 27, 1712 (II, 589).

[11]Trevelyan, *Queen Anne*, III, 216-222, 230-231. Ormonde was somewhat justified in his action because such a confederate attack, if successful, would have cut the Duke's line of communication along the Channel coast with Dunkirk. See especially Articles II and III of "Articles of Impeachment of High Treason, and Other High Crimes and Misdemeanors against James, Duke of Ormonde," *Political State*, X, 154-158.

[12]*Political State*, IV, for July 1712, p. 21.

[13]Sir Henry Bunbury, ed. *The Correspondence of Sir Thomas Hanmer* (London, 1838), pp. 23-24, 132-140. *Political State*, IV, for Aug. 1712, p. 87: "The same Day

lines (at Ostend, Ghent, and Bruges, for instance) suggests that he was kept well apprised of all the Duke's actions.[14] *He* would not be inhibited by Ormonde's modesty, nor would he likely be numbered among those Tories who thought Swift's *History* "too dangerous" to publish. Because he read one of Swift's manuscripts and made "observations," no matter how severe, upon the work between February and May 1713 (at which time, as was noted, Swift renewed work upon his *History*), Hanmer would seem implicitly to have approved of its publication. His own actions of June 1713 opposing two articles of commerce in the peace treaty are indications of his independent thinking in party matters. These notes, in fact, referring to what may be a separable (and certainly a separately paged) manuscript of Book IV, look to me very much like the kind of entries Swift may have made in following up the "observations" of some knowledgeable person like Sir Thomas Hanmer, who in May 1713 appears to have retained Book IV of Swift's manuscript for continued close scrutiny, perhaps of that section devoted to the actions of his friend the Duke of Ormonde, to some of which he had been an eyewitness.

[July 24, 1712] Sir *Thomas Hanmer*, who, as was hinted before, had not been idle all this while, set out from *Brussels*, and in the Evening arrived in the *British* camp [before Ghent], where he conferr'd with the Duke of *Ormond* and the Earl of *Strafford*."

[14]*Political State*, IV, for July 1712, p. 21: "A Report was spread, that the *English* had form'd a Design to seize *Ostend*: Which Rumour was undoubtedly occasion'd by Sir *Thomas Hanmer's* repairing to that Town towards the latter end of *June*, N.S; his causing the Depth of the Harbour to be sounded; and his viewing the Fortifications, with the Burgomaster Bawens, who was suppos'd to be in the *British* Interest. Whether this Surmize was well or ill grounded, Sir *Thomas Hanmer* having spent some days at *Bruges* and *Ghent*, where his Presence was thought necessary to prepare Matters for future Designs, that Gentleman, who from this time began to appear with the Title of the Queen of *Great Britain's* Minister, repair'd to *Brussels;* where the Earl of *Strafford* arriv'd the 11th of *July* N.S. . . ." [on his way to Ormonde's headquarters].

Chapter Three

SWIFT'S LETTER TO A YOUNG LADY
ON HER MARRIAGE

I

HERBERT DAVIS has recently called Jonathan Swift's "A Letter to a Young Lady on Her Marriage" (1723) "in its way a perfect composition."[1] The letter is of the greatest importance both in connection with Swift's general views upon women and marriage and with his own private difficulties over Stella and Vanessa of about this same time.[2] For too long, however, much needless confusion surrounded the identity of the person to whom the letter was supposed to be addressed. As a consequence, there have appeared several well-meant but mistaken interpretations of just what Swift intended. Fortunately, with the rediscovery of a fair copy in Swift's hand at the Huntington Library a generation ago, some of this uncertainty has been cleared up.[3] In the light of recent scholarship the letter needs to be reexamined therefore and, with the manuscript once more before us, some still current notions about it scrutinized more closely. From the time of Lord Orrery's *Remarks* of 1752[4] to recent comments of several American critics, it has been asserted that Swift's letter lends itself to universal application, especially to the condition of all newly married women. This, despite the fact, as Davis has noticed, that "these directions were intended to serve [the addressee] for the rest of her married life."[5] It should also be remarked here that

---

[1]*Prose Writings*, IX, xxx, 83-94, 373-375.

[2]Ricardo Quintana, *The Mind and Art of Jonathan Swift* (London, 1953), p. 355: "It may safely be said that no one who has not studied this *Letter* is qualified to hold any sort of opinion concerning the episodes in Swift's life involving Vanessa and Stella."

[3]See especially Katherine Hornbeak, "Swift's Letter to a Very Young Lady on Her Marriage," *HLQ*, VII (1944), 183-186.

[4]Pp. 102-103; see also Quintana, *Mind and Art of Swift*, p. 355, and T. Scott, *Prose Works*, XI, 114.

[5]*Prose Writings*, IX, xxix.

in 1723 these good counsels were rejected by the "Young Lady" of the title[6] and have been by most women ever since, almost by instinct. Such an intuitive reaction therefore raises the question of just how universal and applicable Swift's advice to a young married woman was, or ever may be.

Connected with this instinctive rejection of Swift's advice is another often expressed assumption and objection, that Swift in his recommendations to the young woman was unfeeling, insensitive, cynical: that he would have his young lady make herself over into a young man if she could.[7] Characteristically, Swift had urged the young woman who received his letter to cultivate to the best of her ability her mental and intellectual powers in order to compensate for the inevitable loss of her youthful beauty. Only thus, and with much good luck and in due time, would it be possible for her to become a friend and companion to her husband. It is often assumed that Swift was asking her to unsex herself: was she not urged to stifle the soft, natural passions of a lover and a mistress which she had experienced or would experience? It is taken for granted that Swift, as a consequence, must have been writing as an embittered antiromantic, as an anti-idealistic, even as a cynical foe to the exalting, rapturous nature of true love and of the happy marriage of romantic sentiment. And yet, near the conclusion of this very letter, in the most passionate terms, Swift went out of his way to warn the recipient at length against allowing herself to become a "Termagant," a virago, the kind of mannish woman that he is so often charged with urging his young lady and others to become.[8] Surely this fact should give pause to some of

---

[6]Pilkington, *Memoirs*, p. 55: "On our return to the Deanery House, we found there waiting our coming Dr Delany and Mr Rochford, to whose wife *A Letter of Advice to a new-married Lady* (published since in the Dean's works) was written, and which, by the by, the lady did not take as a compliment, either to her or the sex. . . ."

Samuel Richardson's coy, marrying minx, Pamela, also resented Swift's contempt of women, which she detected in most of his pieces, ". . . particularly in his *Letter of Advice to a new-marry'd Lady*: A Letter written in such a manner, as must disgust, instead of instructing, and looks more like the Advice of an Enemy to the Sex, and a partial one too, than a Friend to the particular lady" (*Pamela* [London, 1741-42], IV, 383).

[7]See Samuel Johnson's "Swift" in *The Lives of the English Poets*, ed. George Birkbeck Hill, 3 vols. (Oxford, 1905), III, 42: "The reader of Swift's *Letter to a Lady on her Marriage* may be allowed to doubt whether his opinion of female excellence ought implicitly to be admitted; for if his general thoughts on women were such as he exhibits, a very little sense in a lady would enrapture and a very little virtue would astonish him." See also William Makepeace Thackeray's "Swift" (*The English Humourists of the Eighteenth Century*), in *The Oxford Thackeray*, ed. George Saintsbury, 17 vols. (Oxford, 1908), XIV, 499, 505.

[8]*Prose Writings*, IX, 93.

with high hand. In these and a thousand other Cases, it will be prudent to retain as many of their Lectures in your Memory as you can, and then determine to act in full Opposition to them all.

I hope your Husband will interpose his Authority to limit you in the Trade of visiting; half a dozen Fools are in all Conscience as many as you should require, and it will be sufficient for you to see them twice a year, For, I think the Fashion does not exact, that Visits should be payd to Friends.

I advise that your Company at home should consist of Men rather than Women. To say the Truth, I never yet knew a tolerable Woman to be fond of her own Sex I confess, when both are mixed and well chosen, they put their best Qualityes forward, and there may be an Intercourse of Civility and good Will which with the Addition of some degree of Sense can make Conversation or any Amusements agreeable: But, a Knot of Ladyes got together by themselves, is a very School of Impertinence and Detraction, and it is well if those be the worst.

Let your Men-acquaintance be of your Husbands Choice, and not recommended to you by any She

HM 1599, p. 7 (fol. 4ʳ). A Leaf from Swift's "Letter to a Young Lady" (1723). See Chapter III.

A 100^l a year to be preached in any Province but Connaught, of Land not let in Lease above 40 years. Lease not to be for above 21 years. the Tenant bound by penal clause to improve to his successor. The present Tenant, if agreed to be preferred & so &c can but not sink. the Fellow to be chosen by Provost and 7 Senr. Present to hear the casting Voice to be odd just fellows to make up &. & if they refused, the Land to be left to Dr Stephens Colledge. The Fellow to be called Swifts Fellow to go to Eng^d in a Month; to stay ————

All these wrong, as Dr Delany's Scheam; Far more wise to have the the Fellow chosen every year. to have the 100 ^{l} a year —

The Executor to meet once a month about this affair

HM 14346, p. 4. A Draft of Jonathan Swift's First Will (1727).
See Chapter IV.

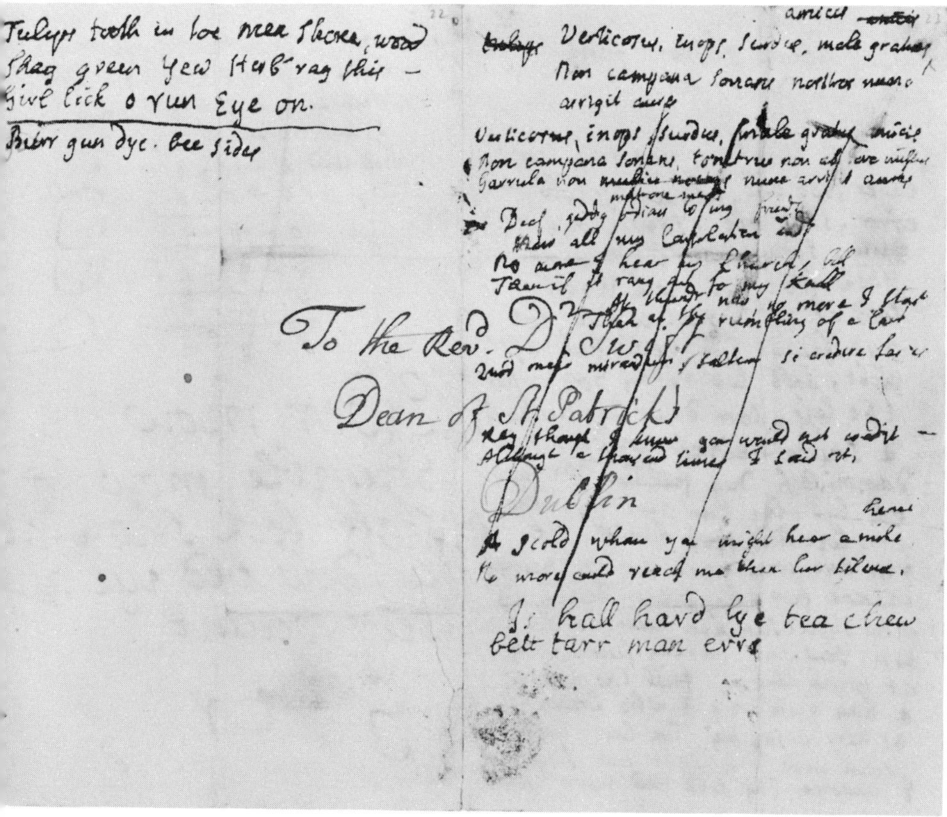
Tulyps tooth in loe mea Ihcore, wood
Shag green Yew Stub rag this —
Girl lick o run Eye on.
Brew gun dye. bee sides
Vertiginosus, inops, surdus, male gratus
Non campana sonans
Deaf, giddy, odious to my friends
To the Rev. Dr Swift
Dean of St Patricks
Dublin
I shall hard lye tea chew
bett tarr man evve

HM 14338, p. 23. An Early Draft of Swift's Autobiographical Poem "*On His Own* Deafness" (1734). See Chapter VI.

Polite.

Methinks *&* a Fire begins to smell well now.

[illegible manuscript lines]

HM 14341, p. D. A Fragment of Swift's *Polite Conversation* in Manuscript (1734-35). See Chapter VII.

Swift's critics and cause them to inquire into the questions more closely, who it was that Swift was addressing, and to what peculiar circumstances of the particular marriage Swift addressed himself. For the marriage was one that was arranged between heads of families, one in which exalted, romantic passions, so much admired and so surely assumed to be present, were not nor were ever likely to be present. It was, in fact, a rational, materialistic, and calculated contract of the kind that is still made today in France and on the Continent, one which matched two possibly congenial persons of different ages and temperaments who were united for the purposes of propagation and of allying similar family interests.

Again, it has quite recently been said that it "really does not matter" what young lady Swift had in mind, "since the proffered advice was intended to be of universal applicability."[9] Working from similar, universal assumptions, Sir Walter Scott, with an incurably romantic and intuitively sympathetic desire to put all women upon pedestals, called attention to Swift's seeming insensitivity and unfeelingness. When he commented upon the presence in the letter of "so little reverence for the individual"[10] addressed, Sir Walter was as much revealing unwittingly his own idealistic and romantic tendency to make all women angels or goddesses as he was defending the right of any individual to be respected as a thinking, feeling being, a proposition with which Swift would have had no quarrel. And when, in her recent psychoanalytic study, so perceptive a critic of Swift's works as Dr. Phyllis Greenacre mistakenly believes that the letter was addressed to another woman, "like several predecessors . . . named Elizabeth," and from this assumption draws some wrong conclusions about the role women played in Swift's life, the precise identity of the recipient does matter, and the circumstances of her marriage become important.[11] When Dr. Greenacre notices that Swift in his letter "warned the girl not to be sentimental, or rapturous," when she concludes (pejoratively, as I understand it) that "of love . . . or spirituality, Swift said nothing; all should be purely reasonable," we may very well ask whether, in the particular circumstances, Swift could reasonably have counseled anything but what he did, or be as insensitive, cruel, and brutally unfeeling as he has sometimes been accused. Given the nature of the marriage, what Swift had to do, in fact, was to teach an

[9]Quintana, *Mind and Art of Swift,* p. 355.
[10]Swift's *Works* (1824), IX, 208*n.*
[11]*Swift and Carroll* (New York, 1955), p. 49.

unworldly and naïve young beauty of nineteen how best to live with a grave, studious husband, twelve years older, in a family-arranged marriage: how to live with it and how to make the best of it. In such a situation, despite the young woman's inclinations, there was from the start little room for the raptures, exaltation, and romantic passions of true love.

If it should prove that the particular woman whom Swift addressed were entering into a marriage which was, as Swift surmised, beset by peculiar temperamental difficulties and unusual hazards of heredity; if that marriage were an arranged one, not a love match; if the young lady should be an unworldly innocent of nineteen, her husband a taciturn, morose man of thirty-one, already set in his ways, for Swift in his letter to have talked of rapturous sentiments, romantic passions, and the spirituality of love would have been, at best, a tactless error, at worst, brutal insensitivity. But if such were the case, the universality claimed for the letter might be discounted, and women's intuitive rejections of Swift's sound but highly specialized advice might be better explained. What may more clearly emerge is the relevance of parts of the letter to Swift's private life in 1723. With the recent rediscovery at the Huntington Library of the dated and signed fair copy of Swift's letter some of these facts and new conclusions begin to fall into place.

II

THE FAIR COPY of "A Letter to a Young Lady on Her Marriage" was one of the last Swift manuscripts to come into Mr. Huntington's possession by purchase from Charles Sessler of Philadelphia in 1925.[12] It is finely bound in cross-grained russet morocco. Stamped in gold on the front cover is the legend "Swift's/Autograph MSS./1723." The work appears to me to be that of an early nineteenth-century English or Irish binder. On the flyleaf and end pages are several penciled notations: a lot number, "457," a price which appears to read "£250-," the figures "18/ 18/-," the present Huntington accession number, "HM 1599," and a price of "$2000.00." Presumably this last was what Mr. Huntington paid for the manuscript.

At least one other collector (of whom Sessler's now have no record) must have owned the manuscript between the time that Mr. Huntington purchased it in 1925 and the early spring of 1849, when

---

[12]A private letter to me of Aug. 1962 from Miss Mabel Zahn of Charles Sessler's, Philadelphia.

the manuscript first came into the hands of Dr. (afterward Sir) William R. Wilde at Dublin, for use in his revised second edition of *The Closing Years of Dean Swift's Life:* "A few months ago we purchased from a person then upon the eve of emigrating to America, Swift's original manuscript of the celebrated Letter upon Marriage, already printed in several editions of his works. It consists of sixteen pages, beautifully and clearly written out, with scarcely an alteration. It is dated 11th February, 1722-3" (p. 181). Sir William's mistake in the total number of pages ("sixteen" should read "eighteen") shows that he was misled by the erroneous pagination of the volume, a mistake which may have occurred when the leaves were bound. The previous owner, then on the point of emigrating to the United States, was very likely one of the last of the dying Rochfort family, among whose possessions the outwardly creased and much-folded letter had been preserved since 1723, when Swift presented it to the new Mrs. John Rochfort for her guidance and constant consultation. For Swift began his essay by noticing that "The Hurry and Impertinence of receiving and paying Visits on Account of your Marriage, being now over;" and ended by expressing the wish that "you will keep this Letter in your Cabinet, and often examine impartially your whole Conduct by it. . . ."

Although the manuscript has recently been collated,[13] it has never been published, and it is therefore reproduced at the close of this chapter. HM 1599 consists of nine leaves of watermarked paper (9 x 7 inches), in the hand of Swift, beginning "Madam" and ending with the signature "Jonath Swift." It is dated from "Deanry-house/ Febr. 11th 1722-3," as Wilde first noticed. The 18 pages have been numbered twice, the second time in darker pencil. By some error pages 8-9 (fols. 4^v and 5^r) were skipped, so that the succeeding pages are misnumbered. Previous folding down the middle before it was bound has damaged the outer leaves of the manuscript a little along the crease, affecting one or two words here and there. Swift also made half a dozen or more corrections or insertions as he wrote. But, in general, this manuscript is a clean, well-preserved, beautifully written specimen of Swift's hand.

In 1944 Katherine Hornbeak published a valuable note upon "Swift's Letter to a Very Young Lady on Her Marriage."[14] It finally

---

[13]*Prose Writings*, IX, 374. The following addition needs to be made to the collation: "Amusement" (p. 88, l. 34 of the printed text) reads "Amusements" in the MS (fol. 4^r).

[14]*HLQ*, VII (1944), 183-186.

cleared up a misunderstanding which had persisted for 165 years, about the precise identity of the "Very Young Lady" to whom the letter was addressed. The difficulty was to know whether she was Lady "Betty" (Elizabeth) Rochfort, née Moore, the younger daughter of Henry, third Earl of Drogheda, whom George Rochfort married on January 24, 1704; or Deborah Rochfort, née Staunton, the only child of Dr. Thomas Staunton, a Master in Chancery and M.P. for the city of Galway from 1727 to 1732, whom John Rochfort, George's younger brother, married on January 19, 1722/3. The confusion was first started by John Nichols in 1779 in a note to his quarto *Supplement* to the *Works* of Swift.[15] Usually a conscientious editor, he, for some reason, initially misconstrued a remark about the recipient of the letter and her reaction to it, recorded by Letitia Pilkington in her *Memoirs* (p. 55). Nichols thereafter repeated his assertion in later editions, that "This letter was addressed to Lady *Betty Moore*, youngest daughter of *Henry* earl of *Drogheda*, on her marriage to Mr. *George Rochfort*." In this error he was followed, however cautiously, by Sir Walter Scott and later nineteenth- and twentieth-century editors and commentators, despite much earlier evidence to the contrary.[16]

Miss Hornbeak verified the respective dates of marriage of George and John Rochfort from John Lodge's *Peerage of Ireland* and noted the clear-cut statement made there, that the letter had been directed to Deborah Rochfort and not to Lady Betty.[17] A clinching argument was the conclusive dating at the end of the Huntington manuscript, which showed that Swift's letter could only have been addressed to Deborah Staunton, now Rochfort, a few weeks after her marriage, at the moment when the honeymoon was ended and just as married life began in earnest. Since Lady Betty Rochfort, as Swift himself mentioned in this very essay,[18] was a horrible example of what

[15]Vol. XIV, p. 675 (note to Vol. II, Pt. II, p. 40).

[16]Swift's *Works* (1824), IX, 208; T. Scott, *Prose Works*, XI, 114; *Swift and Carroll*, p. 49.

[17]London, 1754, III, 378 and n. k.: "To her (Deborah, only Daughter to Thomas Staunton, Esq.) it was, that the ingenious Dean Swift wrote that incomparable Letter for the Conduct of her Life in the Marriage State, printed amongst his miscellaneous Works."

[18]*Prose Writings*, IX, 94; and HM 1599, fol. 9ʳ: ". . . learn to value and esteem your Husband for those good Qualityes which he really possesses, and not to fancy others in him which he certainly has not. . . . But my Caution is occasioned by a Lady of your Allyance, marryed to a very valuable Person, whom yet She is so unfortunate as to be always commending for those Perfections to which he can least pretend."

Swift hoped Deborah would *not* become, John Nichols' mistake about the two women of quite different characters may well have colored some of the late eighteenth- and hostile nineteenth-century interpretations of Swift's letter. Thanks to Miss Hornbeak and Herbert Davis, it now may once more be possible to peruse Swift's letter as it was intended to be read, to add something new about the young girl to whom it was sent, her character and family, the husband she married, and the precise circumstances of their marriage.

Lord Orrery long ago remarked that Swift's "Letter to a Young Lady" has a general and universal application as well as a localized and particular significance.[19] Not the least aspect of our present interest inevitably involves us in an examination of Jonathan Swift's considered views upon women and upon marriage in that crucial year, 1723. At that moment precisely he was suspended between powerful repulsions and attractions: he for them and they for him— of Stella and Vanessa, of Esther Johnson and Esther Vanhomrigh— two of the three women in his life whom Swift might have married. It may be best, however, to begin by further examining the specific circumstances of the family backgrounds, the respective personalities, and the nature of the Dublin society out of which John Rochfort and Deborah Staunton came and into which they returned after marriage, before turning to the wider meanings or the relationship to his own personal dilemma of 1723 of Swift's "Letter to a Young Lady."

III

THE ROCHFORT (sometimes spelled Rochford) family of Westmeath, of French origin, was established in Ireland from the times of Henry III.[20] During the seventeenth and eighteenth centuries they settled at Gaulstown, near Mullingar, County Westmeath, about thirty-seven miles from Dublin. Gaulstown House, a grim, rambling, old brick manorhouse dating from the reign of Edward III, was situated, until torn down by a later owner, by an artificial lake and upon an extensive, well laid-out, beautifully kept-up demesne.[21] During the period when Robert Rochfort (1652-1727), in turn the Attorney General of Ireland, Lord Chief Baron of the Exchequer, a longtime

[19]*Remarks*, p. 103; see also *Prose Writings*, IX, xxx: ". . . addressed to a private person on a particular occasion."

[20]Digested from *Peerage of Ireland*, III, 369-381: "Rochfort, Earl of Belvedere."

[21]Ball, *Corresp.*, II, 280, n.2, and facing III, 96, a photograph of Gaulstown and gardens as they were in the late nineteenth century.

M.P. for Westmeath, and sometime Irish Privy Counselor, was head of the family, Gaulstown was as famous locally as Moor Park had been under Sir William Temple. In the times of James II, Robert Rochfort, the then popular Recorder of Londonderry, a staunch Whig and a loyal Protestant, was forced to flee to England, and, in 1689, his estate was sequestrated, himself proscribed. The next year, however, he returned to Ireland with the forces of William III, at first as one of the three Commissioners of Oyer and Terminer, and, soon after, as one of the three Commissioners of the Great Seal of Ireland.

Swift may have become acquainted with Robert Rochfort and his family through the Temples, possibly as early as 1690 or perhaps in 1695.[22] For it was through the influence of the Temple family, and—more particularly—by means of a private treaty with Sir John Temple, his predecessor in office, that Robert Rochfort was appointed Attorney General in 1695. In August 1695 he was once more reelected M.P. for Westmeath, and almost immediately thereafter he was elected Speaker of the Irish House of Commons. In 1703, when the second Duke of Ormonde came over as the new Queen's Tory Lord Lieutenant, Rochfort anticipated Swift and changed political parties.[23] Thereafter he became more Tory than the Queen. As a reward he was elevated to the rank of Chief Baron in 1707, a post he lost in 1714 upon the accession of George I. And yet the fortunes of his family continued to flourish; they grew even greater in the times of the second and third Georges in the persons of the first and second Earls of Belvedere, Robert's grandson and great-grandson. It has been truly said that until 1814 the Rochforts had "ruled Westmeath with a rod of iron for nearly a century and a half."[24] With the death of the childless second Earl of Belvedere, the fortunes of the Rochfort family declined rapidly.

[22]F. Elrington Ball, *The Judges in Ireland, 1221-1921*, 2 vols. (London, 1926), II, 4. Swift was in Ireland from June 1690 to mid-Aug. 1691, for some of that time in the service of Sir Robert Southwell, Secretary of State for Ireland (Ball, *Corresp.*, I, 3, n.3). The three commissioners also traveled in Southwell's entourage. See also *Calendar of State Papers, Domestic Series, . . . 1695* (London, 1908), p. 339 and p. 119: "[Dublin Castle, Dec. 7, 1695. Lord Capel to Mr. Vernon.] My concerning myself in the attorney general's place between the old [Sir John Temple] and the new [Robert Rochfort] is upon desire of Lady Gifford [Giffard] and Sir John Temple, and a 'wholy' submission in Mr. Rochford to my award of what formerly has been in treaty between them." In Dec. 1695 Swift visited Dublin from his cure in Northern Ireland (*Corresp.*, I, 18, n.2).

[23]*Judges in Ireland*, II, 3-4, 28.

[24]James Woods, *Annals of Westmeath* (Dublin, 1907), p. 69.

Old Robert Rochfort died at Gaulstown on October 10, 1727, aged 75, and was buried there. George Rochfort (1682-1730), the elder of his two sons by Hanna Handcock, sister of Sir William Handcock, succeeded his father as head of the family but died three years later in July 1730. John (sometimes called "Nim" or Nimrod), the second son, about whom more will be said, was born in 1692 and died in 1771. Like his father (and like Swift himself) he lived a long life. In January 1704, as he was determined to do for both his sons, Robert Rochfort arranged a marriage between George and Lady Elizabeth ("Betty") Moore, who bore her husband five sons. At the time of his marriage George Rochfort was given Gaulstown by his father, and so Lady Betty became mistress of the estate.[25] On April 7, 1708, no doubt through the influence of his father, George Rochfort was also appointed Chief Chamberlain of the Court of Exchequer, a sinecure he held until his death. After his father died in 1727, George represented Westmeath in Parliament for the next three years, and at his own death he was succeeded there by his eldest son, Robert, who was, in turn, raised to the peerage in 1737 as Baron Belfield, in 1751 becoming Viscount Belfield, and in 1756 was created the first Earl of Belvedere.

The second Robert Rochfort (1708-1771), George's eldest son, was educated at the Dublin school of Swift's closest Irish friend, Dr. Thomas Sheridan, and at Trinity College, Dublin.[26] In August 1736 he married as his second wife the beautiful Mary Molesworth, eldest daughter of Richard, Lord Viscount Molesworth.[27] She was sixteen and he was twenty-eight, a discrepancy in age of twelve years, as was also the case in 1723 with the marriage between Deborah Staunton and John Rochfort. In 1744, after his wife had borne him three sons and a daughter, Robert, the arrogant and suspicious future Earl of Belvedere, suspecting his still youthful wife of having incestuous criminal relations with his younger brother Arthur, immured her at Gaulstown and held her virtually a prisoner there for

[25] *Judges in Ireland*, II, 68; and Ball, *Corresp.*, II, 280, n. 2.

[26] Burtchaell, p. 712.

[27] What follows is digested mostly from Woods's *Annals of Westmeath*, pp. 69-72. Yet as early as 1732, at the time of the death of the young first wife of "such a young Villain" as Robert Rochfort even then appeared to Swift to be, Swift wrote to Charles Ford from Dublin on June 30, 1732, to say that already the future first Earl of Belvedere "hath shown himself the most avaricious, unnatural undutifull Rogue you ever heard of . . ." (*The Letters of Jonathan Swift to Charles Ford*, ed. D. Nichol Smith [Oxford, 1935], p. 138).

the next thirty years. The baronet himself moved to his new estate of Belvedere, a mile or so away. As a result of forged letters and a rigged trial he was also awarded £20,000 damages from his brother. When Arthur fled Ireland because he was unable to pay and then later returned, heartless Robert Rochfort had him arrested and put in prison, where he remained until his death. It was this ruthless, cruel, and avaricious streak in the Rochfort family, in which old Robert, his sons, and grandsons shared,[28] that Swift may have had in mind when composing his letter for Deborah Staunton's guidance.[29] Obviously Swift could not there mention to a new young wife what he was later to say about the less admirable characteristics of his friend John Rochfort in private letters to Dr. Sheridan and others. But these inherited family characteristics of the Rochforts should be kept firmly in mind when judging the tone and manner with which Swift addressed the "Very Young Lady" of his letter.

As an interesting aside, it might usefully be noticed here that in the 1890's when the young James Joyce was a student at Belvedere College, Dublin, built by the second earl in 1775, he became so fascinated by this eighteenth-century love tragedy of the Rochfort family that he some years later contemplated writing a small book about the matter, as Richard Ellman has noticed.[30] Eventually Joyce incorporated the theme of the incestuous younger brother and the adulterous wife into his theory of Shakespeare's life and art, so brilliantly developed by Stephen Dedalus in the "Scylla and Charybdis" chapter of *Ulysses*. It is also remarkable that Sir Walter Scott, without knowing as much about the Rochfort family as Joyce did, detected, with his usual compassion and intuition, the seriousness of tone and admonitory manner of Swift's letter. Sir Walter remarked upon the "so little reverence for the individual . . . addressed, and such a serious apprehension expressed lest she may fall into the worst of the errors pointed out. . . ."[31] The point here is that Swift knew in-

[28]*Corresp.*, IV, 465 (Swift to Sheridan from Dublin, March 2, 1735): "I doubt the Rochforts, both Male and Female, have a very sharp sense of feeling, upon the score of Avarice. . . ."

[29]*Corresp.*, IV, 501 (Swift to Sheridan from Dublin, June 5, 1736): "except that damn'd vice of Avarice, he is a very agreeable man." Yet Sheridan, in an earlier reply (*Corresp.*, IV, 462), nicknamed the gossipy Lady Betty Rochfort "Lady Betty Tattle" and John Rochfort "*John Solemn*," and he threatened, if he were not paid forthwith, to lampoon them both under these names in a manner that suggests Swift's *Polite Conversation* of 1738.

[30]*James Joyce* (New York, 1959), pp. 35-36.

[31]Swift's *Works* (1824), IX, 208.

timately the strain of moroseness and cruelty that ran in the family and the avarice of heart of his thirty-one-year-old friend John Rochfort, the "Nim" or Nimrod of the Gaulstown days, when Swift visited there almost annually from 1715 to 1721.[32] He also knew of the complete unworldliness, innocent beauty, and spoiled-child vanity of Deborah Staunton in 1723 when he addressed his letter to this nineteen-year-old young lady. Swift thus may have feared a similar tragic outcome to that marriage, in which arrangement he may also have had a hand.[33]

IV

DEBORAH STAUNTON (1703-1737) was the only child of Swift's life-long friends Thomas and Bridget Staunton (sometimes spelled Stanton). At the commencement of his "Letter to a Young Lady" Swift recalled that "I have always born an entire Friendship to Your Father and Mother." The family came originally from England and then from Galway, but at the time when Swift first knew the Stauntons, they were residing at Dublin.[34] With a friendship of such long standing it seems to be quite possible that Swift may have known Deborah Staunton from birth or have been acquainted with her since she was a little girl. At the time of her marriage to John Rochfort she was nineteen and a half years old, just five or six months short of her twentieth birthday, and twelve years younger than her husband, exactly the same difference in age that existed in 1736 between the first Earl of Belvedere and his youthful bride of sixteen. For Deborah Staunton was born late in June or possibly on the first of July 1703, and her baptism was recorded on July 2, 1703, in the *Register* of St. Audoën's Parish, Dublin: "1703, July 2nd, Deborah the dautr. of Jon: Staunton Esq & Bridgatt his wyf bt."[35] As Swift was later to

[32]See especially *Poems*, I, 276-283.

[33]HM 1599, fol. 1r: "I have always born an entire Friendship to Your Father and Mother; and the Person they have chosen for Your Husband hath been for some Years past my particular Favorite. I have long wished You might come together. . . ." Fol. 5r: "yours was a Match of Prudence and common good Liking, without any Mixture of that ridiculous Passion, which has no Being but in Play-books and Songs."

[34]*Journal to Stella*, I, 188 (Feb. 10, 1710/1): "I send a letter this post to one Mr. Staunton, and I direct it to Mr. Acton's in St. Michael's Lane. He formerly lodged there. . . ." A. Martin Freeman, *Vanessa and Her Correspondence with Jonathan Swift* (London, 1921), hereafter referred to as *Vanessa and Swift*, pp. 193-195, first printed the letter to Staunton mentioned by Swift in the *Journal to Stella*. In it Swift says of Staunton (p. 193), "you were a person I had long known."

[35]I am much indebted to Canon G. S. McPhail of St. Werburgh's Vestry, Dublin, for discovering and copying out for me this baptismal entry.

mention, his friends the Stauntons were at about that same time living in rented lodgings in St. Michael's Lane near St. Audoën's where he had visited them.[36] John Staunton, Thomas' brother, sometime Recorder of Galway City and M.P. for the same, was exactly Swift's age and had attended Trinity College from 1685 to 1689, when Swift was an undergraduate there.[37] It may have been through John Staunton that Swift became acquainted with his brother Thomas, then a rising young lawyer.

Although Swift had somewhat lost touch with the Stauntons between 1703 and 1710, he was always ready to do them a good turn when he was able, and Thomas Staunton did the same for Swift in return. For instance, in 1710-1711, when Swift was high in the favor of the Tory ministry of Oxford and Bolingbroke at London, with the help of one hundred guineas by way of an emolument from Staunton, Swift was able to procure a position for his friend under Henry Temple, later Viscount Palmerston.[38] The job, a legal one, may have been connected with Temple's sinecure as First Remembrancer of the Irish Exchequer, of which Robert Rochfort was Chief Baron until 1714. In 1726, when Swift quarreled bitterly with Palmerston about another matter, the Dean mistakenly accused the Viscount of firing Staunton from the position. As it turned out, the prudent and ambitious Staunton had quit because he had not received an expected or requested raise in pay.[39] In 1716 he and Captain John Pratt, Deputy Vice-Treasurer of Ireland, good-naturedly undertook to supervise some of the debts and investments of the new Dean of St. Patrick's. By that time Staunton was well enough off, or enough Swift's friend, to refuse payment for his help, a kindness which a little embarrassed Swift, who hated to be in debt to anyone.[40] Much later, in 1725, when all of Swift's by then considerable fortune of £1,200 was in danger through the defalcation of Captain John Pratt, Thomas Staunton once more protected Swift's financial interests and helped to recover most of the sum for his friend.[41] Thus, each man helped the other in generous ways and at various times. I believe that Swift

[36] *Journal to Stella*, I, 188; *Vanessa and Swift*, pp. 193-195.

[37] Burtchaell, p. 766.

[38] *Vanessa and Swift*, p. 194; *Corresp.*, III, 298.

[39] *Corresp.*, III, 123, 124, 126.

[40] *Corresp.*, II, 201, 202, 229.

[41] *Corresp.*, III, 47, 64.

also helped arrange the marriage of Deborah Staunton and John Rochfort and may have felt some personal responsibility for its success. "I have long wished you might come together," he wrote in the first paragraph of his letter. Both Thomas Staunton and old Robert Rochfort were, after all, his close friends of long standing, and both their children he had known for many years.

The alliance by marriage with the rich and powerful Rochfort family as well as his own considerable legal talent and great personal integrity appear almost at once to have helped to advance the career of Deborah Staunton's father. The family was now well enough off to move to Usher's Quay, a fashionable address not far from where Stella then lived.[42] In June 1727 Thomas Staunton was appointed one of the four Masters in Chancery.[43] Later in the same year he was elected Member of Parliament for Galway City in the first parliament of George II.[44] On March 5, 1728, he was also awarded an honorary LL.D. from Trinity College; thereafter he was called "Dr. Staunton."[45] He died on March 5, 1731/2, a few days before the end of the third session of Parliament, in which he served with John Rochfort, his son-in-law, and other Tories on several important committees. His death seems to have been a great loss to the Irish bar as well as to the cause of good government in Ireland, and he was mourned by more than his family.[46]

After her husband's death the Honorable Mrs. Staunton moved in to live with her only child and her son-in-law John Rochfort. In his notes and letters of 1735-1736 to "Nim," Swift sometimes remembered to send his regards to both mother and daughter.[47] By that time

[42] *Vanessa and Swift*, pp. 198, 199.

[43] Rowley Lascelles, comp. *Liber munerum publicorum Hiberniae*, 2 vols. (London, 1852), I, Pt. II, 22. Staunton's patent was dated June 12, 1727. See also James L. Hughes, *Patentee Officers in Ireland, 1173-1826* (Dublin, 1960), p. 123.

[44] *The Journals of the House of Commons of the Kingdom of Ireland*, 21 vols. (Dublin, 1763-65), V, 418, 636; VI, 6.

[45] I am indebted to H. W. Parke, vice-provost and librarian of T.C.D., for the following, copied from the College Register for March 5, 1728: "The same day ye grace of ye house for an Honorary Degree of Dr. in Laws to Mr. Thomas Staunton and Mr. Colley Lyons."

[46] *Pue's Occurrences*, Vol. XXIX, No. 20, for Sat., March 4–Tues., March 7, 1731/2: "Dublin, March 7. On Sunday Night [March 5, 1731/2.] died Thomas Staunton, Esq; one of the Masters in Chancery, and Member of Parliament for the Town of Gallway, he was a Gentleman of great Integrity, and much esteemed by all, who had the Pleasure of his Acquaintance, so that his Death is universally lamented."

[47] *Vanessa and Swift*, p. 207.

John Rochfort's growing family was settled in a fine town house on Jervais Street, Dublin, and (as an inheritance from old Robert Rochfort) in the summers at a country estate at New Park, six miles north of the city.[48] Although "Nim" Rochfort had been one of Stella's executors in 1728 and was to be one of the commissioners who inquired into Swift's lunacy in 1742, the long friendship between the two men meanwhile showed signs of cooling. About 1735-1736 Swift appears to have a little resented the fact that he was not invited to spend part of the summer at New Park, a hunter's paradise, as he had done at Gaulstown earlier.[49] At this same time trouble also arose between Dr. Thomas Sheridan at his new school in Cavan and his old friend of Gaulstown days about payment of tuition for the education and for the costly actions of a delinquent younger son of the deceased George Rochfort.[50] His brother John had assumed jointly with the ailing Lady Betty Rochfort, who died in March 1736, the responsibility for educating the boy.[51] Swift took Sheridan's side in the quarrel and had several times to touch up Rochfort about paying the debt with a severity that could only have been estranging. Yet Swift was able to write to Sheridan in 1736 that "except for that damn'd Vice of Avarice . . . [John Rochfort] is a very agreeable Man."[52]

In 1723, the year of her marriage, Deborah Staunton bore her first child Robert, who died young and unmarried. Another son was born in 1735; in the following year, her first daughter. A second daughter, born probably early in 1737, completed the family.[53] On November 27, 1736, Deborah, her mother, and John Rochfort were in a carriage accident at Dublin; both ladies as well as the coachman were injured, according to the *Dublin Evening Post*:

Last Saturday Night ——— Rochfort, Esq; his Lady and her Mother, driving in their Coach through Pill-lane, something gave the Horses a Fright, which by the suddeness of the Shock pitch'd the Coachman out of the Box, and the Horses having then no Guide, ran without any Person being able to stop them till they went to Barrack-street: the two Ladies

---

[48]*Corresp.*, IV, 493 and n. 1.

[49]*Corresp.*, IV, 501.

[50]*Corresp.*, V, 40 and n. 2. The son in question was probably George's youngest, William Rochfort (*Peerage of Ireland*, III, 379).

[51]*Peerage of Ireland*, I, 331, "Moore, Earl of Drogheda."

[52]*Corresp.*, IV, 501.

[53]*Peerage of Ireland*, III, 379.

jump'd out of the Coach and were both very much hurt, and the Coach-man so bruis'd that his Life is despair'd of.[54]

Injuries received in this accident may well have hastened the prema-ture death of Deborah Staunton a year later, aged thirty-three. She died on November 12, 1737, less than two weeks after her cardplay-ing friend Lady Anne Acheson, the "Modern (Dublin) Lady" of Swift's satiric poem of 1729.[55] At the time of her death Deborah Staunton was but two years older than her husband had been when he married her in 1723, fourteen years before. In 1746 John Rochfort married the widow of a clergyman from Westmeath. He died a few months after the death of this second wife on January 30, 1771.[56] So far as can be known now, John Rochfort's marriage to Deborah Staunton had proved to be a reasonably happy and fruitful union, despite the fact that it had been arranged by their families.

V

THE FIRST of the two opening paragraphs by way of preamble in Swift's letter concludes by promising to instruct the "Young Lady" of its title about "how you are to act" and "what you ought to avoyd" (fol. 1ᵛ).[57] These positive and negative counsels thus become the complementary double theme of the following account. With the second of these advices, the "don't's" of married life, the letter proper begins and so continues for ten paragraphs of admonition. The sec-ond ten paragraphs of more positive exhortation, the "do's" of Dub-lin life, then follow. Three paragraphs are added before the closure, and they appear to be reflective afterthoughts. They hold up to view as horrible warnings a couple of particularized local examples drawn from observations of some contemporary Dublin marriages with which the newly married young lady would be familiar. The first ex-ample may have in mind someone like Thomas Sheridan's shrewish termagant of a wife, "Mrs. Mac" (MacFadden, her maiden name), chief of the "Tribe of bold, swaggering, rattling Ladyes" in Dublin

[54]Vol. V, No. 42, for Saturday, Nov. 27–Tuesday, Nov. 30, 1736; see also Vol. V, No. 43, for Nov. 30–Dec. 4, 1736: "Mr. Rochfort's Coachman who was last Week pitch'd from the Coach-Box in Pill-lane, died on Monday last of the Bruises he then receiv'd."

[55]*Poems*, II, 443-453.

[56]*Peerage of Ireland*, III, 379, and *Notes and Queries*, 8th Ser., II (July–Dec. 1892), 46. John Rochfort died in the house he still maintained in Jervais Street, Dublin.

[57]References within the text are to HM 1599.

(fol. 8ᵛ), whom Swift had satirized in verse not long before.[58] The next paragraph refers to the public but ill-judged enthusiasms of Lady Betty Rochfort for qualities which, in fact, were lacking in her good-natured husband, George Rochfort. Only the fair copy at the Huntington alludes to "a Lady of your Allyance" (fol. 9ʳ) rather than to "a Lady of your Acquaintance" as the printed versions have it;[59] it is certain that Swift had in mind here Lady Betty Rochfort, the mistress of Gaulstown. The third paragraph hints in a veiled way that would be understood by the young woman at the avarice and tight-fistedness of her new husband. The short closure of the letter ends with a warning and a blessing, to consult these counsels often in the hope that it will be an exemplary marriage if the advice is followed.

Something of this same two-part structure, this invidious comparison made between men and women in general, between the positive and negative aspects of contemporary Dublin marriages, and—most noticeably—between the few slight virtues of Deborah Staunton and the many talents of her paragon of a husband, is to be found everywhere throughout the letter. As it ranges from the general to the particular, the effect, upon me at least, is one of caricature, so gross are the comparisons. In the letter Swift twice chose to single out to praise above all else in Deborah Staunton's character, in contrast to that of her husband, "the Goodness of your *own* Disposition," as the fair copy alone expresses it (fols. 1ʳ, 5ʳ).[60] With youthful good looks, she was further characterized as an unworldly, romantically inclined but virtuous young woman of limited education, a girl still a little possessed by "that violent Passion for fine Cloaths so predominant in Your Sex" (fol. 2ᵛ). Both Stella and Vanessa were modest, sometimes even careless dressers, and they were the sickly, fatherless older daughters of large families. By contrast, it would appear that according to Swift, Deborah Staunton's chief attributes, her good nature and her virtuousness, were of a much lower order than Stella's humane spirit, her trained intelligence, and wider worldly experience, or Vanessa's greater physical charms, higher spirits, and warmer nature. Untutored and sheltered as she was from life, Deborah Staunton appears in Swift's letter as a healthy, beautiful, likable, but somewhat

---

[58]*Poems*, I, 219-221. See also III, 954-955. Faulkner subtitled his version of Swift's satire, "A quiet Life, and a good Name" (1719), "*To a Friend, who married a Shrew*."

[59]See, for instance, *Prose Writings*, IX, 94.

[60]Italics mine. See *Prose Writings*, IX, 85: "the Goodness of your Disposition."

spoiled only child. Like the youthful Emma Bovary whom she seems at moments to resemble, this young lady, as Swift perceived, at nineteen displayed a similar dangerous tendency toward what was much later to be called *bovarysme*: romanticizing erotic love, idealizing married life, and giving too much thought to dress and pretty clothes.[61] In these respects, after marriage, she might have been tempted into some of Stella's youthful extravagances or into Vanessa's uncurable romanticizing. Of these pitfalls Swift dutifully warned her.

In fact consciously or otherwise, Swift may have deliberately underrated Deborah Staunton's many other good qualities in order to pique her pride and to deflate her romanticizing nature, just as he seems, quite consciously, to have exalted and idealized in an irritatingly masculine way the superior virtues of her husband, so that "you might in time make your self worthy of Him" (fol. 1ʳ). It is easy to imagine what Stella's witty or Vanessa's fiery reply to this assumption of natural male superiority might have been. Swift characterized John Rochfort as "a wise man" (fol. 1ᵛ), "a Man of good Education and Learning, of an excellent Understanding and an exact Tast" (fol. 4ᵛ), all of which, no doubt, he was. But in view of what Swift had afterward to say of Rochfort, when he here portrays him as a man of "great modesty" and of "a most amiable Sweetness of Temper," with "an usuall Disposition to Sobriety and Virtue" (fol. 5ʳ), we may well ask whether these may not be glossings over of John Rochfort's taciturnity, moroseness, grave manner, and avarice. When Swift writes that "he is not capable of using you ill" (fol. 5ʳ), the pen falters in the fair copy,[62] and we, recalling John Rochfort's later shabby treatment of Dr. Sheridan and the characteristically ruthless Rochfort manner in which his nephew the first Earl of Belvedere treated his two young wives, may be allowed to be a bit skeptical about this assurance.

In view of his own continuing high regard for both Stella and Vanessa, even in the crisis of 1722-1723, should we not discount somewhat in this letter Swift's inflation of the masculine virtues and his correspondingly vigorous devaluation of those of the generality of womankind? If Swift literally believed what he here had to say about

---

[61]See, for instance, Harry Levin's brilliant discussion of *bovarysme* in *The Gates of Horn* (New York, 1963), pp. 249-250.

[62]Swift wrote "ill," then "will," crossed out both and wrote "ill" again, which he let stand.

women in general, how could he have preserved so much as a modicum of respect for even a Stella or a Vanessa? For in this letter men are presented as being wise, well-bred, of good sense, masterly, learned, modest, gentle-natured, brave, possessors of many good qualities, and, like John Rochfort, wanting in "so very few Accomplishments" (fol. 9ʳ). By contrast, women are represented as being not fond of their own sex (fol. 4ʳ), as employing "more Thought, Memory, and Application to be Fools, than would serve to make them wise and usefull," as "a Sort of Species hardly a Degree above a Monkey" (fol. 6ʳ⁻ᵛ).⁶³ He remarks (what surely has been made abundantly clear at this point) upon the "little Respect I have for the generality of your Sex" and upon "all the Nonsense and Frippery of your own Sex" in conversation (fols. 5ᵛ, 6ʳ⁻ᵛ). Women, Swift says, through no fault of their own are illiterate, and yet those called "Learned women" are impertinent, talkative, and conceited (fol. 7ʳ). In a passage which might especially have offended Vanessa if ever she saw the letter, Swift summed up: "Pray observe how insignificant Things are the common Race of Ladyes when they have passed their Youth and Beauty; how contemptible they appear to the Men, and yet more contemptible to the younger [Part] Sort of their own Sex . . ." (fol. 7ᵛ). But he quickly added, in a passage which might have mollified Stella if she ever read it, "Whereas I have known Ladyes at sixty, to whom all the polite Part of the Court and Town payd their Addresses without any further View than that of enjoying the Pleasure of their Conversation" (fol. 8ʳ).⁶⁴ Yet all of this must have been cold comfort to the lively, lovely, newly married nineteen-year-old Deborah Staunton.

A letter upon a woman's role in marriage in 1722-1723 would of course have been of the greatest interest to a curious Stella or Vanessa. But could either or both of them, if they read it, believe that she, and she alone, was exempted in Swift's mind from the otherwise sweeping censure of the generality of her sex? In Vanessa's case, since she had only very recently received in letters from Swift almost identical

---

⁶³A dozen years later Swift, in an Anglo-Latin phrase, formulated this notion, that apes imitate humans, humans apes, but with more malice, so as to include both men and women. See "Swift's Games with Language in Rylands English MS. No. 659," *Bulletin of the John Rylands Library*, XXXVI (March 1954), 437, 446.

⁶⁴*Journal to Stella*, II, 558 (Sept. 18, 1712), records Swift's and others' great pleasure in conversing with the still charming but aged Lady Orkney, William III's mistress, who Swift said was "the wisest woman I ever saw."

counsel,[65] the doubt raised may have been great, possibly great enough to require the reassurance which Swift was unable to give. If on the other side, the young woman to whom the letter was addressed were submissive, gullible, or even stupid enough to accept without question the unflattering evaluation that Swift made of herself and her sex, why should such a paragon as John Rochfort or any sensible man have wished to marry her? If, however, no matter how sheltered and unworldly she was, she possessed a normal amount of pride and even a moderate degree of intelligence, she could not but reject Swift's characterization of herself and her sex and with it some of his well-meant advice. According to Mrs. Letitia Pilkington, Deborah Staunton, although no Stella or Vanessa, *did* resent and reject Swift's counsels. It is hard to see how she or any other self-respecting woman could have done otherwise.

But this response on the part of the recipient raises the question of why Swift, in his "Letter to a Young Lady," bore down so heavily, even heavy-handedly, upon women in general and upon Deborah Staunton in particular. Why was John Rochfort, who had his personal faults, or were men generally, let off so lightly here by Swift, the misanthrope? Surely he must have known Deborah Staunton well enough to guess that she would not readily accept all that his letter to her had to say about herself and her sex. It is possible that Swift suspected that she might grow indignant and rouse up in her own defense, a goal to be desired. In an arranged marriage a youthful and inexperienced Deborah Staunton had quickly to be saved from what later was called *bovarysme*, and that required forceful methods. Swift also knew that to be docile or overly submissive was disastrous for the wife of a Rochfort. It may also be that about 1722-1723 Deborah Staunton was associated in Swift's mind with the similarly passionate and sometimes embarrassingly romantic importunities of Vanessa, which troubled Swift and about which he wrote to her in an identical vein.[66] It may be, too, that Swift, who was often charged (although unfairly) with the same traits of avarice, undue gravity,

[65] *Vanessa and Swift*, pp. 134-135 (Swift to Vanessa from Clogher, June 1, 1722): "Remember I still enjoin you reading and exercise for the improvement of your mind and health of your body, and grow less romantic, and talk and act like a man of this world." See also p. 139 (July 13, 1722) and p. 142 (Aug. 7, 1722). Cf. *Prose Writings*, IX, 88, 90.

[66] See *Vanessa and Swift*, pp. 113, 135, for Swift's advice to Vanessa about the cleanliness of her person and her romantic tendencies. Cf. *Prose Writings*, IX, 87, 89, for similar advice to Deborah Staunton.

moroseness, and refined cruelty of heart as were actually or potentially a part of John Rochfort's nature, unconsciously identified himself with his young Gaulstown favorite and so tended to conceal
Rochfort's faults from his own eyes by a kind of idealization and self-
deception.

Yet Swift, even in his old age, was nothing if not clear-eyed and
hardheaded. He was never much given to self-deception, possibly
because, as a satirist, he observed so much of it in others. In 1722-1723,
at which time *Gulliver* was begun (echoes of it appear in this very
letter),[67] *The Drapier's Letters* soon to be written, and at the height
of his powers, Swift can hardly have misjudged completely the effect
that his letter might have upon its recipient, the only daughter of an
old and trusted friend. Nor could he have hoped for long to have
deceived himself, his friend John Rochfort, or "Nim's" young wife,
about shortcomings in the husband's character with which he was
well enough acquainted. Can it be that Swift, then, knowing the
nature of Dublin society of that time, actually had in mind a wider
audience than merely Deborah Staunton?

The two women in Dublin who in early 1723 would have had the
greatest interest in and curiosity about Swift's thoughts on marriage
were Stella and Vanessa. It was just about the time that Swift composed his letter that his dilemma over the two women was approaching a climax. Of the two, Stella, older and more self-possessed, might
be more reassured by the letter, since she seems to have best lived up
to the high standards Swift there set down. To the degree that *she*
may have felt that she was being addressed, as well as Deborah Staunton, Vanessa would probably have been as wounded and piqued as
the recipient was. And all three, to the degree that they were women
of different ages but thinking, feeling human beings, with some justice might well have resented what Swift chose here to say about their
sex. Although Swift's letter is not, to my mind, "universally applicable" to all newly married young women, since few then or since
have been matched in arranged marriages of just this kind, it may

---

[67]Cf. the full title and contents of *Gulliver's Travels* and the following from HM
1599, fols. 6v-7r: "If they . . . [Men of Breeding as well as Learning] talk of the Manners and Customs of the severall Kingdoms of Europe, of Travells into remoter Nations; of the State of their own Country, of the great Men and Actions of Greece and
Rome. . . . Or of the Nature and Limits of Virtue and Vice. It is a Shame for an English Lady not to relish such. . . ." See also Swift's recommendation (fol. 5v) that the
young lady read "a Collection of History and Travells," and compare his mention to
Vanessa of reading the same, *Vanessa and Swift*, p. 139.

have had, temporarily, a wider local application and a momentarily broader significance to the Dublin society of 1722-1723. If it were seen by Stella or Vanessa at that time, it would have had immediate bearing upon the crisis and dilemma which confronted Swift in his relationship with these two women, might, for instance, account for Vanessa's violent reaction in changing her will totally not long before her death early in June 1723,[68] or explain Stella's resentful estrangement from Swift in the summer of 1723, which she passed at Charles Ford's estate of Wood Park outside Dublin[69] and Swift's lonely and moody "ramble" on horseback to the south and west of Ireland all that summer.[70]

By the time of his return in September 1723 Vanessa was dead. Early in October he and Stella, who was now without a rival, were reconciled happily for the years of life that remained to her. As for the still youthful Deborah Staunton (now Rochfort) soon to bear her first child, the events that now engaged her probably so occupied her time that she had little concern just then with Swift's advice about married life.

A LETTER TO A YOUNG LADY ON HER MARRIAGE

HM 1599

(fol. 1ʳ)   1 Madam

The Hurry and Impertinence of receiving and
5 paying Visits on account of your Marriage, being now
over; You are beginning to enter into a Course of Life
where you will want much Advice to divert you from
falling into many Errors Fopperyes and Follyes to
which your Sex is subject. I have always born an entire
10 Friendship to Your Father and Mother; and the Person
they have chosen for Your Husband hath been for some
Years past my particular Favorite. I have long wished

---

[68] *Vanessa and Swift*, p. 189. Vanessa's will is dated May 1, 1723; it was proved on June 6, 1723.

[69] *Corresp.*, II, 456. See also *Letters of Swift to Ford*, p. 198.

[70] *Corresp.*, II, 453 and n. 3.

<that> You might come together, because I hoped, that
from the Goodness of Your own Disposition, and by
15 following the Council of wise Friends, you might in time
make your self worthy of Him. Your Parents were so
far in the right, that they did not produce you much into
the World, whereby you avoided many wrong Steps which
others have taken, and have fewer ill Impressions to
20 be removed. But, they failed, as it is generally the
Case, in too much neglec[t]ing to cultivate your Mind,
without which it is impossible to acquire or preserve

(fol. 1ᵛ) 1 the Friendship and Esteem of a wise Man, who soon grows
weary of acting the Lover, and treating His Wife like a
Mistress, but wants a reasonable Companion and a true
Friend through every Stage of his Life. It must be
5 therefore your Business to qualify your self for those
Offices, wherein I will not fayl to be your Director, as long
as I shall think you deserve it, by letting You know how
you are to act, and what you ought to avoyd.
And beware of despising or neglecting my Instructions,
10 whereon will depend not only your making a good Figure
in the World, but your own real Happyness, as well as that
of
the Person who ought to be dearest to you.
I must therefore desire you in the first Place, to be
very slow in changing the modest Behavior of a Virgin. It
15 is usuall in young Wives before they have been many
Weeks marryed, to assume a bold, forward Look, and
manner of talking; as if they intended to signify in
all Companyes, that they were no longer Girls, and
consequently that their whole Demanor before they got a
20 Husband, was all but a Countenance, and Constraint
upon their Nature. Whereas I suppose, if the Votes of
Wise Men were gathered a very great Majority would
be in favor of those Ladyes, who after they have entered

(fol. 2ʳ) 1 into that State, rather chuse to double their Portion of
Modesty and Reservedness.
I must likewise warn you strictly against the
least Degree of Fondness to your Husband before any
5 witness <. .> whatsoever, even before your nearest Relations;

(fol. 1ʳ)   L. 13: "that" canceled.
           L. 21: "neglecting" holed.
(fol. 1ᵛ)   L. 19: "their" inserted above the line by a caret.
(fol. 2ʳ)   L. 5: two letters are canceled; undecipherable.

or the very Maids of your Chamber. This Proceeding
is so very odious and disgustfull to all who have either
good Breeding or good Sense, that they assign two very
unamiable Reasons for it, the One is gross Hypocrisy,
10 and the other has too bad a Name to mention. If there
is any Difference to be made, Your Husband is the
lowest Person in Company either at home or abroad, and
every Gentleman present <in the Company> has a better
Claim to
all Marks of Civility and Distinction from you. Conceal
15 your Esteem and Love in your own Breast, and reserve
your kind Looks and Language for private Hours,
which are so many in the four and twenty that
they will afford Time to employ a Passion as exalted
as any that was ever described in a French Romance.
20   Upon this Head I should likewise advise you to
differ in Practice from those Ladyes who affect
abundance of Uneasyness while their Husbands are
abroad, start with every Knock at the Door, and ring
(fol. 2ᵛ)   1 the Bell incessantly for the Servants to let in their
Master; will not eat a Bit of Dinner or Supper if the
Husband happens to stay out, and receive him at his
Return with such a Medly of Chiding and Kindness
5 and catechising him where he has been, that a Shrew
from Bilingsgate would be a more easy and
eligible Companion.
     Of the same Leaven are those Wives, who when
their Husbands are gone a Journy must have a
10 Letter every Post upon Pain of Fitts and Histericks,
and a Day must be fixed for their Return home,
without the least Allowance for Business, or Sickness,
or Accidents or Weather. Upon which I can onely say,
that in my Observation, those Ladyes who were apt
15 to make the greatest Clutter upon such Occasions
would liberally have payd a Messenger for bringing
them News that their Husbands had broken their
Necks on the Road.
     You will perhaps be offended when I advise you
20 to abate a little of that violent Passion for fine
Cloaths, so predominant in Your Sex: It is a little
hard, that Ours for whose Sake you wear them are

L. 13: "present" inserted above the line by a caret.
L. 19: "any that" inserted above the line by a caret.

(fol. 3ʳ) 1 not admitted to be of Your Council. I <will> may venture
   to assure you that we will make an Abatement at any
   time of ten Pounds a Yard in a Brocade, if the Ladyes
   will but allow a suitable Addition of Care in the
 5 Cleanlyness and Sweetness of their Persons. For, the
   Satyricall Part of Mankind will needs believe that
   it is not impossible to be very fine and very
   filthy; and that the Capacityes of a Lady are
   sometimes apt to fall short in cultivating
10 Cleanlyness and Finery together. I shall onely add
   upon so tender a Subject, what a pleasant Gentleman
   said concerning a silly W[o]man of Quality, that nothing
   could make her supportable but cutting off her Head,
   for his Ears were offended by Her Tongue, and His Nose
15 by her Hair and Teeth.
      I am wholly at a Loss how to advise you in
   the Choice of Company, which however, is a Point
   of as great Importance as any in Life. If your
   generall Acquaintance b[e] among Ladyes who are
20 your Equalls or Superiors, provided they have nothing
   of what is commonly called an ill Reputation, you
   think you are safe, and this in the Style of the

(fol. 3ᵛ) 1 world will pass for good Company. Whereas, I am afraid
   it will be hard for you to pick out one femal
   Acquaintance in this Town, from whom you will not be
   in manifest Danger of contracting some Foppery,
 5 Affectation, Vanity, Folly, or Vice. Your onely safe
   way of conversing with them is by a firm
   Resolution to proceed in your Practice and Behavior
   directly contrary to whatever they shall say or do.
   And this I take to be a good generall Rule with
10 very few Exceptions. For instance, in the Doctrines
   they usually deliver to young marryed Women for
   managing their Hus[ban]ds, their severall Accounts
   of their own Conduct in that Particular, to
   recommend it to your Imitation; The Reflections
15 they make upon others of their own Sex for acting
   differently; Their Directions how to come off with
   <Difficulty> Victory upon any Dispute or Quarrell you

(fol. 3ʳ)   L. 1: "will" canceled.
         Ll. 12, 19: words with brackets holed or stained.
(fol. 3ᵛ)   L. 12: word holed, letters supplied in brackets.
         L. 17: "Difficulty" canceled.

may have with Your Husband, The Arts by
which you may discover and practice upon his
20 weak Sides; When to work by Flattery and Insinuation
when to melt him with Tears, and when to engage
(fol. 4ʳ) 1 with high Hand. In these and a thousand other Cases, it
will be prudent to retain as many of their Lectures in
your Memory as you can, and then determine to act in
full Opposition to them all.
5 I hope Your Husband will interpose his Authority to
limit you in the Trade of visiting; half a dozen Fools are
in all Conscience as many as you should require, and it
will be sufficient for you to see them twice a year; For,
I think the Fashion does not exact, that Visits should
10 be payd to Friends.
I advise that your Company at home should consist
of Men, rather than Women. To say the Truth, I never
yet knew a tolerable Woman to be fond of her own Sex.
I confess, when both are mixed and well chosen, they put
15 their best Qualityes forward, and there may be an
Intercourse of Civility and good Will which with the
Addition of some degree of Sense can make Conversation
or any Amusements agreeable: But, a Knot of Ladyes got
together by themselves, is a very School of Impertinence
20 and Detraction, and it is well if those be the worst.
Let your Men-acquaintance be of Your Husband's
Choice, and not recommended to You by any She
(fol. 4ᵛ) 1 Companions, because they will certainly fix a Coxcomb
upon You, and it will cost You some Time and Pains <b>
before you <will> can arrive at the Knoledge of
distinguishing
such a one from a Man of Sense.
5 Never take a Favorite waiting-Maid into your Cabinet
Council, to entertain you with Historyes of those Ladyes
whom she hath formerly served, Of their Diversions and
their Dresses, of the Arts they used to govern their
Husbands; to insinuate how great a Fortune you brought,
10 and how little you are allowed to squander; To appeal to
her from Your Husband, and be determined by her
Judgment, because you are sure it will be always for
You: To receive and discard Servants by her Approbation
or Dislike: To engage you by her Insinuations into

(fol. 4ᵛ) L. 2: "b" written, then canceled—at end of the line.
L. 3: "will" canceled.

15 Misunderstandings with Your best Friends; To represent
all Things in false Colors, and to be the common
Emissary of Scandal.

But the grand Affair of Your Life will be to gain
and preserve the Friendship and Esteem of Your
20 Husband. You are marryed to a Man of good
Education and Learning, of an excellent Understanding
and an exact Tast. It is true, and it is happy for You

(fol. 5ʳ)   1 that these Qualityes in him are adorned with great
Modesty, a most amiable Sweetness of Temper, and an
unusuall Disposition to Sobriety and Virtue. But,
neither good Nature nor Virtue will suffer him to esteem
5 You against his Judgment; and although he is not
capable of using You <ill will> ill; yet you will in time
grow a Thing indifferent, and perhaps contemptible, unless
you can supply the Loss of Youth and Beauty, with more
durable Qualityes. You have but a very few years to be
10 young and handsom in the Eyes of the World, and as few
Months to be so in the Eyes of a Husband, who is not a
Fool: For I hope you do not still Dream of Charms
and Raptures, which Mar[r]iage ever did and ever will put
<an> a sudden End to: Besides, yours was a Match of
Prudence and
15 common good Liking, without any Mixture of that
ridiculous Passion, which has no Being but <onely[?]> in
Play-books and Songs.

You must therefore use all Endeavors to attain to
some Degree of those Accomplishments which your
20 Husband most values in other People, and for which
he is most valued himself. You must improve your
Mind by closely pursuing such a Method of Study

(fol. 5ᵛ)   1 as I shall direct or approve of. You must get a Collection
of History and Travells which I will recommend to You,
and spend some Hours every day in reading them, and
making Extracts from them, if your Memory be weak.
5 You must invite Persons of Knoledge and Understanding
to an Acquaintance with you, by whose Conversation you
may learn to correct Your Tast and Judgment; and
when you can bring your self to comprehend and to relish

(fol. 5ʳ)   L. 6: two words canceled.
L. 13: "Marriage" holed.
L. 14: "an" canceled; "a sudden" inserted by a caret.
L. 16: word canceled.

the good Sense of others, you will arrive in time to
10 think rightly your Self, and to become a reasonable
and agreeable Companion. This must produce in your
Husband a true rationall Love and Esteem for You
which old Age will not diminish. He will have a
Regard for your Judgment and Opinion in matters of
15 the greatest Weight. You will be able to entertain
each other without a third Person to relieve you by
finding Discourse; The Endowments of your Mind will
even make Your Person more agreeable to Him; And
when you are alone, your Time will not ly heavy upon
20 your Hands for want of some trifling Amusement.

    As little Respect as I have for the generality of your
(fol. 6ʳ) 1 Sex, it hath sometimes moved me with Pity to see the
Lady of the House forced to withdraw immediatly after
Dinner, and this in Familyes where there is not much
drinking, as if it were an established Maxim, that
5 Women are uncapable of all Conversation. In a Room
where bothe Sexes are met, if the Men are discoursing
upon any generall Subject, the Ladyes never think
it their Business to partake in what passes, but in
a separate Club entertain each other with the Price
10 and Choice of Lace and Silk, and what Dresses they
liked or disapproved at the Church and the Playhouse.
<But> And when you are among your selves, how
                              naturally
after the first Compliments do you apply your Hands to
each others Lappets, and Ruffles, and Mantues, as if
15 the whole Business of your lives, and the publick Concern
of the World, depended upon the Cut and Colour of your
Dress. As Divines say, that some People take more Pains
                              to be
damned, than it would cost them to be saved, So your Sex
employs more Thought, Memory, and Application to be
                              Fools,
20 than would serve to make them wise and usefull. When
I reflect on this, I can <hardly> not conceive you to be
                              human
Creatures, but a sort of Species hardly a Degree above a

(fol. 5ᵛ)   L. 20: "trifling" inserted above the line by a caret.
(fol. 6ʳ)   L. 12: "But" canceled; "And" inserted above line.
            L. 13: "first" inserted above the line by a caret.
            L. 21: "hardly" canceled; "not" inserted above the line by a caret.

(fol. 6ᵛ) 1 Monkey, who has more diverting Tricks than any of You,
         is an Animal less mischievous and expensive, might in time
         be a tolerable Critick in Velvet and Brocade, and for ought
         I know would equally become them.

      5   I would have you look upon Finery as a necessary Folly,
         as all great Ladyes did whom I have ever known, I do not
         desire you to be out of the Fashion, but to be the last
         and the least in it; I expect that your dress shall be one
         degree lower than your Fortune can afford; and in your
     10 own Heart I would wish you to be an utter Contemner of
         all Distinctions which a finer Petticoat can give you;
         because it will neither make you richer, handsomer, younger
                                                              [,]
         better natured, more virtuous or wise, than if it hung
         upon a Peg.
     15   If you are in Company with Men of Learning,
         although they happen to discourse of Arts and Sciences out
                                                       of your
         Compass, yet you will gather more Advantage by listning
         to them, than from all the Nonsense and Frippery of your
         own Sex. But if they be Men of Breeding as well as
     20 Learning, they will seldom engage in any Conversation
         where you ought not be a Hearer, and in time have your
         Part. If they talk of the Manners and Customs of the
         severall Kingdoms of Europe, of Travells into remoter

(fol. 7ʳ) 1 Nations; of the State of their own Country, of the great Men
         and Actions of Greece and Rome. If they give their
                                                   Judgment
         upon English and French Writers either in Verse or Prose;
         Or of the Nature and Limits of Virtue and Vice. It is
      5 a Shame for an English Lady not to relish such
         Discourses and improve by them, and endeavor by reading
         and Information to have her Share in such an
         Entertainment, rather than turn aside, as it is the usuall
                                                        Custom,
         and consult with the Woman who sits next her, about a
     10 new Cargo of Fans.
             It is a little hard that not one Gentleman's Daughter in a
         thousand should be brought to read or understand her own
         naturall Tongue, or be judge of the easyest Books that are

(fol. 6ᵛ) L. 12: comma not visible because of binding?
         L. 16: "to discourse" inserted above the line by a caret.

(fol. 7ʳ) L. 8: "than" inserted above the line by a caret.

written in it, as any one may find who can have the Patience
15 to hear them, when they are disposed to mangle a Play or
a Novell, where the least Word out of the common Road
is sure to disconcert them: And it is no wonder, when they
are not so much as taught to spell in <the> their Childhood,
nor can
ever attain to it in <yo> their whole Lives. I advise you
20 therefore to read aloud more or less every day, to your
Husband if he will permit you, or to any other Friend
(but not a female one) who is able to set you right. And
as for Spelling, You may compass it in time by making
(fol. 7ᵛ) 1 'Collections from the Books you read.

I know very well, that those who are commonly called
Learned women, have lost all Manner of Credit by their
impertinent Talkativeness, and Conceit of themselves. But
5 there is an easy Remedy for this, if you once consider, that
after all the Pains you may be at, you never can arrive in
point of Learning, to the Perfection of a Schoolboy; But
the Reading I would advise you to is onely for Improvement
of your own good Sense, which will never fayl of being
10 attended by Discretion. It is a wrong Method, and ill
Choice of Books, that makes those Learned Ladyes just so
much worse for what <ha> they have read. And therefore
it shall be my Care to direct you better, which is a Task
I take my self to be not ill qualifyed for, because I have
15 spent more time, and have <ma> had more
Opportunityes
than many others, to observe and discover from what
Sources the various Follyes of Women are derived.
Pray observe how insignificant Things are the common
Race of Ladyes when they have passed their Youth and
20 Beauty; how contemptible they appear to the Men, and yet
more contemptible to the younger [Part] Sort of their own
Sex,
(fol. 8ʳ) 1 and have no Relief but in passing their Afternoons in Visits
where they are never acceptable, and their Evenings at Cards
among each other, while the former Part of the Day is spent
in Spleen and Envy, or in vain Endeavors to repair by Art
and

L. 18: "the" canceled; "their" inserted above by a caret.
L. 19: "yo" canceled.
(fol. 7ᵛ) L. 12: "ha" canceled.
L. 15: "ma" canceled.
L. 21: "Part" written first; "Sort" written over it.

5 Dress, the Ruins of Time. Whereas I have known Ladyes
at sixty, to whom all the polite Part of the Court and
Town payd their Addresses without any further View than
that of enjoying the Pleasure of their Conversation.

I am ignorant of any one Quality that is amiable in
10 a Man, which is not equally so in a Woman; I do not
except even Modesty and Gentleness of Nature. Nor do I
know one Vice or Folly which is not equally detestable
in both. There is indeed [o]ne Infirmity which seems to
be generally allowed you, I mean That of Cowardice:
15 Yet there should seem to be something very capricious
that when Women openly profess their Adorations for a
Collonell or <an> a Captain on Account of their Valor,
they
should fancy it a very gracefull becoming Quality in
themselves to be afraid of their own Shadows; to scream
20 in a Barge when the Weather is calmest, or in a Coach
on the Ring, to run from a Cow at a hundred yards'
distance, to fall into Fits at the Sight of a Spider, an
Earwig, or a Frog. At least, if Cowardice be a <Sn> Sign

(fol. 8ᵛ) 1 of Cruelty, as it is generally granted, I can hardly think
it an Accomplishment so desireable as to be <improved by>
thought worth improving by Affectation.

And, as the same Virtues equally become both Sexes, so
5 there is no Quality whereby Women endeavor to distinguish
themselves from Men, for which they are not just so much
the worse, except onely that one of Reservedness, which
however, as You generally manage it, is nothing else but
Affectation or Hypocrisy: For, as you cannot too much
10 discountenance those of our Sex who presume to take
unbecoming Liberty before you; So you ought to be
wholly unconstrained in the Company of deserving Men,
when you have had sufficient Experience of their
Discretion.
15 There is never wanting in this Town, a Tribe of bold,
swaggering, rattling Ladyes; whose Talents pass among
Coxcombs, for Wit and Humor; their Excellency lyes in
rude chocquing Expressions, and what they call running

(fol. 8ʳ) L. 13: "one" holed in first letter.
L. 17: "an" deleted.
L. 18: "becoming" first written "become," then altered.
L. 23: "Sn" canceled.

(fol. 8ᵛ) L. 2: "improved by" deleted.

a Man down. If a Gentleman in their Company happens
20 to have any Blemish in his Birth or Person, if any
Misfortune hath <happened to> befell His Family or
himself, for
which he is ashamed, they will be sure to give him broad
Hints of it without any Provocation. I would recommend
You

(fol. 9ʳ) 1 to the Acquaintance of a common Prostitute, rather than
to that of such Termagants as these. I have often thought
that no Man is obliged to suppose such Creatures to be
Women, but to treat them like insolent Rascals disguised
5 in Female Habits, who ought to be stripped and kicked
down
Stairs.
     I will add one Thing, though it be a little out of
Place, which is to desire that you will learn to value and
esteem your Husband for those good Qualityes which he
10 really possesses, and not to fancy others in him which he
certainly has not. For although this latter is generally
understood to be a Mark of Love, yet it is indeed nothing
but Affectation or ill Judgment. 'Tis true, he wants so
very few Accomplishments, that you are in no great
15 Danger of erring on this Side. But my Caution is
occasioned by a Lady of Your Allyance, marryed to a
very valuable Person, whom yet She is so unfortunate
as to be always commending for those Perfections to
which he can least pretend.
20   I can give You no advice upon the Article of
Expence, onely, I think you ought to be well informed
how much Your Husbands Revenue amounts to, and to be so
good a Computer as to keep within it, in that Part of the

(fol. 9ᵛ) 1 Management which falls to your Share; and not to put your
self in the Number of those politick Ladyes, who think they
gain a great Point, when they have teazed their Husbands, to
buy them a new Equipage[,] a laced Head, or a fine
5 Petticoat, without once considering what long Scores
remain
unpayd to the Butcher.
     I desire you will keep this Letter in your Cabinet, and
often examine impartially Your whole Conduct by it. And
so God bless you, and make you a fair Example to your

L. 21: "happened to" deleted; "befell" inserted above by a caret.

10 Sex, and a perpetuall Comfort to Your Husband and
Your Parents.
I am with great Truth and Affection
Madam
Your most faithfull Friend,
15 Deanry-house   and humble Servt
Febr. 11th 1722-3.   Jonath Swift

Chapter Four

SWIFT'S FIRST WILL AND THE FIRST USE OF THE PROVOST'S NEGATIVE AT T.C.D.

I

JONATHAN SWIFT, in 1686 a bachelor of arts of Trinity College, Dublin, until late in life maintained a strong interest in the welfare of the university from which he had graduated. It appears that one reason for Swift's visit to Ireland in 1690-1691 was to sit for a junior fellowship. In a letter of May 29, 1690, Sir William Temple recommended his protégé to the new Secretary of State for Ireland, Sir Robert Southwell, for a junior fellowship at T.C.D. Since the college was then just recovering from the disastrous policy of James II, no fellowships were held until May 1692, by which time Swift had returned to Moor Park by way of Oxford, where instead he took his Master's degree.[1] In October 1692 St. George Ashe, Swift's college tutor, was appointed provost of Trinity College; and it was through such friends as Ashe, who were senior or junior fellows of T.C.D., that Swift continued to follow with considerable interest the fortunes of the college.

As we learn from the *Journal to Stella*, one of Swift's later friends and occasional companions in London from 1710 to 1714 was another provost of Trinity College, Dr. Benjamin Pratt, a loyal Tory. When in February 1715/6, the Duke of Ormonde was attainted for treason, the Prince of Wales was elected chancellor in his place as part of the political reorientation that followed the Queen's death. Soon afterward in 1717, the Tory Provost Pratt was replaced by Dr. Richard Baldwin, a violent Whig. Swift, however, found that he still had many friends left among the senior and junior fellows, men like Dr.

[1]Williams, *Corresp.*, I, 1-2, 11-12, and notes; Stubbs, *History*, pp. 135-136.

[69]

Patrick Delany, one of his closest Dublin friends, Dr. Richard Helsham, Swift's personal physician, Dr. Robert Clayton, later Bishop of Clogher, and the promising young junior fellow, James Stopford. Like them Swift watched with growing indignation the arbitrary and highhanded exercise of his powers for political ends of the new provost, Dr. Baldwin.

With the appearance in Dublin in 1724 of the new English Whig Primate of Ireland, Dr. Hugh Boulter, Dr. Baldwin's ruthlessness seemed to increase. Supported from England by the Archbishop of Canterbury and by the Duke of Newcastle, Secretary of State, Archbishop Boulter early determined that all important places in the Church, on the Bench, at the Bar, and in the college should go to loyal Whigs, preferably English Whigs; and that Trinity College, Dublin, should not longer be permitted to remain the "seminary of jacobitism" he believed it to be.[2] Soon a strong Tory opposition developed among Swift's friends in the college. After some successful preliminary skirmishes in 1724 and 1725 with Dr. Delany, Swift's friend and the leader of the Tory opposition among the senior fellows, Provost Baldwin with Archbishop Boulter's backing was emboldened to act even more outrageously in the fellowship elections in 1727 and to exercise, probably for the first time, the provost's negative in the fellowships of that year.

To Provost Baldwin belongs the dubious distinction of being the first to use the provost's negative, about which so much has been written.[3] According to Stubbs, it has been used upon only three occasions, twice by Provost Baldwin and once by Provost Hely-Hutchinson.[4] Finally upon this last occasion which occurred in December 1790, the vice-chancellor, Lord Clare, after lengthy hearings in August 1791, decided against Hutchinson's claims, and the provost's

[2]*Letters Written by His Excellency Hugh Boulter, ... to Several Ministers of State in England*, 2 vols. (Oxford, 1769-70), I, 13, 21, 54, 146, 182, 183, 191, 208. See also I, 16-18, 40-41, 48-49, 54-55, 58, for Delany's opposition to Baldwin. Hereafter cited as Boulter, *Letters*.

[3]*Corresp.*, III, 218, 220, 221. See the pamphlets of 1727-28 described below. Also see [Matthew Young], "An Enquiry How Far the Provost of Trinity College, Dublin, is Invested with a Negative ... Dublin, 1790"; William B. S. Taylor, *History of the University of Dublin* (London, 1845), pp. 248-251, 282, 289-290; Wilde, *Closing Years*, pp. 89-90; Stubbs, *History*, pp. 97-166, 166n, 248-253, 416-419; *The Book of Trinity College, Dublin: 1591-1891* (Belfast, 1892), pp. 56-57, 79-80; Constantia Maxwell, *A History of Trinity College, Dublin: 1591-1892* (Dublin, 1946), p. 113.

[4]Baldwin exercised his negative in 1727 and again, upon one later occasion, the date of which I have been unable to ascertain. Provost Hutchinson negatived Stack and nominated Brinckley in 1790. Stubbs, *History*, pp. 97, 248.

negative has never been in use since. The whole vexed question arises from the interpretations of an ambiguous phrase in the Laudian revisions of the college statute of 1637 which has to do with the method of electing a junior fellow: *"una cum Praeposito, vel eo absente Vice-Praeposito...."* The Latin is usually taken to mean that a majority of the board of eight senior fellows, of which the provost is one, elects the new junior fellow. Provosts Baldwin and Hutchinson took the words to mean that the senior fellows should be at one with the provost's nomination, which otherwise overrules through his power to negative an opposing candidate even though that candidate has a majority of the votes of the other senior fellows present.

The immediate situation which occasioned the first use of the provost's negative was the election in May 1727 of one of nine candidates to a vacant junior fellowship. When the Reverend William Rowan, a Whig and the most senior of the junior fellows, entered into what has been called "a Precipitant Marriage," he was obliged according to the statutes to resign his fellowship. Examinations for the place thus vacated were duly announced, and the public examinations, attended by many leading Dublin citizens and by most of the collegians, were held on the four days preceding Trinity Sunday which fell in 1727 on May 28. Before the next day, Trinity Monday, on which date the board of senior fellows was to meet by statute to elect the new junior fellow, it was generally agreed in Dublin and at the college that only five of the nine candidates had been outstanding enough in their public examinations to be considered real contenders. It was also generally agreed that Arthur Ford, whose tutor was Dr. Delany, and who was a Tory in politics, easily stood at the head of those being examined. Two other candidates, John Obins and Henry Hamilton, were also considered to have answered well. Both these men were subsequently elected junior fellows in 1728. John Pellisier, a leading Whig candidate whose tutor was Dr. Gilbert, the vice-provost, was not generally considered to be among the five leading candidates.[5]

John Pellisier (his surname is variously misspelled Pallisier, Palliseer, Pelessier, Paliseer, Pelishere) matriculated at T. C. D., as a pensioner from Dr. Lloyd's school, on April 25, 1719, aged sixteen. Although he was born in Clonygown, Queen's County, according to college records, he was thought to be somewhat "Frenchified" in his manners if not a downright foreigner. He was the son of a French-

[5]*A Short History*, passim and marginal annotations

man, Abel Pellisier, who had, however, served under William III as an officer in the army in Flanders and in Ireland. Pellisier was elected a scholar in 1721, took his B.A. in 1723, his M.A. in 1726. Once before, probably in the fellowships of 1726, he had been an unsuccessful candidate. As well as the traditional subjects in which he and the others were examined—dialectics (logic), mathematics, natural and moral philosophy, Latin, and Greek—Pellisier understood Hebrew and Chaldee and some Syriac, languages which were not at the command of most of the senior fellows who were the examiners. In the examinations Pellisier displayed a quick intelligence and a ready tongue in guessing at some of the more difficult questions. Until his previous and unsuccessful candidacy, he had lived in the college and kept his college duties faithfully, even in vacation, and he never ran into debt. Since the previous year, however, he had lived away from the college outside the city with the family of a certain Colonel Oliver. His modesty and civility were insisted upon by his friends, and by them he was appreciatively called "a true and honest Whig."[6]

Pellisier's enemies, however, maintained that his command of languages was pedantry and that his facility in the examinations was mere glibness and shrewd guesswork, that his living away from the college was a neglect of his duties, and that his civility and friendliness were but the fawning Gallic obsequiousness of a "Foreigner." They added that in age and standing, as well as by public demonstration, Pellisier was inferior in all respects to the leading "native" candidate Arthur Ford.[7]

Arthur Ford matriculated on November 11, 1718, aged sixteen, coming to T.C.D. from Dr. Thomas Sheridan's school in Dublin. In December 1717 Swift may have seen or met Ford performing in the Greek play put on by the leading scholars of his close friend, Dr. Sheridan, one performance of which play Swift appears to have attended.[8] Ford took his B.A. in 1726 and his M.A. in the summer of the same year. He was native born, the younger son of a squire of either County Down or County Armagh and was the descendant of English forebears who had lived in Ireland for several generations. In the public examinations Ford did not guess at questions to which

[6]Burtchaell, p. 659. *The Protest* and *An Answer*, passim.

[7]*A Short History, An Humble Remonstrance, The Protest*, passim.

[8]*Corresp.*, II, 301, n. 1, and Forster No. 510 ("Account Book, Nov. 1st 1717-Nov. 1st 1718"), p. 12b; "Decbr 11th [1717] at the Greek play 5s 5d."

he did not know the answers, but in all subjects he answered well and often brilliantly, so that he was generally believed, in Dublin and in the college, to be the obvious choice for the fellow's place. He was modest and well liked, and he lived in the college and was regular in his college duties. He was intimate with some of the senior fellows, especially with such friends of Swift as Dr. Delany and Dr. Helsham, and he was described by them as being "a Youth of the best Life and Accomplishments; a native of [Ireland], the son of Natives; of an Ancient and Honourable Family; as Eminent for his Morals, as his Learning."[9] Even Ford's enemies had only good to say of him. But, alas, he was a Tory and thus was passed over in the fellowships of 1727, and Pellisier was elected by the first exercise of the provost's negative.

A distinction should be made between the provost's power to *nominate* a junior fellow and the power illegally assumed by Provosts Baldwin and Hutchinson to *negative* the election of a candidate preferred by a majority of the board. For example, as his enemies in 1727 were quick to remind him, Dr. Delany was himself nominated a fellow in 1709 by Provost Peter Browne, despite the fact that "all the Senior Fellows voted against him" (Stubbs, *History*, pp. 327-328). According to *The Protest* (p. 14), "There are two ways appointed for filling up a vacant Fellowship: One by the Joint-Election of the *Provost, and the Major part of the Senior Fellows*; the other by the Nomination of the *Provost alone*." The pamphlet goes on to say that the extraordinary power to nominate "has been very rarely made use of by any *Provost* but the present," but that the number of nominations made by Baldwin since his promotion to provost in 1717 exceeded the number of all nominations made since the founding of the college in 1591. *An Humble Remonstrance* (pp. 4-5) also concedes the provost's extraordinary power to nominate his own candidate if he and a majority of the board cannot make up their difference within the statutable number of scrutinies. One objection, then, of the dissenting fellows in 1727 was that Provost Baldwin had strained a legal right by using it too frequently and upon ordinary occasions. Baldwin seems not to have been intimidated; in 1738 he nominated James Knight and in 1746 John Stokes as junior fellows (Taylor, *History*, p. 282).

[9]Burtchaell, p. 297, and *An Humble Remonstrance, The Protest, An Answer*, passim, and especially *A Short History*, from which the characterization quoted is taken. The annotator of *A Short History* identified "Phordaios" in the margin as "Mr. Ford, of the County of Down." Burtchaell says that Ford came from County Armagh.

The provost's negative, first used by Baldwin in 1727, constituted *negativing*, or voting directly against the candidate (Ford) who had the votes of the majority of the board, thus knocking him out of the running. The provost then used his rightful but extraordinary power to nominate his own candidate (Pellisier) and to elect him a fellow, despite the fact that he had only the votes of Baldwin and his vice-provost. The Whig author of *An Answer* (p. 1) concluded lamely concerning the provost's newly found negative: "as I do not pretend to understand that Matter thoroughly, I shall omit Consideration of that. . . ." In 1727 the Tories considered Provost Baldwin's first use of his negative to be unprecedented, and an "arbitrary," "exorbitant," and "enormous" power—one that was "tyrannically" assumed, as Lord Clare termed it in 1791. But as Swift expressed it, Provost Baldwin, in his own time, had the law on his side (*Corresp.*, III, 221). The matter was not finally settled until the vice-chancellor, Lord Clare, disallowed the use of the provost's negative by his decision of 1791 (Stubbs, *History*, p. 253).

II

ABOUT HALF the known documents, most of them violently partisan, are still extant to describe the actions of the provost and senior fellows on Trinity Monday, May 29, 1727. One such is the Latin entry in the College Register for that date, of which the short character of Arthur Ford, given above in English, is an approximate translation of the conclusion.[10] This censure of the provost's highhanded action in negativing Ford and nominating Pellisier was caused to be entered into the College Register by Dr. Delany and the four other senior fellows who voted for Ford. Dr. Delany also sent off to Swift in England this Latin censure which the Dean translated and forwarded along with "a whole State of the Case," by way of protest to the Prince of Wales as chancellor of the university (*Corresp.*, III, 218).

A second document, undated, but probably printed soon after the fellowships of 1727, because of the immediacy with which it de-

[10]The Registrar of Trinity College kindly supplied me with the following transcription from the College Register (p. 552): "1727. Die Lunae post Dominicam Trinitatis, Praepositus nominavit Johannem Pellisier, e stirpe adventitia ortum in Socium Juniorem hujusce Collegii, nemine Sociorim Seniorum tunc praesentium, excepto Doctore Gilbert, Tutore nominati, suffragante aut consentiente. Caeteris quinque Sociis Senioribus, viz. Doctore Helsham, Doctore Delany, Mag. Thompson, Doctore Clayton, et Magistro Rogers, qui tunc temporis adfuerunt, suffragia sua conferentibus in Magistrum Arthurum Forde, optimae spei juvvenem, indigenam, parentibus indigenis generosis prognatum, et non minus morbius quam eriditione conspicuum."

scribes them, is an anonymous broadsheet entitled *A Short History of the Eight Philosophers of the Island Cos*.[11] It is a detailed—and, in many places, verbatim—account of the proceedings, told in the humorously transparent terms of Greek history in which Ireland becomes Cos and England the oppressive neighboring island of Rhodes. In tone it is strongly pro-Ford and Tory and states, more or less openly, that Provost Baldwin's negative was exercised for political purposes by direct collusion with Archbishop Boulter. This charge is further reinforced by the annotations on the margins of a copy now in Trinity College Library made somewhat later by a contemporary who seems to have had detailed information about the fellowships of 1727.[12] This broadsheet is in all probability "the inclosed Print" for which Swift thanked Sheridan in a letter of June 24, 1727, from London.[13]

The five dissenting senior fellows, Drs. Delany, Helsham, Thompson, Clayton, and Rogers also had printed, either in 1727 or between January and March 1727/8, a seven-page pamphlet to which they signed their names entitled *The Protest of all the Senior-Fellows in Trinity College, Dublin, (except one)*.[14] The senior fellow excepted was, of course, Dr. Gilbert, the vice-provost, who voted with Baldwin against Ford and for the nomination of Pellisier, his pupil. The eighth senior fellow, Dr. Elwood, was absent in France. *The Protest* gave seven cogent reasons why the dissenting fellows were so strong in their opposition to the unprecedented use of the provost's negative.

Another anonymous pamphlet of nine pages, dated 1727/8, is printed with *The Protest* but seems to have been written independ-

[11]Trinity College Pamphlet, Press. A.7.20. No. 14.

[12]Although the annotator is writing in 1742 or after, he noted in the margin about two of the five leading candidates, "Doctor Obins, and Mr. Hamilton, afterwards Fellows, sat at yt time." Both were elected fellows in 1728; Obins became a doctor of divinity in 1740. In my opinion, the hand of the annotator resembles that of Dr. John Lyon, Swift's keeper in his old age and a graduate of the college.

[13]*Corresp.*, III, 399. "Print" was in use in Swift's time to mean a single sheet printed for sale, a paper less than a pamphlet.

[14]Bradshaw Collection, University Library, Cambridge. Hib. 7.727.12, pp. 10-16. Wilde, *Closing Years*, pp. 89-90, refers to this pamphlet and adds in a footnote, "We are indebted to our learned friend, P. V. Fitzpatrick, for this rare tract." Stubbs printed the pamphlet as Appendix XXXVI of his *History*, pp. 416-419, with no indication as to source, although dating it 1727 and employing a slightly different title. On the present title page the pamphlet is called "a *Protest* of all the *Senior Fellows in Trinity College, Dublin*, (Except one) against the *Provost*." On an interior page it is titled as cited above, in the text. There are one or two variant readings when Stubbs's regularized version is compared with the one followed here.

ently of it, to judge from a postscript (p. 9).[15] Some, however, like the author of *An Answer*, suspected "that the same Hand wrote the Remonstrance that wrote the Protest" (*An Answer*, p. 2). It was printed by Sarah Harding, a printer whom Swift used for political pamphleteering between 1725 and 1730. Its full title is *An Humble Remonstrance in the Name of the Lads in all the Schools of Ireland, where Latin and Greek are taught: And of the young students now in the University of Dublin.*[16] Like *The Protest* it sets forth ten specific reasons why the provost's power should be restrained, and in its final paragraphs (pp. 8-9) it becomes a direct petition to the Irish Parliament then assembled (November 1727–May 1728) to inhibit "by a Law" the provost's precedent in using his "Enormous" and "Exorbitant Power."

A final pamphlet in this paper war, this time one of four double-column pages, appeared belatedly in 1728 to argue at tedious length in formal logic the case for Pellisier. Its title explains its sympathies and purpose: *An Answer to the Remonstrance of the Scholars, and the Protest of Five of the Senior Fellows of Trinity College, against the Reverend Dr. Baldwin, their Provost, on Account of His Electing Mr. Pellessier a Junior Fellow, etc, with a Defence of Mr. Pellessier against several Calumnies in that Paper.*[17] The annotator of *A Short History* noted in the margin that "Doctor Gilbert, then Vice-Provost, who was Pellisier's Tutor, was the only one of the Board, who join'd The Provost, & he far from strenuously." The author of *An Answer* seems at times to argue as strenuously for another candidate, "Sir [Henry] Hamilton," as he does for Pellisier, and it is possible that the author of *An Answer* may have been someone like Dr. Gilbert himself, or a friend of Pellisier among the junior fellows.

It is clear from the pamphlets described above that the threefold plan of the senior fellows was to protest strongly through Swift, at that time in England, to the Prince of Wales as chancellor; to make such representations as are contained in *The Protest* to the two col-

[15]"*P.S.* Since the writing of this, we have received a Copy of the *Protest* made by the five *Senior Fellows* against the *Provost*, upon chusing the above-named *Pallisier* into a Fellowship, contrary to their unanimous Opinion.

"Some of the Arguments above-made use of, are touched at in the following Protest: But this being gone to the Press, it was too late to make any Alterations."

[16]Bradshaw Collection, University Library, Cambridge, Hib. 7.727.12, pp. 1-9.

[17]Trinity College Library Pamphlet E. 4.7a, No. 55. For calling my attention to this pamphlet, as well as *A Short History*, and for supplying me with photostats, together with permission to quote from these two rare pamphlets, I wish to thank Trinity College Library and especially H. A. Parke, librarian and vice-provost.

lege visitors, the vice-chancellor, John Stearne, Bishop of Clogher, and the Archbishop of Dublin, William King; and to pursue the matter with the Irish Parliament when it met in the winter of 1727-1728, as is done in the *Remonstrance*. Among the unpublished correspondence of Archbishop William King now in the Trinity College Library there are two references to the matter which show how King viewed the situation and how he exerted his influence.[18] The death of King George I and the legal opinion of Samuel Molyneux, M.P. for the university in the Irish Parliament and secretary to the Prince of Wales, may be two main reasons why the Irish Parliament declined to consider limiting the provost's power. As Swift wrote to Sheridan in a letter from Twickenham dated July 1, 1727: "I took Dr. D—— [Delany's] Paper to the K—— when he was Pr; he and his Secretary [Molyneux] are discontented with the Provost, but they find he has Law on his Side. The King's death hath broke that Measure" (*Corresp.*, III, 221).

Swift's correspondence in 1727, some of it lost, also allows us to follow or to infer how deeply he was concerned with the welfare of his college, and how resolutely he attempted, even at a distance, to help his Tory friends among the fellows combat the influences of Provost Baldwin and of Archbishop Boulter. Since Swift appears to have received his letter (now lost) sometime during the first week of June 1727, or at least while the new King was still Prince, Dr. Delany must have written his urgent appeal for Swift's help in the disputed fellowship on or soon after the day on which the election was held, May 29, 1727. Writing from London on June 24, to Sheridan, Swift said:

[18]Mr. O'Sullivan of Trinity College Library has kindly transcribed the following entries for me from Archbishop King's Letterbook, 1725-27 (MS. N.3.8):

William King to Samuel Molyneux Esq., Dublin, 30th May, 1727:
I send enclosed a copy of an entry made in the College Registrey on the last ellection, it makes a great noise there and in town, which is a grief to me and to all that wish well to that Society. If you desire it I will get a full account of the matter and send it to you.
In my opinion it would not be amiss if his Highness as Chancellor would oblige the visitors to execute the statute for Triennial visitations, but I am not for any visitation upon a complaint, for the one being a thing of course would make no great noise, but the other would and in all probability have ill effects, but I mention this with submission to better judgements (p. 201).

William King to the Bishop of Clogher, Dublin, 28th June, 1727:
[Discussing the king's continuing to hold the chancellorship] "... pray hast to Dublin as fast as you can, for you are much wanted to help settle things in the College that go very much amiss" (p. 220).

I desire you will let Dr. D—— [Delany] know that I transcrib'd the Substance of his Letter, and the Translation of what was Register'd [in the College Register], and added a whole State of the Case, and gave it to Mrs. H——d [Howard] to give to the Prince from me, and to define that as Chancellor, he would do what he thought most fit. I forgot to ask Mrs. H——d [Howard] what was done in it, the next Time I saw her, and the Day I came to Town [Wednesday, 14 June] came the News of the K——'s [King's] Death. . . . (*Corresp.*, III, 218)

It is possible that Swift forgot to ask Mrs. Howard about the matter when next he saw her, because that was the day on which Swift presented to her his penetrating "Character of Mrs. H[owar]d," dated June 12, 1727.[19] Another letter "with the inclosed Print," now lost, from Sheridan and dated in all probability about June 15 was acknowledged by Swift in his letter of June 24.

Possibly the most lamentable loss is that of the memorandum which Swift prepared and forwarded through Mrs. Howard to the Prince of Wales before he became King. In all likelihood it was as forceful and as vigorous an account of the actions of Provost Baldwin and of his motives in exercising his negative as any we now have. And all the more so, because Swift himself was seemingly even more directly involved with the fellowships held at Trinity College, Dublin, in 1727 than has hitherto been suspected.

III

HM 14346 consists of two leaves (6¼ x 3⅞ inches) with notations in the hand of Jonathan Swift on the first two pages, and again, written upside down, on the last page. Page three is blank.

The first two pages contain headings for what was probably intended to be a political prose pamphlet entitled "Proposal for Virtue." Sir Henry Craik first printed the notes from the Theophilus Swift papers, then in the possession of Frederick Locker-Lampson, in the second edition (1894) of his *Life of Swift* (II, 166-167). Both Craik and Temple Scott, who referred to and quoted Craik's note in his *Prose Works* (VII, 375-376), believed that a "Proposal" was written in England during Swift's last visit there from April to September 1727. A reference in the manuscript to the "late K——" makes it seem almost certain that Swift noted down his thoughts at some time soon after the death of King George I on June 11, 1727. The

---

19 T. Scott, *Prose Works*, XI, 147.

news of the King's death in Osnabrugge reached London at almost the same moment that Swift came up to the city on June 14, 1727.[20] Whatever the case, it seems certain that Swift had the folded sheet of paper with him in England during his last visit there in 1727.

The last page, reproduced below, contains seventeen lines of memorandum written in the hand of Swift and noting down what appears to be the draft of a will, almost certainly Swift's own. The notes, written hurriedly and in places difficult to decipher because of the foldings of the paper, sketch out a considerable endowment in land to Trinity College, Dublin, to establish a junior fellowship there, the recipient to be known as "Swift's Fellow." The first eleven lines lay down the conditions of sale and leasing of the land to be purchased, the method of selecting the fellow, and the direction that the land should be left to Dr. Steevens's Hospital should the college refuse the gift intended. Some of the legal formulas here used are similar to those employed by Swift in his own later will and codicils and to the conditions specified by Stella when she drafted her will a month before her death on January 28, 1727/8. The next four lines of the draft are set off by a diagonal stroke, suggesting an afterthought, and are concerned with some differences between "Dr. Delany's Scheam" and "mine." The last two lines are again set off by double diagonal strokes and add a further condition, "The Executors to meet once a month about this affair." The size of the gift, the legal form, and some of the expressions ("Executors," for example) are those of a will.

HM 14346, page 4

1   A 100 ll a year to be purchased in any Province
but Connaught, of Land not let in lease above 40
years. Lease not to be for above 21 years. the Tenant
bound by penl clauses to improve [?] &c. No fine taken [?]
5 The Present Tenant, if requird [?] to be preferrd [?] G 8 pr
cent <but> but not Sinck. The Fellow to be chosen by
Provost and 7 Senrs. Provost to have the casting Voice
or to elct junr fellow to make up 9. <A> if this
refusd, the land to be left to Dr Stephens hospitll

[20]*Corresp.*, III, 218 (June 24, 1727, to Sheridan): "The Day I came to Town came the News of the K___'s Death. . . ." Abel Boyer, ed. *Political State of Great Britain*, XXXIII (1727), 549: "On *Wednesday*, the 14th of June, about three a clock in the afternoon, a Messenger brought the surprizing News of the King's Death to Sir *Robert Walpole*, then at *Chelsea*, who immediately carried it to the Prince and Princess of *Wales* at *Richmond*; Whereupon their Royal Highnesses came, with all Speed to *Leicester-House*."

10 The fellow to be called Swift's Fellow To go to
  Engld in a Winter [?] to stay

                            /

  All this wrong on Dr Delany's
  Scheam; For mine was to have <the>
15 <an> the Fellow chosen evry year, to have
  the 100 ll a year

                          //

  The Executors to meet once a month
  about this affair

Many questions come to mind at once about the generous fellowship here proposed in Swift's handwriting. When were the notations
made? Was Swift proposing to establish a fellowship at T.C.D. from
his own resources, or was he helping to draft a will for someone else?
Why was he establishing a fellowship and one which allowed the
recipient to travel? Such questions may be tentatively answered by
examining the internal evidences of the memorandum in detail and by
referring them to the external evidence connected with the disputed
election of a fellow at T.C.D. in 1727, as well as to certain facts of
Swift's life.

From what has been said above, it is clear that Swift would not have
established in his own right nor encouraged anyone else to establish
for him a junior fellowship bearing his name, after he had learned of
the arbitrary action of Provost Baldwin in the fellowships held in
May 1727. Therefore the will must have been sketched out before
that time. If we may assume for the moment that the will is Swift's
own, it is also possible to settle upon a date before which it is most
unlikely that Swift would have had available the considerable amount
of money required to establish the terms of the will. In the summer
of 1725 Swift was visiting at Quilca, Dr. Sheridan's country house in
Cavan, where the Dean busied himself with final revisions of *Gulliver's Travels*. In May 1725, by the defalcation of his friend John
Pratt, deputy vice-treasurer and brother of the former provost of the
college, Swift appeared about to lose over £1,200: "Something more
than all I had in the world."[21] Although Swift faced his impending loss
stoically, he appeared relieved to learn by mid-July 1725 that somehow he was to get back all but a few pounds through the efforts of
the Reverend John Worrall and through the honesty of Pratt himself.

[21]David Nichol Smith, ed. *The Letters of Jonathan Swift to Charles Ford* (Oxford,
1935), p. 121. See also *Corresp.*, III, 64, 74, 75.

Writing from Quilca on July 9, 1725, to thank Worrall, Swift also directed him to "inquire where the money may be safely put out at six pounds *per cent*" (*Corresp.*, III, 74). It is clear, then, that in spite of the near disaster to his total fortune, Swift had available in July 1725, ready to reinvest, although this time more safely, the sum of £1,200, a sum which was just about what would be needed to return the amount of £100 per year called for by the Swift fellowship. By her will, for example, Stella left £1,000 in reversion to establish a chaplainship at Steevens's Hospital; in 1783 it was returning £107 per year, and in 1803, £121.[22]

Not only did Swift have the necessary sum in hand after mid-July 1725, he had also, as a letter of July 9, 1725, to Archdeacon Walls shows, recently declared his intention of making at some time a public benefaction of the £1,200, or whatever constituted his fortune.

I find there is some Expedient found out relating to my Business with Mr Pratt, and that I shall not be wholly undone. I have Witnesses enough, that I behaved my self with sufficient Temper in that Matter, neither was I in Raptures, to find I had saved something out of that Shipwreck, by which the Publick would have been greater Losers than I. What I had I came honestly by, and if it should please God to disappoint me of doing publick Service with it, I must submitt, and he will not lay the Defect to my Charge. (*Corresp.*, III, 73)

Although such "publick Service" seems here still to be only intended or contemplated, Swift may have been enough frightened by the near loss of his fortune to begin active plans for establishing his intended public benefaction as soon as he returned to Dublin in late September or early October 1725.

A worthy and deserving object of his proposed "publick Service" may also have occurred to Swift at this time—the welfare of the neglected scholars of Trinity College. At the very moment that his own fortune was seemingly lost, on July 3, 1725, Swift was writing in unselfish terms to Lord Carteret, the new Lord Lieutenant, to recommend deserved preferments for several worthy clergymen and "Natives," fellows of T.C.D. (*Corresp.*, III, 70-72). Again in April 1726 Swift made the lack of preferment of "Natives" and fellows of T.C.D. a point of discussion in his presentation of Irish grievances to Sir Robert Walpole (*Corresp.*, III, 132-133). On November 26,

[22]Wilde, *Closing Years*, p. 118, and J. Warburton, J. Whitelaw, and R. Walsh, *History of the City of Dublin*, 2 vols. (London, 1818), II, 684.

1725, Swift wrote from "Wretched Dublin, in miserable Ireland" to James Stopford, then traveling abroad, that Provost Baldwin and "such beasts" had given away all of the junior fellow's pupils (*Corresp.*, III, 115). About the same time Baldwin with Archbishop Boulter's help successfully prevented Dr. Delany from obtaining a necessary royal dispensation of a college statute, thereby denying him a lucrative living in Dublin that had been offered by Christ Church Cathedral (Boulter, *Letters*, I, 48). In April 1727 Swift stopped off at Oxford on his way to London and visited his old friend Stratford. Stratford noted that Swift railed at the Lord Lieutenant because he had recently denied Delany a preferment promised "because he was suspected to be somewhat of a Tory."[23] From such discouragements, done through political motives, to the advancement of native scholars, Swift may have recognized the need of T.C.D. for additional benefactions that would be above the power of the provost to distribute politically, benefactions such as the fellowship created in the draft of a will.

After mid-July 1725, then, and before June 1727, Swift had in hand the amount needed to establish the fellowship mentioned; in this same period he also stated his intention of making a public benefaction with his fortune; and more and more he perceived that the neglected welfare of the graduates and fellows of T.C.D. was a worthy and deserving object of such benefactions, especially in the face of such increasing discouragements as were suffered by some fellows, because of partisan politics.

Much of the internal evidence in the draft of a will supports the biographical and circumstantial evidence. Dr. Delany's name is mentioned there in what seems to be an afterthought and in such a manner as to suggest that, although Swift and Delany differed over how the fellowship was to work, they had consulted together in drawing up the will. In so momentous an affair it is logical that Swift would seek the advice of his friend, the leading Tory among the senior fellows. There were, however, between July 1725 and June 1727 only two periods of about six months each during which Swift and Delany could have consulted together directly in Dublin. Swift returned from Quilca to the city in late September or early October 1725. He left for his first visit to England in early March 1726, returning in September of the same year. Again in early April 1727 he left once

[23]Historical Manuscripts Commission, *Manuscripts of His Grace the Duke of Portland*, VII (London, 1901), 446-447.

more for England. So far as we know, Dr. Delany was not in communication with Swift during his two English visits except in connection with the disputed fellowships of 1727, nor had he himself ever been to England until his visit of July 1727.[24] If Swift conferred directly with Dr. Delany about establishing the Swift fellowship, he must have done so the easiest way, by consulting him in Dublin between October 1725 and early March 1726, or between September 1726 and early April 1727. Since Dr. Delany was consulted in the matter, he very likely was intended to become one of the "Executors" mentioned, as he later became one of the executors of Swift's will of 1740.

The question remains whether the draft contained in HM 14346 is Swift's own will. It is written in his hand, establishing a fellowship bearing his name, in a scheme called "mine." Prior to embarking upon two successive voyages to England would be a good time for a man approaching sixty to make his will, if he had not already done so. And the making of wills was on Swift's mind at the time. In a letter to John Worrall from England dated July 15, 1726, Swift urged the ailing Stella to make her will. For some reason Stella did not do so until December 1727. The same letter went on to say that: "Her intentions are to leave the Interest of all her Fortune to her Mother and Sister during their Lives, and afterwards to Dr Stephens's Hospital, to purchase Lands for such Uses there as she Designs" (*Corresp.*, III, 141). This statement of intention on Stella's part would seem to me to rule out the possibility that the draft of a will here presented was drawn up by Swift on Stella's behalf, since she had not yet made a will, and had intentions of leaving her fortune to Dr. Steevens's Hospital and not to the college. Apart from Stella, there would be few other people in Dublin at the time close enough to Swift to establish a fellowship in his name with enough money to lay out for such a benefaction. It seems to me more likely that Swift suited his action to his words of advice to Stella and drew up his own will as example to her, before going to England on one of his two visits there in 1726 and 1727.

Again, the draft of a will contains conditions of land tenure and legal provisos that are characteristically Swiftian. The prohibition

---

[24]F. Elrington Ball, *Swift's Verse* (London, 1929), p. 232, says that Delany first came to London as one of a delegation from Trinity College to present an address of loyalty to the new King George II on his accession. Swift remarked, in a letter of Oct. 26, 1731, to the Countess of Suffolk, that he had presented Dr. Delany to the then Mrs. Howard at Marble Hill, presumably in 1727 (*Corresp.*, III, 50).

against purchasing land in Connaught appears both in Swift's last will in the same terms and in Stella's will of 1727, which Swift may have helped draft. A limit of twenty-one years for leases of land purchased is also a restriction in which Swift believed firmly—a notion made into law for lease of church lands by a statute of the time of Charles the First in order to prevent lands being leased for lives or in perpetuity during which time the buying power of the cash income might diminish or "sink."[25] The binding of the tenant to improve the land by means of penal clauses should he fail to do so; the stipulation that no fines be taken in lieu of increases in the amounts of lease; and the general preferential treatment of the present tenant, are all typical rewards and punishments by which Swift believed careful husbandry and continuous improvement of the land were encouraged.[26] Similar conditions appear also in Stella's will of 1727. All embody characteristic lessons connected with land tenure which Swift had learned from his experience as an administrator of church lands and from his disastrous experience with the leases set by other earlier church administrators who had not taken such care as Swift of the investments in land entrusted to their care.

Other provisos of the will are characteristically his, and they seem to me to point to the period between September 1726 and April 1727 as the time when the will may have been drafted. The method of electing "Swift's Fellow," the "Provost to have the casting Voice," resembles very closely the election of a fellow as recommended in the *Remonstrance* of 1727-1728, which proposed in one place (p. 7) that the provost's power be lessened, "leaving him only a casting Voice." Besides leaving the provost a vote decisive only in case of a tie, another alternative here proposed in the draft of a will and one that was sometimes employed by the board in fellowships when not enough senior fellows were present, was to elect a junior fellow (usually the one most senior) so that, in this case, there would be nine voters and hence no ties. Such a double-barreled condition implies that Swift, at the time of drafting the will, already had strong doubts about the fair-mindedness of Provost Baldwin, a suspicion that would exist in 1725-1726 and would be further strengthened by 1726-1727. An ad-

---

[25]See Swift's *Some Arguments against Enlarging the Power of Bishops* (1723); *Prose Writings*, IX, 46. See also Louis A. Landa, *Swift and the Church of Ireland* (Oxford, 1954), p. 100.

[26]*Prose Writings*, IX, 45-55; Landa, *Swift and the Church of Ireland*, especially Chap. III, 96-123.

ditional condition, that the land was to go to Dr. Steevens's Hospital should the college refuse to accept the endowment of a fellowship under the conditions specified, also implies a strong distrust of Provost Baldwin, and it tends in the direction of Stella's will of December 30, 1727, which left the bulk of her estate to establish a chaplaincy at the same hospital.

The difference between "Dr. Delany's Scheam" and "mine" is also a characteristic one. Delany and Swift differed on a similar point when the question of the election of fellows to the Erasmus Smith Professorships arose in January 1727/8 (*Corresp.*, III, 259, and notes). In the present case Swift apparently wanted the new fellow to be chosen each year and to receive the full £100. By implication Dr. Delany appears to have favored, as he did in the question of the Smith Professorships, giving the fellowship to someone who was already a junior fellow to hold as long as he was a member of the society as an additional perquisite, or to have elected the "Swift Fellow" as an additional member of the society without limit of time.

In what seems to be a clause that allowed the Swift Fellow to go to England for some definite period ("a Winter"?), Swift may be showing the influence of one of his most respected young Tory friends among the junior fellows, James Stopford, who returned to Dublin in the spring of 1727 after two years of travel in England and on the Continent. Stopford had been helped by a loan from Stella to make an earlier trip abroad and this time was encouraged by Swift, who wrote high praise of him in letters of introduction to Lord Bolingbroke, Pope, Gay, and Arbuthnot.[27] Swift's own delight in his visits to England in 1726 and 1727 may also have led to this proviso of the will.

To sum up, then, we may assume from the biographical and internal evidence of HM 14346 that the draft of a will there blocked out is Swift's own will, drawn up in Dublin after consultation with Dr. Delany between July 1725 and March 1726, or, more probably, between the time of Swift's return from England in September 1726 and before his departure once more for England in April 1727, at which time Swift carried with him the draft of his will establishing a Swift's fellowship at T.C.D., a paper upon which he also made notations for a prose pamphlet, in London sometime after the King's death in June 1727.

Several passages in two of the pamphlets mentioned above seem to

---

[27]*Corresp.*, III, 199, 201-202, 202. Swift called Stopford "The most valuable young man of this Kingdom" (*Corresp.*, III, 22).

support the internal evidence of HM 14346 that the will drafted there was Swift's own will, probably his first. Archbishop Boulter suspected Dr. Delany of being "a great influence in these parts" (Boulter, *Letters*, I, 49). *The Protest* of the five dissenting senior fellows was the work chiefly of Dr. Delany. The author of *An Answer* also thought that *The Protest* was the work of a single hand, and he further suspected that the same hand wrote the *Remonstrance*. This last surmise need not necessarily be accepted, since the apology at the end of the *Remonstrance* (p. 9) for covering some of the same ground as did *The Protest* sounds sincere. Yet both were printed together, and by Sarah Harding, a printer who also did work for Swift, Delany, Sheridan and other Tories from the college or from the circle of Swift's Dublin friends between 1725 and 1730, and both pamphlets follow a similar line of argument. It is possible that the author of the *Remonstrance* was someone as close to Swift as Delany, the originator of *The Protest*, and someone, moreover, were he writing between January and March of 1728, who may have had Swift's own version of the affair to work with. Dr. Sheridan seems to me to be a likely possibility, since, as a Tory schoolmaster, he was professionally interested, and as the instructor of Arthur Ford and the friend of Swift he was personally involved.

As one of its seven reasons *The Protest* said:

Fourthly, Because we are of Opinion that the Exertion of this absolute Power [of a negative] in the *Provost*, may prevent future Benefactions to the *College*, particularly with regard to the Foundation of *new Fellowships*. And we take this Opinion to be well grounded for many Reasons sufficiently evident, but more especially this; that a Person who lately intended a considerable Donation to the Society for founding a *new Fellowship*, and advised with some of us upon that Head, has on account of the late Nomination, as we have too much reason to believe, altered his Intentions, and determined his Benefaction another way to the great loss of the Society. (p. 13)

An Humble Remonstrance twice mentions, and with even greater detail, a similar benefaction which was withdrawn:

[Concerning the unprecedented use by Baldwin of the provost's negative] . . . the bad Consequences whereof have already been a great Discouragement to Gentlemen of Fortune from sending their Sons to this University, as well as to Benefactors, from founding any new *Fellowships*, where the choice is to depend upon the Passions of any single Man, whether they will be rightly disposed of or no. (pp. 5-6)

It is manifest, that nothing is more likely to discourage Charitable and generous Spirits from becoming Benefactors, than the deserved Reproach of such infamous Practices. It is not unknown that a certain Person, who had applied great Part of his Fortune towards founding a *Fellowship* in this University, with a more ample Income than usual; did, upon the notice he received of the *Provost's* Demeanour, in this flagrant Case, immediately tear all the Papers relating to that Settlement, with a Resolution never to dispose of one Farthing in favour of the Society. (p.7)

The unidentified benefactor mentioned in both pamphlets, then, "lately" intended to establish a new junior fellowship at T.C.D. "with a more ample Income than usual." The amount intended to be given was "a considerable Donation" and would have involved for the unknown benefactor a "great Part of his Fortune." Since the junior fellows at T.C.D. were receiving in the 1720's about £60 per year,[28] a fellowship of £100, as set out in the draft of a will, would be both generous and "ample"; if the donor were Swift, a benefaction of about £1,200 would be both a "considerable" gift and one that would have taken, in 1725-1727, the greater part of his private fortune. According to *The Protest*, the unknown benefactor "advised with some of us," and most likely with Dr. Delany, the author of that pamphlet. According to the *Remonstrance*, the unknown benefactor also "received notice" of the provost's actions, which suggests that he was at some distance from Dublin at the time of the disputed fellowships, and "did . . . immediately tear all the Papers relating to that Settlement, with a Resolution never to dispose of one Farthing in favour of the Society." This reaction may explain why only the draft of a will remains, and why so little has been heard of the matter since. But the description of a violent reaction and the immediate resolution (in which the would-be benefactor's very words seem still to echo) suggest also that the unknown benefactor was probably a Tory, or at least someone who had good previous reason to become highly incensed at the provost's first use of his negative for political purposes. These implications, taken together with the internal evidence of the manuscript cited above, it seems to me, support the assumption that the unknown benefactor described in *The Protest* and the *Remonstrance* could only be Jonathan Swift; that the "new Fellowship" "lately" contemplated could only be the "Swift's Fellow" proposed in the draft of a will in Swift's hand contained in HM 14346; and that the draft itself is all that remains of the first will that Swift—in all

28Stubbs, *History*, pp. 209-210, 230.

probability—ever made, a will which disposed of a major part of his own fortune to create a generous fellowship at his old college; and one which Swift destroyed in anger when he learned of the arbitrary exercise by Provost Baldwin of the provost's negative.

IV

IT WAS, of course, while Swift was staying with Alexander Pope at Twickenham that the disputed fellowships of 1727 were held. Word of the surprising outcome apparently reached Swift in a letter written by Dr. Delany about the time of the Trinity Monday elections, May 29, 1727. Dr. Sheridan appears to have followed up with additional details, including, in all probability, some such printed matter as *A Short History*. Sometime before June 14, when the news of King George I's death carried them to London, and at the time the Prince and Princess were at Richmond Park and Mrs. Howard still at Marble Lodge, Swift digested Delany's information about Baldwin's first use of the provost's negative; translated from the Latin the censure which Delany and his fellows had caused to be entered into the College Register; and "added a whole State of the Case" to be forwarded as a memorandum, probably before June 12 through Mrs. Howard to the Prince as chancellor and to Samuel Molyneux, his secretary and M.P. for the university, by way of protest. It was somewhat guiltily that Swift confessed to Sheridan in his letter of June 24: "I forgot to ask Mrs. H——d [Howard] what was done in it, the next Time I saw her, and the Day I came to Town came the News of the K——'s [King's] Death .." (*Corresp.*, III, 218).

In an undated note to Mrs. Howard, which very likely—out of guilt—was written on the same day (June 24) as the letter to Sheridan, Swift asked Mrs. Howard for more information about the protest presented to the Prince (*Corresp.*, III, 220). In the same note Swift started the question of who should become the new chancellor of the university now that the Prince was King. Very delicately Swift scouted the possibility that Frederick, the new young Prince of Wales, would be appointed, by lightly crossing out yet leaving still easily legible, the clause "who I doubt is too young." Then he mentioned his real candidate and Pope's friend, the Earl of Scarborough (*Corresp.*, III, 220). A short while later, however, writing to Sheridan from Twickenham on July 1, he said, "I propos'd the Pr. of *Wales* to be Chancellor, and I believe so it will go" (*Corresp.*, III, 221)—as it did.

The pressures and influences at work upon Provost Baldwin in the fellowships of 1727 at first may have been only suspected by Swift, at least until he heard from his friends in Dublin. But Swift appears to have sized up accurately the situation developing in Dublin. The motives which led Baldwin to exercise his first negative may now, however, be traced through the pamphlets mentioned above. In *The Protest* Delany and the fellows could only hint broadly, by way of ironical hypothesis, what Swift called "putting cases." For example, the fellows' second reason for rejecting the influence exerted upon Provost Baldwin concluded ironically: ". . . supposing us equally good Judges of the Merits of the Candidates, and equally upright as well as unprejudiced with *Dr. Gilbert*, and as little liable to be influenced of any kind as the *Provost . . .*" (p. 11). The seventh heading also returns in irony upon the subject of "Arbitrary and Absolute Power" being exercised "in the Reign of *King George*, in an Age of Liberty and Learning..." (p. 15).

The anonymous *Short History*, a copy of which Swift may have received from Sheridan, was even more outspoken. It has Balderdashinus [Baldwin] say baldly:

Phordianus [Ford] is indeed a Scholar, and an honest Young-Man I allow, but this is not an Age for either Learning or Virtue. I have a mind to quit this troublesome Life, and would fain be chosen a Pontifex [bishop]; which I cannot be, except I make choice of one recommended to me by some of the Rhodian [English] Governours, under whose Jurisdiction we are. I'll do as I please this time, I hope to leave you before the next, and then you may do as you Please, Gentlemen. I must ask your pardons, if I set a higher value upon a good Preferment, than a good Conscience. I would rather go to Tartarus drawn in a fine Chariot, than walk bare-foot to Olympus. (p. 2)

A few lines farther the influence of Archbishop Boulter is indicated directly: "It was owing to the Influence of an *Archimagus* [an archbishop] who spirited away his Reason and Conscience the night before."

A later annotator wrote boldly over the title of *A Short History*: "An Account of the Proceedings at Fellowships, when Doctor John Pellisier was nominated, by the Provost, a Fellow; by the Influence of Doctor Boulter, then Lord Primate."

With Boulter's influence sustained, the college's case against Provost Baldwin now dismissed, his candidate for the chancellorship of the university already defeated, Swift may have begun to sense, as early as July 1, 1727, which way the political wind was going to blow, so far as Ireland was concerned. Within a week or so he went off with Lord Oxford and Pope for a long ramble to Cambridgeshire, only to be afflicted upon his return in early August by an attack of giddiness and deafness and not long after by the painful news that Stella was dying in Ireland. All further thoughts of Trinity College and of Irish politics were driven from his head.

Not so, however, with Swift's Whig enemies in Dublin. As soon as commencement at Trinity College was over, Archbishop Boulter sent Provost Baldwin off to London, the bearer of a letter to the Archbishop of Canterbury dated July 6. Boulter wrote:

There has lately been an election of a fellow in the College, which has occasioned a quarrel there, in which he [Baldwin] has been very much misrepresented and abused: and he has been threatened with their [the Tory party's] preferring a petition to the King, and having the power given him by the statutes reduced. The power he has is indeed beyond any thing any Head of a College has in *Oxford*, but is all little enough to keep the College here from being a seminary of jacobitism: through the strength of a faction in the College against him. (Boulter, *Letters*, I, 180)

By early August, however, Boulter seemed relieved to learn that already the Tory opposition to the exercise of the provost's negative had come to nothing; on August 10 he wrote again to the Archbishop of Canterbury, "I thank your Lordship for your kind reception of Dr. *Baldwin*, and your intention to support him, if there be occasion" (Boulter, *Letters*, I, 190). Needless to say, there was no further occasion to do much about the matter; the Irish Parliament, meeting from November 1727 to May 1728, appears not to have taken cognizance of the petition made in the anonymous *Remonstrance* that the provost's power should be limited by law.

One of the sad duties facing Swift when he returned to Ireland in late September or early October 1727 was to help Stella, now in her last illness, to draw up her will. The will, which has been reprinted, is dated December 30, 1727, about a month before her death.[29] Swift's influence is probably at work in such, by now, familiar provisos as the land to be purchased in any county but Connaught; penal clauses to insure improvement and proper use of the land by the tenant; the land to be leased for a specific period of time (forty-one years) and not let for lives or in perpetuity; and preferential treatment provided for the

[29]Wilde, *Closing Years*, pp. 97-101.

present tenant if a good husbandman. These provisos follow closely the same conditions laid down in the draft of Swift's will contained in HM 14346.[30]

The conditions by which the chaplain was chosen seem to show Swift's immediate influence, since they create a position that favors Trinity College by devising what amounts to another junior fellowship for a graduate of that college. Some of the conditions laid down also suggest that the lesson learned by Swift and his friends from the disputed fellowships of 1727 was incorporated into this part of Stella's will. For example, the chaplain is to be "native" born, to be a Master of Arts specifically of T.C.D., and like the fellows there, to be in orders, to live celibate, with specific duties of attendance that resemble college duties. The income per year was to be a little more than that received by a junior fellow at the college. Significantly, the Dean of St. Patrick's, as well as the provost of the college, although not governors of the foundation, were ex officio each to have a vote in electing the chaplain, thus canceling each other's power, if they were (as they continued to be for some time) such violently opposed persons as Dean Swift and Provost Baldwin.[31] Since Stella's will, in effect, creates a chaplaincy at Dr. Steevens's Hospital that is very much like the fellowship proposed but withdrawn by Swift in the draft of his first will (with the exception of the provision about going to England), and since the chaplaincy is established in such a way as to check Baldwin's exercise of his arbitrary power, it accomplishes, in some degree, what Swift had hoped for in his proposed fellowship at the college. Thus, from 1731 onward, when Swift came to draft his next will, he could turn to another public benefaction that became even more useful and famous, the establishment of a hospital for idiots and lunatics.

The total defeat of the Tory opposition to Provost Baldwin, which he had led, seems utterly to have crushed the spirit of Dr. Delany and others of the fellows. In January 1727/8, a few weeks before Stella's death, through the influence of Swift and Lord Carteret, the Lord Lieutenant, Delany was presented the college living of Derryvullen and the chancellorship of Christ Church Cathedral in Dublin.[32] A

---

[30]Stella's will is somewhat more specific than HM 14346 about increasing rent when new leases are made, and about new leases being negotiated only in the last two years of the expiring lease (Wilde, *Closing Years*, p. 100).

[31]Ibid., pp. 98-99.

[32]*Corresp.*, III, 259, n. 1.

passing remark by Swift in his ironic *Vindication of his Excellency, the Lord Carteret* (1730) seems to indicate that Dr. Delany made up his mind to resign from the society soon after the first exercise of the provost's negative, and possibly as a result: "Three or four Years ago, the Doctor grown weary of an Academick Life, for some Reasons best Known to the Managers of the Discipline in that Learned Society (which it may not be for their Honour to mention) resolved to leave it; although by the Benefit of his Pupils, and his Senior-Fellowship with all its Perquisites, he received every Year between Nine Hundred and a Thousand Pounds" (*Prose Writings*, XII, 165). Although Swift went on to calculate that Delany had reduced his income by at least two-thirds in resigning his fellowship in February 1727/8, the future Dean of Down did not actually suffer unduly from it. By gradually and skillfully changing his politics (a shift which caused some coolness between Swift and himself for a time), by devoting his attention more and more to safely learned theological subjects instead of politics, and by means of two careful marriages, Dr. Delany prospered.[33]

Within a year of Delany's resignation both Dr. Helsham and Dr. Clayton had resigned as senior fellows. Since James Stopford, another victim of Baldwin, had resigned his junior fellowship in 1727, Swift found by 1730 that he had few friends left in the college. The Whig power under Baldwin was triumphant. Although later in 1734 Swift interested himself in the low state of discipline at the college and in dispensations for fellows to hold livings while still members of the society, his influence and interest diminished with the defeat and dispersal of his friends among the fellows of the college (*Corresp.*, IV, 273-274; 284-287).

The later careers of John Pellisier and Arthur Ford, the rival candidates about whom the disputed fellowships of 1727 centered, read very much like the brief histories of Eugenio and Corusodes which Swift recounted in an *Intelligencer* (No. VII) of 1728.[34] Satirically, Swift there furnished parallel case histories of two young Oxford students and clergymen, one of whom, Corusodes, the "man of discretion," was well rewarded by the world, while Eugenio, a man of virtue and true learning, was neglected and sank finally into obscurity.

[33]Boulter, *Letters*, II, 20, says, in a footnote, that "Dr. *Delany* in the latter part of the Primate's time, made as much court to him as ever he had done before to Dean *Swift*."

[34]*Prose Writings*, XII, 41-45.

Pellisier followed almost exactly in the footsteps of his college tutor and mentor, the vice-provost, Dr. Gilbert. In 1738 he became a Doctor of Divinity and was appointed in the same year the Donegal Lecturer, a post once held by Dr. Gilbert. Like Gilbert he was, in 1746, appointed Professor of Divinity; in the previous year he had been made vice-provost under Baldwin. Like Gilbert, Pellisier quit the society in 1752 to accept a lucrative college living as Rector of Ardstraw. He died in January 1781, aged seventy-eight. Before leaving the college, Pellisier became the tutor of the young Edmund Burke and had the honor of examining him for entrance.[35]

After the fellowships of 1727 relatively little more is heard of Arthur Ford. Like Swift's Eugenio, he ended "utterly undistinguished and forgotten" as a minor clergyman, being collated a canon in the diocese of Kildare in January 1736/7 and finally as a prebendary of Dromore in September 1748.[36] He died in 1768. Appropriately, the last time that Ford's and Pellisier's names appeared together was in 1735 when both were listed as subscribers to George Faulkner's Dublin edition of Swift's works.

The negativing of Ford and the nomination of Pellisier came as the climax to a lengthy struggle among the senior fellows, between Swift and the Tory faction in the college and the Whig faction backed by Archbishop Boulter. Eventually, through Swift's endeavors, the disputed fellowship elections of 1727 reached the notice of the Prince of Wales at the moment when he became the new King of England. The intervention of Archbishop Boulter involved the Archbishop of Canterbury. As Swift was quick to realize, and as he indicated when he destroyed his first will which was to establish a new fellowship in his name at the college, the outcome of the fellowship elections of 1727, in which Baldwin first exercised with impunity the negative, demonstrated conclusively the dominance of the provost over his senior fellows, of Whig over Tory, of "foreign" or English-born place-seekers over competent "natives," of England over Ireland, to make, as Archbishop Boulter and the Whigs desired, Ireland an absolute English dependency. As sometimes happens, university politics became an example and a mirror of national politics.

[35]Stubbs, *History*, pp. 203-204; Burtchaell, p. 659.

[36]Henry Cotton, ed. *Fasti ecclesiae Hibernicae* (Dublin, 1848-49), II, 249; III, 303.

Chapter Five

"RAGE OR RAILLERY": TRANSCRIPTIONS OF *AN EPISTLE TO A LADY* AND *ON POETRY: A RAPSODY*

I

THE RARE BOOK COLLECTION at the Huntington Library includes a finely made four-volume octavo edition of Jonathan Swift's works (No. 81494) published by subscription in 1735 at Dublin by George Faulkner. Volume II, which contains the bulk of Swift's poetry printed to that date, has tipped in between pages 456 and 457 a gathering of eight leaves numbered 1-14 by way of pagination (the last leaf is not numbered). On these fourteen pages, carefully transcribed in a neat contemporary hand that is *not* Swift's, are a hitherto unnoticed version of *An Epistle to a Lady* (1733) and some passages of political satire prudently omitted from *On Poetry: A Rapsody* (1733). Soon after the publication in mid-November 1733 of *An Epistle*, the printer, the publishers, and two of Swift's Irish friends, the Rev. Matthew Pilkington and Mrs. Mary Barber, were arrested because of their part in the publication of that poem. Sir Robert Walpole is said by Thomas Sheridan to have been so angered by *An Epistle* and *A Rapsody*, published at the end of December 1733, that he had sworn out—until otherwise persuaded—a warrant for the arrest of Swift himself.[1] When *A Rapsody* was reprinted in Dublin soon after, several printers and publishers there were arrested.[2]

Although (or perhaps because) the two poems were considered libelous in their time, they have since come to be valued among the best of Swift's major political satires in verse. Probably in composition and revision, certainly in publication, as well as in afterfame, these two poems have always been linked together. Examined criti-

[1]Sheridan, *Life*, pp. 276-278.
[2]*Poems*, II, 640.

cally and in relation to each other, they furnish almost perfect examples of complementary forms: the one of *raillery*, which turns seeming blame to praise sincerely meant; the other of *mock panegyric*, which turns seeming praise to blame by the extended use of verbal irony. So expertly was the irony of *A Rapsody* sustained, that, as Swift himself said, "Queen Carolina was pleased"—at first.[3]

The uniqueness of these transcriptions of (possibly) libelous matter, the sumptuous bindings of all four volumes, the quality and watermarking of the paper in Volume II, the contemporary Irish bookplate in each volume, all suggest the likelihood that Mr. Huntington obtained them from an Irish source; and that they were originally, perhaps, one of only a few sets—a special job struck off by Faulkner and especially bound as a presentation copy for one of Swift's great or close friends in Dublin. It is also possible that Faulkner may have kept or disposed of this set himself.[4]

At first glance, the appearance of the volumes is the most striking thing about them. All four are still in their original bindings of dark-blue morocco, handsomely gilt at the edges and expertly tooled on front, back, spine, and edges. The unusual design of the tongues of flame and alternating crowns of the roll resembles very closely work from the tools of a craftsman whom Maurice Craig, in his recent book *Irish Bookbindings: 1600-1800* (London, 1954), identifies as "The College Binder." The Huntington bindings are very like Plate XXI in Craig's work, an example from "The College Binder" dated 1733-1737 (Pine's *Horace*).[5] It seems to me, then, that the bindings of the Huntington volumes are the work of "The College Binder," finished probably in early 1735 soon after the date of publication, at which time the two poems mentioned above were still politically—and legally—hot. The gathering of eight leaves upon which the transcriptions are made appears to have been bound in at the same time. These pages bear the "Strasburg Lily and Bend" watermark of the fine laid paper of the rest of the volume, and their edges were gilt along with the rest of the printed matter.

[3]See below (p. 113) the hitherto unpublished dialogue in the Anglo-Angli "language" from Forster No. 530.

[4]In his advertisement for the 1735 edition Faulkner mentions "A few Copies are Printed on Royal Paper, at Forty Shillings in Sheets, or Two Guineas Bound," of which this set may be one (Ball, *Corresp.*, V, 449).

[5]Mr. Harold M. Nixon of the British Museum staff has kindly examined the bindings with me and agrees generally with my opinion, although, of course, he is in no way responsible for my conclusions.

The early eighteenth-century bookplate is engraved with the crest of the Tisdalls of Charlesfort, County Meath.[6] Three Tisdalls (or Tisdel[l]s) subscribed for Faulkner's original edition: Charles, Philip, and William, the last, Swift's sometime friend and an early suitor for Stella's hand. It seems unlikely that the bookplate is his, since the Rev. William Tisdall died on June 8, 1735. For political and professional reasons Philip Tisdall would also seem to be ruled out. He was an ardent Whig, a lawyer who eventually became Attorney General for Ireland. In 1739 as a Whig M.P. for the university, he was involved in a disputed election in which Swift engaged against him. More likely the owner was Charles Tisdall of County Meath, scion of the Charlesfort family and a man precocious enough to matriculate at T.C.D., aged fourteen, September 14, 1734, as a fellow commoner. Whichever Tisdall came into possession of the volumes, it seems certain that he was not the first owner. Most clearly—but disappointingly—the original bookplates, wider and longer than the present ones, had been removed (the marbled end papers show signs of scrubbing and removal) before the present bookplates were pasted in. Two leaves of the preliminary matter (A2, A3) in Volume II have also been cut away, the stubs still visible. Each was written upon in ink by some former owner, as the remaining loops of letters show.

The volumes were purchased by Mr. Huntington from William H. Robinson's Sales Catalogue No. 14 (1926), *The Library of Mrs. Elizabeth Vesey 1714-1791 . . . With Other Literature of the Eighteenth Century*. They were offered with the "Other Literature" as item No. 1121 (p. 90) and were described as follows:

1121. *Swift* (Jonathan) WORKS. *Large and Thick Paper Copy of the Surreptitiously printed First Edition*. Portraits and plates to Gulliver's Travels. 4 vols., 8vo., very fine copy in CONTEMPORARY BLUE MOROCCO, *elaborately gilt, g.e.* Dublin: George Faulkner, 1735. An original subscriber's copy, with his bookplate in each volume.

Items No. 1118 and 1119 were two original letters from Swift to Samuel Gerrard dated April 7, 1733, and February 6, 1734/5. For his edition of 1824 Sir Walter Scott made a transcript of them, preserved now in Huntington Acc. No. 141696, Volume II. At that time they were in the possession of the Gerrard family in Ireland. One may

---

[6]Laurence Butters, ed. *Fairbairn's Crests* (Edinburgh, [1860]), I, 473, 591: "out of a ducal coronet, or, an armed hand, erect, ar., charged with a pellet, holding an arrow, ppr. . . . *Tutantur tela coronam* (*Weapons protect the crown*)."

guess that the four volumes of Huntington No. 81494 came from the same source, or at least, out of Ireland.

II

THE TRANSCRIPTIONS bound into the Huntington copy have all the appearance of being a contemporary job done at about the time of publication of the volume, or soon after, when the set was bound up. Since Faulkner promised delivery of three of the volumes on November 27, 1734, and the fourth on January 6, 1735, the transcriptions probably were made about that time. The transcriber carefully ruled light guidelines in pencil and numbered the pages consecutively 1-14. The passages omitted from *A Rapsody* take up pages 1-3, and they follow immediately after the printed version of that poem; *An Epistle* runs from pages 4 to 14. The transcriber observed the breaks in the latter poem, but they differ from the breaks in all other printed versions of *An Epistle*. He gave as catch phrases the tag end of the preceding line for the passages from *A Rapsody*. Someone (possibly at a later date) has lightly checked in pencil the places in the printed text where the omitted passages belong. The transcriber rarely capitalized or punctuated his copy except haphazardly and by moments.

The passages omitted from *On Poetry: A Rapsody* begin, without heading, on the first page of the gathering. There are six separate passages, and they run in length from two to thirty-six lines. The unique circumstance is that all six passages are to be found in the one manuscript. Sir Harold Williams, in his edition of Swift's poems (II, 658-659), gave versions of the six passages, taking his text from a manuscript transcription found among Lord Orrery's papers at Harvard College Library (MS. Eng. 218.2, III, 114-116); from Sir Walter Scott's versions (printed without indication of source) in the second edition of 1824 of Swift's works (XIV, 328-346); or from both. In several places the Huntington transcript varies significantly from that of Orrery or Scott; the chief and only omission is of the second couplet, found only in Scott, of the four lines intended to follow line 186 in the folio.

First of the omitted passages is a couplet to follow line 164 in the text and is found only in the Orrery manuscript, with which it agrees except for the lack of punctuation noted above. The second passage is a couplet to follow line 186. It is found only in Scott's text of 1824 (XIV, 334), where are also two additional lines which do not appear in the Huntington transcript or elsewhere. In the second line the

Huntington transcript has the unusual variant of "well" for Scott's "ill." "Well," which changes the sense of the line to its opposite, may here be used ironically; but "ill" is an apter description of Stephen Duck's, the thresher poet's, rhyming ability. The transcript has "Rhime" for Scott's "rhyme." The third omission is eight lines to follow line 190 and is found both in Scott and in Orrery, whom Sir Harold Williams follows. There are the usual differences in capitalization, and "Extoll" in Orrery is spelled "Extol" in the transcription. Orrery's use of the old-fashioned "ye" for the definite article is not followed here or elsewhere throughout. The fourth omitted passage is a couplet to follow line 202 and is found only in Scott (XIV, 335). The Huntington version has "ceast" (l. 1) for Scott's "ceased"; "he's grown" (l. 2) for Scott's "He grows"; "and Beast" for Scott's "or beast," with other differences in capitalization. The sixth omission is a couplet to follow line 416 and is found only in Orrery from which it differs slightly in capitalization and punctuation.

The fifth addition is by far the longest. It consists of 36 lines to follow line 410 and is found in both Scott and Orrery, whom Sir Harold Williams follows. Apart from capitalization and spelling there are almost a dozen differences between Lord Orrery's version and that of the Huntington, which has "Quire" for "Choir" (l. 3); "for Flatt'ry; True" for "of flattery true" (l. 5); parentheses (l. 12); "would" for "Wou'd" (l. 16); "Burden" for "Burthen" (l. 20); "through" for "Thro'" (l. 22); "for" for "to" (l. 24); "wor'st" for "worst" (l. 26); "cou'd" for "could" (l. 26); "which" for "That" (l. 30); "Neb'chadnezzars" for "Nebuchadnazzars" (l. 35).

Of these six passages, four were intended to fit in after what are now lines 164-190 of the printed texts. They attack the King twice, the Queen (by implication) as the encourager of Stephen Duck, the House of Lords, and the Bench of Bishops—in other words, the reigning monarch, his consort, and the lords temporal and spiritual—any or all of whom might take swift and powerful legal action against such open and violent attacks. Hence, they must have been omitted by Swift, or by Pilkington, Motte, or Gilliver, as potentially libelous. The last two omissions, one a passage of 36 lines, were to go after lines 410 and 416. Since the longer passage compares kings to the vilest of animals, it, too, was probably considered to be libelous or even treasonable. The last omission, a couplet, may have been omitted as much on artistic grounds as for political or legal reasons. It was to follow line 416, would come at the height of a magnificently sustained pas-

sage of ironic, tongue-in-cheek, mock panegyric, and would seem
to me to add little to the passage. In general, however, one must
agree with Lord Orrery's heading for the omitted passages, "which
ought to have been inserted in the Rhapsody, if it had been safe to
print them."

(p. 1) ———— Den of Thieves
1 A House of Peers or Gaming Crew
A Griping Monarch or a Jew

———— Best at Court
1 And may you ever have the luck
to Rhime almost as well as Duck

———— Workman on the Nail
1 Display the Blessings of the Nation
and praise the whole Administration
Extol the Bench of Bishops round
who at them rail. bid G—d confound
5 To Bishop-haters answer thus
(the only Logick us'd by us)
what tho' they don't believe in Christ
deny them Protestants—thou ly'st

———— his Death confuted
1 his Panegyricks then are ceast
he's grown a Tyrant, Dunce, and Beast

———— that Nurses both
1 Perhaps you say Augustus shines
immortal made in Virgil's Lines
and Horace brought the tunefull Quire
to sing his Virtues on the Lyre
5 without reproach for Flatt'ry; True
because their Praises were his due
(p. 2) For in those ages Kings we find
were Animals of human kind
but now go search all Europe round
10 among the savage Monsters crown'd
with Vice polluting every Throne
(I mean all Kings except our own)
in vain you make the strictest view
to find a King in all the Crew

15 with whom a Footman out of place
 would not conceive a high Disgrace
 a burning Shame a Crying Sin
 to take his Morning Cup of Gin
 thus all are destin'd to obey
20 some beast of Burden or of Prey
 'tis sung Prometheus forming man
 through all the brutal species ran
 Each proper Quality to find
 adapted for a human mind
25 A mingled Mass of good and bad
 the wors't and best that cou'd be had
 then, from a Clay of mixture base
 he shap'd a King to rule the Race
 endow'd with Gifts from every Brute
30 which best the Regal nature suit
 thus, think on Kings, the Name denotes
 Hogs, Asses, Wolves, Baboons, and Goats
(p. 3) To represent in figure Just
 Sloth, Folly, Rapine, Mischief, Lust
35 O, were they all but Neb'chadnezzars
 what Herds of Kings wou'd turn Grazers

—————— Magnanimity of Spirit
1 How well his publick Thrift is shewn
 all Coffers full except his own

III

THE HUNTINGTON LIBRARY transcription of *An Epistle to a Lady* also seems to be a unique version of the poem, since it contains seven or eight variant readings not found elsewhere, as well as four additional couplets, three of which were first printed by Faulkner in 1746. The half-dozen or so variants of single words, when compared with the text printed by Sir Harold Williams (*Poems*, II, 628-638), are of no great moment and are given below in a footnote. They may represent tinkerings for the sake of better sound or sense.[7] Line 80 reads "kindly entertains their friends" for "Kindlier entertains her Friends?"—a more drastic change from that of all other printed ver-

[7] L. 6 reads "is" for "was"; l. 19, "so" for "too"; l. 67, "your" for "our"; l. 134, "Neighbour" for "Neighbours"; l. 182, "hoise 'em" for "hoyse 'em"; l. 191, "Senate" for "Senates"; l. 267, "Parnassus's" for "Parnassus" or "Parnassus'."

sions. Line 153 follows Lord Orrery's hitherto unique manuscript variant,[8] "where a Monkey wore a Crown." In line 206 the word "Scour" for "sour" is probably a miscopying on the part of the transcriber, as is surely the case with the omission of an "a" five lines later; otherwise the line is short by a syllable.

Of the various printed versions of the poem, notably the folio pamphlet of November 15, 1733, which Sir Harold Williams follows for his text, *A New Miscellany for the Year 1734, Part I,* and Faulkner's text of 1746, the Huntington transcript resembles more closely the latter which, according to Sir Harold Williams, may have come from "an authentic source, perhaps a copy of the folio edition corrected by Swift himself" (*Poems*, II, 629). The folio of 1733 furnished a poem of 274 lines; Faulkner in 1746 printed a poem of 286 lines; the Huntington transcript runs to 280 lines. It agrees with Faulkner by including the extra couplets which follow lines 80, 148, and 192 in the folio text; and with Faulkner preserves such inversions as "have I" (l. 2) and "not me" (l. 58), and such readings as "live" (l. 102) and "the" (l. 106). At lines 245 and 252 it fills out the dashes for proper names in approximately the same way as Faulkner's text. The Huntington transcription, however, omits six lines printed by Faulkner to follow line 132 in the folio, but it also furnishes lines 149-154 of the folio, three couplets printed by Faulkner in asterisks probably because they were the very lines objected to in 1734 as libelous. The transcription also supplies a couplet at lines 219-220 in the folio which Faulkner and later editors omitted until Sheridan restored them in 1784. In a few places the Huntington transcription disagrees with Faulkner's text of 1746 on single words and agrees with *A New Miscellany for the Year 1734*, except for elision, or lack of it.[9]

As copied into the Huntington volume, the poem is divided into fourteen sections by staggering the position of the verse paragraphs on the page. There are only about two-thirds the number of divisions in the printed versions, and sometimes the breaks come without too much regard for the speaker or for the logical structure of the poem at that point. For example, a break is indicated at line 272 for no apparent reason, and yet there is none at line 134 (l. 132 in the folio version) where logically the structure calls for one.

---

[8]Houghton Library, Harvard University, MS. Eng. 218.14, opp. 327.

[9]L. 3 reads "cou'd" for "wou'd"; *New Miscellany* reads "could." L. 40 reads "continued" for "continual"; *New Miscellany* reads "continu'd."

Punctuation is entirely neglected in the transcript except for a rare comma or parenthesis within the line or an occasional question mark or dash at the end. Sometimes the initial letter of a line is capitalized and sometimes not, with no great consistency. "Should" is almost always elided and "would" only rarely; "could" may be elided or not. "Ev'ry" is preferred to "every," and "e'er" or "ne'er" to "ever" and "never." Elision is generously used to catch the slurrings of the human voice, as are such colloquialisms as "tho'," "'till," "'tis," and "'em." Spelling is sometimes old-fashioned;[10] yet modern spellings appear.[11] "Triffle" (l. 61) is possibly a misspelling on the part of the copyist. "Enuff" (l. 131) is a spelling Swift insisted upon when he revised copy for Faulkner's edition of 1735.[12] A few words ("Compleat," "enuff") are consistent with Swift's own peculiar usage. It seems unlikely, however, that the transcriber was copying from one of Swift's own manuscripts but more likely from a copy or a revised printed text, as Sir Harold Williams surmised was the case with Faulkner's version of 1746. The title, "A Letter to a Lady," may be an earlier or abbreviated Irish form later expanded for purposes of publication in England to the lengthy descriptive title under which the poem was first published there: *An Epistle to a Lady Who Desired the Author to Make Verses on Her, in the Heroick Stile.*

A Letter to a Lady

(p. 3)   1 After venting all my Spight
          tell me what have I to write
          Every Error I cou'd find
          thrô the Mazes of your mind
        5 have my busy Muse employ'd
          'till the Company is cloy'd
          are you positive and fretful
          heedless ignorant forgetful
          these and twenty follies more
       10 I have often told before
                  Hearken what my Lady says
                  have I nothing then to praise?

[10]As with "begg" (l. 49); "spightfull" (l. 65); "omitt" (l. 73); "witt" (l. 74); "easy'r" (l. 146); "noysom" (l. 181); "Duce" (l. 185); "submitt" (l. 192); "compleat" (l. 194); "Ruine" (l. 194); "Jockies" (l. 207); "chuse" (l. 266).

[11]As with "Beaus" (l. 42); "Style" (l. 50); "Rhyme" (l. 58); "Pultney" (l. 179); "hoise" (l. 182); "dullness" (l. 210).

[12]See *Poems*, II, 448*n.*

(p. 4) Ill it fits you to be witty
        where a fault shou'd move your pity
15   if you think me too conceited
        or to Passion quickly heated
        if my wandring head be less
        Set on Reading than on dress
        if I always seem so dull to 'ye
20   I can solve the diffi-culty
        you would teach me to be wise
        truth and honour how to prize
        how to shine in Conversation
        and with Credit fill my Station
25   how to relish Notions high
        how to live and how to dye
        but it was decreed by fate
        Mr. Dean you come too late
    Well I know you can discern
30 I am now too old to learn
    follies from my Youth instill'd
    have my Soul entirely fill'd
    in my head and heart they Center
    nor will let your lessons enter
35   bred a fondling and an heiress
        drest like any Lady May'ress
(p. 5) Cockered by the Servants round
        was too good to touch the Ground
        thought the Life of every Lady
40   shou'd be one continued Play' day
        Balls and Masquerades and Shows
        Visits Plays and Powder'd Beaus
        thus you have my Case at large
        and may now perform your Charge
45   those Materials I have furnish'd
        when by you refin'd and burnish'd
        must that all the World may know 'em
        be reduc'd into a Poem
        but I begg suspend a while
50   that same paultry Burlesque Style
        drop for once your constant rule
        turning all to Ridicule
        teaching others how to ape ye
        Court nor Parliament can scape ye

55   treat the Publick and your friends
               both alike while neither mends
Sing my Praise in Strain Sublime
treat not me with doggrel Rhyme
'tis but just you shou'd produce
60 with each fault each faults excuse

(p. 6)   Not to publish ev'ry triffle
and my few perfections stifle
with some Gifts at least endow me
which my very foes allow me
65 am I spightfull proud unjust
did I ever break my trust
which of all your modern Dames
censures less or less defames
in good manners am I faulty
70 can you call me rude or haughty?
did I e'er my Mite with hold
from the impotent and old
when did ever I omitt
due regard for men of witt
75 when have I esteem exprest
for a Coxcomb gaily drest
do I like the Female tribe
think it witt to fleer and Gibe
who with less designing ends
80 kindly entertains their friends
with good words and Count'nance sprightly
Strive to treat them all politely
           Think not Cards my chief diversion
           'tis a wrong unjust aspersion
85   never knew I any good in 'em
           but to doze my head like Lodanum

(p. 7)   We by play as men by drinking
           pass our Nights to drive out thinking
           from my Ailments give me leisure
90   I shall read and think with pleasure
           Conversation learn to relish
           and with books my mind embellish
              Now methinks I hear you cry
              Mr. Dean you must reply—
95   Madam I allow 'tis true
all these praises are your due

you like some acute Philosopher
Ev'ry fault have drawn a Gloss over
placing in the strongest light
100 all your Virtues to my Sight
though you lead a blameless Life
live an humble prudent Wife
answer all domestick Ends
what is this to us your friends
105 though your Children by a Nod
Stand in awe without the Rod
though by your obliging Sway
Servants love you and obey
though you treat us with a Smile
110 clear your looks and Smooth your Style
load our Plates from Ev'ry dish
this is not the thing we wish.
(p. 8) Col'nel ———— may be your Debtor
we expect Employment better
115 you must learn if you would gain us
with good Sense to entertain us
Scholars when good sense describing
call it tasting and imbibing
Metaphorick meat and drink
120 is to understand and think
we may Carve for others thus
and let others carve for us
to discourse and to attend
is, to help yourself and friend
125 Conversation is but carving
carve for all yourself is Starving
give no more to Ev'ry Guest
than he's able to digest
give him always of the prime
130 and but little at a time
Carve to all but just enuff
let them neither Starve nor Stuff
and that you may have your due
let your Neighbour carve for you
135 to Conclude this long Essay
pardon if I disobey
nor against my Nat'ral vein
treat you in Heroic Strain
I, as all the Parish knows

140 hardly can be grave in Prose

(p. 9)   Still to lash and lashing Smile

     ill befits a lofty Style

     from the Planet of my Birth

     I encounter Vice with Mirth

145 wicked Ministers of State

     I can easy'r Scorn than hate

     and I find it answers right

     Scorn torments them more than Spight

     all the Vices of a Court

150 do but Serve to make me Sport

     were I in some foreign Realm

     which all Vices overwhelm

     where a Monkey wore a Crown

     must I tremble at his frown

155 Could I not thro'all his Ermin

     Spy the strutting chattring Vermin

     Safely write a smart Lampoon

     to expose the brisk Baboon

            When my Muse officious ventures

160   On the Nations representers

            teaching by what Golden Rules

            into Knaves they turn their fools

            how the Helm is rul'd by W——le

            at whose Oars like Slaves they all pull

165   let the Vessel split on Shelves

            with the freight enrich themselves

            Safe within my little Wherry

            all their madness makes me merry

(p. 10)   Like the Watermen of Thames

170   I row by and call them Names

            like the ever laughing Sage

            in a Jest I spend my Rage

            though it must be understood

            I would hang them if I could

175   if I can but fill my Nitch

            I attempt no higher Pitch

            leave to D'Anvers and his Mate

            Maxims wise to rule the State

            Pultney deep. Accomplish't St. Johns

180   Scourge the Villains with a Vengeance

            let me tho' the smell be noysom

            Strip their Bums, let Cabeb hoise 'em

then apply Alectos whip
till they wriggle howl and Skip
185 Duce is in you Mr. Dean
what can all this Passion mean
Mention Courts you'll ne'er be quiet
on Corruptions running Riot
End as it befits your Station
190 come to use and application
nor with Senate keep a fuss
I submitt and answer thus
if the Machinations brewing
to Compleat the publick Ruine
(p. 11) 195 Never once could have the power
to affect me half an hour
Sooner would I write in Buskins
Mournful Elegies on Bluskins
if I laugh at Whig and Tory
200 I conclude a fortiori
all your eloquence will scarce
drive me from my favourite farce
This I must insist on for as
it is well observ'd by Horace
205 Ridicule has greater power
to re form the World than Scour
horses thus, let Jockies Judge else
Switches better guide than Cudgels
Bastings heavy dry obtuse
210 only dullness can produce
while [a] little gentle Jerking
sets the Spirits all a Working
        Thus I find it by Experiment
        Scolding moves you less than merriment
215   I may Storm and rage in vain
        it but stupifies your Brain
        but with Raillery to Nettle
        Sets your thoughts upon their mettle
        give Imagination Scope
220   never lets your mind elope
(p. 12)   Drives out Brangling and Contention
        brings in Reason and Invention
        for your Sake as well as mine
        I the lofty Style decline

225 I should make a figure scurvy
  and your head turn topsy turvy
   I who love to have a fling
   both at Senate House and ———
   that they might some better way tread
230 to avoid the publick hatred
   thought no method more commodius
   than to shew their Vices odious
   which I chose to make appear
   not by anger but a Sneer
235 As my method of re forming
  is by laughing not by Storming
  (for my friends have always thought
  tenderness my greatest fault)
  wou'd you have me change my Stile
240 on your faults no longer Smile
  but to patch up all our Quarrells
  quote you Texts from Plutarchs Morals
  or from Solomon produce
  Maxims teaching Wisdoms use
245 If I treat you like a Cr——d H——d
  you have cheap enough compounded
(p. 13) Can you put in higher Claims
  than the Owner of St. J——s
  you are not so great a grievance
250 as the hirelings of St. St——s
  you are of a lower Class
  than my friend Sr. R——t Brass
  none of these have mercy found
  I have laugh'd and lash'd them round
255 have you seen a Rocket fly
   you could Swear it pierc't the Sky
   it but reach'd the middle Air
   bursting into pieces there
   Thousand sparkles falling down
260 light on many a Coxcomb's Crown
   See, what mirth the sport creates
   Sindges hair but breaks no pates
   thus, should I attempt to climb
   treat you in a Style Sublime
265 such a Rocket is my Muse
   Shou'd I lofty Numbers chuse

E'er I reach'd Parnassus's top
I shou'd burst and bursting drop
all my fire would fall in Scraps
270   give your head some gentle raps
only make it smart a while
then cou'd I forbear to Smile
(p. 14)   When I found the tingling pain
entring warm your frigid Brain
275 make you able upon Sight
to decide of wrong and right
talk with sense whate'er you please on
learn to relish truth and Reason
thus we both shou'd gain our Prize
280 I to laugh and you to grow wise.

IV

IT IS CLEAR that Faulkner in Dublin had available to him about 1734-1735 in manuscript or in a revised printed text (as with the Huntington transcriptions) more complete versions of *An Epistle to a Lady* and *On Poetry: A Rapsody* than he eventually printed. Although *A Rapsody* appeared in Volume II of the *Works* (1735), it omitted such passages as are found tipped into the Huntington volume and are recorded elsewhere. In spite of his desire to publish accurately all that he could of Swift's acknowledged poems, it is evident that Faulkner did not dare to print *An Epistle to a Lady* until 1746, and then only with six lines of an offensive and libelous passage that had led to legal action earlier left in asterisks, and with six additional (but inoffensive) lines added elsewhere. The same is probably true of the omitted passages in *A Rapsody*, in itself a far more offensive piece. For when that poem appeared in folio on December 31, 1733, *An Epistle to a Lady* had been in print for a month and a half, with no action as yet having been taken against it. Moreover, when the printer John Wilford was the first to be arrested on January 4, 1734, it was ostensibly because of the libelous nature of *An Epistle*, and yet the much more libelous *Rapsody* surely must have been the final cause for legal action. The omissions from *A Rapsody*, by whomever made, were a kind of tacit admission that *An Epistle* had given offense enough, as well as a recognition that even stronger abuse occurred in these passages of *A Rapsody*.

Wilford incriminated Swift's protégé, the Reverend Matthew Pilkington, who in turn gave away Lawton Gilliver, one of the publishers, and Mrs. Mary Barber, a struggling Dublin poetess whom Swift befriended and to whom (according to Mrs. Pilkington) he gave the manuscripts of *An Epistle* and *A Rapsody* to convey to Pilkington in London.[13] Gilliver panicked and in turn incriminated his fellow publisher Benjamin Motte. Motte's letter to Swift of July 31, 1735, furnishes a good account of the affair.[14]

Although Motte and Mrs. Barber were released on bail soon after their arrest, the government (especially Sir Robert Walpole) was enraged enough to want its full pound of flesh. Swift's biographer Sheridan probably did not exaggerate Walpole's rage or the consequences for Ireland, had the Prime Minister sent a king's messenger to arrest Swift himself in order to bring him to trial in England.[15] Frustrated in this, the government seems to have made as much difficulty as possible for Swift's friends Motte and Mrs. Barber. According to Motte, charges against the two were not finally dismissed until "the last day of the last term" (*Corresp.*, IV, 370), or about the end of June or early July 1735, both having been arrested in late January 1734. From his letter to Swift of July 31, it is apparent that Motte had been compelled to lead a circumspect and cautious existence in the meanwhile. The same was probably true of the luckless Mrs. Barber, the publication of whose long-awaited subscription volume of *Poems on Several Occasions* seems also to have been hindered by the charge against her.[16]

[13]*Memoirs*, p. 98. Mrs. Pilkington had no reason to love her former husband when she was writing her *Memoirs*, but she then (p. 105) maintained that he was not, as was commonly supposed, the informer.

[14]*Corresp.*, IV, 370-374.

[15]The following news item from the *Gentleman's Magazine* for Sept. 1734 (IV, 509) shows the temper of the Kevan Bail at this time: "*Sunday*, 22 [*Sept*.]. As *Paul Farrell*, alias *Gallows Paul*, a noted Constable at *Dublin*, was carryed Prisoner to *Kilmainham* for a Misdemeanour, the Mob, bearing him an old Grudge for being active in apprehending the late riotous Weavers, seiz'd him, cut out one of his Testicles, cut off his Underlip, hacked him in several Parts of his Body, and then hang'd him on a Tree, where he remain'd till 12 o'Clock next Day."

[16]Although dated 1734, Mrs. Barber's volume of verse did not appear until the spring of 1735 and was then distributed by her son. The (London) *Daily Courant* for Friday, Jan. 17, 1735, reported: "December 19. 1734. Those Persons who have done Mrs. Barber the Honour to solicit A Subscription for her, and have not yet given in their Lists, are intreated to send them immediately to Mr. Charles Rivington, Bookseller in St. Paul's Church-yard, or to Mr. Leake, Bookseller at Bath.

"The Books will be delivered to the Subscribers the 1st of March next, or any Day after, by the Author's Son, Rupert Barber, at Mr. Pond's, Painter, in Covent Garden, from Ten in the Morning to Six in the Afternoon.

"N.B. Whereas many Receipts have been lost by Persons to whom they were deliv-

It is little wonder, then, that Faulkner, when he came to issue the last of his four volumes of Swift's works in early 1735, with charges against Motte and Mrs. Barber still to be heard, proceeded cautiously in the matter of *A Rapsody* (although technically it had not been complained of as libelous) and was eminently cautious, even as late as 1746, in printing *An Epistle*, although he had undoubtedly had manuscripts or revised texts of both poems in hand in 1735 at the time he was printing Swift's works. Faulkner may also have profited by the delay in printing *An Epistle*, perhaps obtaining from Swift himself the additional six lines which the edition of 1746 first included, as well as other minor corrections and improvements.

An Epistle to line 132 is a fine example of raillery, the skillful kind of panegyric in which Swift took such great pride. The poem to this point is in dialogue form, and as it opens, Lady Acheson, the "Lady" of the title, may be supposed to have just finished importuning Swift to write something in heroic style to make up for the lambasting he had given her in *The Journal of a Modern (Dublin) Lady* (1729). It is to this earlier poem that Swift seems to refer in the first ten lines of *An Epistle*. Although he manages to avoid writing in a heroic vein about her virtues, Swift still achieves a deft and graceful praise of Lady Acheson's many good qualities in an indirect and backhanded way that is raillery of the best sort, especially lines 65-90 and 99-110. After line 132 and for the remainder of the poem it becomes practically a monologue of abuse directed against the King and his ministers. As Sir Harold Williams surmised, the first part of the poem with its brilliant raillery was probably composed at the Achesons'

---

ered, 'tis hoped those who demand Books, whose Names are not in the List of Subscribers, will not be offended, if they are asked to whom they Subscribed."

It is of some interest perhaps to notice that Swift, in one of the MSS he gave Mrs. Barber to carry to London, seems to be poking fun at a passage in one of her own poems that he had seen in manuscript and which he would not have liked, since it was profuse flattery addressed to the son of the prime minister.

"*An Invitation to* Edward Walpole, Esq; upon Hearing He Was Landed in Dublin," *Poems on Several Occasions* (London, 1734), pp. 196-197:

> I expect not a Place, nor hope for a Pension.
> The Love of the Muse is my only Pretension.
> I hate to abuse—and I never can flatter:
> I write for no Party, nor either bespatter.

On Poetry: A Rapsody, in *Poems*, II, p. 655, ll. 411-414:

> Fair *Britain* in thy Monarch blest,
> Whose Virtues bear the strictest Test;
> Whom never *Faction* cou'd bespatter,
> Nor *Minister*, nor *Poet* flatter.

estate of Market Hill in 1729 or 1730. The second part of the poem —the libelous portion—was probably composed in 1732 or in the first half of 1733.

A Rapsody was probably composed at about the same time as the latter half of *An Epistle*. It is in the same, or even huger, vein of abuse, this time, however (reversing the formula of raillery), moving by moments to rhapsodies of fulsome praise that by a continuous and masterly use of irony turns all to dispraise, especially lines 411-480.[17] But the greatest irony of all was that Queen Caroline at first was taken in by the surface meaning of the poem, until Lord Hervey taught her to look for the opposite of what was said. We have always had to take the word of Reverend Dr. William King, Swift's young Oxford friend, for Queen Caroline's initial confusion about *A Rapsody*, even though the poem's title with its slangy double-pun upon "a rapp" or counterfeit coin and a "rap" or knock on the head should have warned of its true content.[18] Recently, however, I have

[17]The following unpublished passage from Forster No. 530, pp. 67-68, shows that by about 1735 Swift was adept enough at mock-panegyric to write it even in "Anglo-Latino":

Cumbo is, laetus trito beas meri as ama
id at fore te en, or as ager manat—
anno ver e'ver aro a ringat toris
o vera poto Mummi na sto-ve: O, i
fis parum inani timeor placeor o portu
niti, Ima sono fato ad, apis mire, orto
se more stilla citi Zeno fano ver.
And dy et Siriam alo i alma nas
ani; I rore alo udas as i passo vere
veri guttur at nite, Hi fora [Georgio]
fore ver. His favo rite Si Robur time an
is a pri minis ter fit for a nempe—
rore; his Quin is ago des. His sonat—
tuenti is fit fora do Zeno fine Ladi
sto pro duce ab as tarde veri forti nite
An ange lis notas feras e veri da uter
tecum aro undas ut hinc fit: In fine, asto
Hanno veri an Boo bis here tequ mi
cane at ani time; fors uritis nos in at alto
beatum forti times a de, ormo re . . . Alimenti sto do
aliquando fora sis ter omine in abusi
nes o vim portans. at anno ver. Quin
Caro linis reddito favo rus; fuimus
tonare hera quales. . . . Euro pisto narro fors o
miti a nempe rore asso ursis His quin Caro linis
offas hi a rasas e ver sat in atro—
ne. Os odi vina nani mali sto bea
do reddas an ange lis; Abite Abite,
Itis qui te a re verso falli sed.

[18]King's account is to be found in his *Political and Literary Anecdotes* (London, 1818), p. 15. Swift used the word "raps" to signify a counterfeit half-penny in his po-

come upon the following passage in a dialogue written by Swift and Dr. Thomas Sheridan in "Anglo-Angli," one of their privately concocted Anglo-Latin "languages" of 1734-1735. The dialogue was probably written late in 1735 when Swift visited Sheridan at Cavan. It is among the unpublished Anglo-Latin writings preserved in the Forster Collection (Forster No. 530, pp. 22-23), and it seems to acknowledge, in Swift's own words, that Queen Caroline was indeed deceived by the irony of *A Rapsody*:

　1　[Sheridan] They cap tack [?] nose yew
　　　two bee ann ay nay me
　　　Isle Scene o mower.
　　　[Swift] I've all you no tea vile tongs, Eye
　　　maw law yawl Deign toe hiss
　　　Madge ease tye a swell ass thick
　　　ween. [Sheridan] Youth inck sow o Knack
　　　Count of fewer pan a jeer rick
　　　Inn ewer raps odd he Ice
　10　up hose. [Swift] Note a tall; <Cue e'en
　　　Carroll in a> Fork ween Carol in
　　　a wasp leased[19]

The Huntington transcriptions differ from Lord Orrery's or Scott's versions of the passages omitted from *A Rapsody*, and yet

---

ems of 1724-25, "A Serious Poem Upon William Wood" and "*Wood, an Insect*" (*Poems*, I, 335, 352), poems he may have been looking over in 1732 or 1733 for inclusion in Faulkner's edition. Concluding an extended simile at the end of *An Epistle* (l. 270), he spoke of "gentle raps," or knocks on the head. The word would then have been on his mind—in all its punning meanings—when he came to choose a title for *On Poetry: A Rapsody*.

Two poems appeared almost at once to answer *A Rapsody*. "On Reading the Rhapsody on Poetry" was printed in the *London Magazine*, III (Jan. 1734), 42, and in the *Gentleman's Magazine*, IV (Jan. 1734), 45. The second picked up the pun in its title and was announced in "The Register of Books publish'd in January, 1734" of the *Gentleman's Magazine*, IV, 55, as "A Rap at the Rapsody. Price 6d."

19
　　　　1 (Sheridan) the captack [?] knows you
　　　　　to be an enemy
　　　　　I'll say no more.
　　　　　(Swift) I value not a' vile tongues, I'm
　　　　　a loyal Dean to his
　　　　　Majesty as well as the
　　　　　Queen. (Sheridan) You think so
　　　　　on account of your panegyric
　　　　　in your *Rapsody* I
　　　　10 suppose. (Swift) Not at all; <Queen
　　　　　Carolina> For Queen Carolina
　　　　　was pleased.

they include all six omitted passages. *An Epistle*, with some differences, resembles most closely the poem as printed by Faulkner in 1746. In showing what Faulkner had available to print in early 1735 but dared not do so for fear of legal consequences, both transcriptions are of value. As examples of the great pains Swift took in composing and later revising his work, they also represent a stage of development in two of his major poems in 1735, at a time and in a form when these poems circulated privately among Swift's closest Dublin friends.

Chapter Six

SWIFT'S MANUSCRIPT VERSION OF

"ON HIS OWN DEAFNESS"

I

IT WAS ONLY in 1861 or 1862 that Ménière's disease was first described as an affection of the inner ear.[1] About sixty years ago, Bucknill, writing in *Brain*, was the first to diagnose properly as Ménière's disease the affliction from which Jonathan Swift suffered for most of his lifetime.[2] Such eminent physicians and surgeons as Sir Walter R. Brain[3] and Dr. Thomas G. Wilson[4] have commented upon the consequences for Swift's life and art of his devastating illness, which we have only recently been able to cure. It is principally from these accounts, as well as from Swift's own writings about himself, that I derive what follows about the origin and nature of his disease.

The chief characteristics of Ménière's disease are its totally unpredictable and often lengthy attacks of giddiness, deafness, nausea, and what Swift called "Flux," or diarrhea. Singly or in combination, these are its symptoms and effects; its causes are less well understood. The giddiness, a form of vertigo, results from a diseased or abnormal condition of the inner ear and hence affects one's sense of balance, causing the sufferer to stagger, lurch about, and even to fall like a

[1]Thomas G. Wilson, "The Mental and Physical Health of Dean Swift," *Medical History*, III, No. 3 (July 1958), p. 176. See also Thomas G. Wilson, "Swift and the Doctors," *Medical History*, VIII, No. 3 (July 1964), p. 201.

[2]John C. Bucknill, *Brain*, IV (Jan. 1882), 493-506. Bucknill recognized that Swift's illness was Ménière's disease, an infection of the labyrinthine canal of the inner ear, and so he termed it also "labyrinthine vertigo."

[3]"The Illness of Dean Swift," *Irish Journal of Medical Science*, 6th Ser. (1952), 337-345.

[4]"Swift's Personality," *Review of English Literature*, III (July 1962), 37-58. A report to the *New York Times* of Sept. 29, 1964, from the Science Service of Chicago mentions that high frequency sound waves have been successful in 80 per cent of the cases treated in an attempt to find a cure for Ménière's disease.

drunkard. The deafness brings with it, often, a ringing and clanging in one's ears that make it impossible to hear any but the most high-pitched voices, normally those of women only. The nausea produces retching and vomiting not unlike that of airsickness and sea-sickness. The nature of Ménière's disease can best be understood by those who suffer from epilepsy, with which the disease was long confused.[5] To any sensitive and sociable person, the unpredictable, awkward timing of attacks and the humiliating and incapacitating effects of Ménière's disease are degrading enough. To Swift, the fact that they also cut him off from almost all communication with those about him was, in addition, spiritually isolating.

At various times in his life and in several different places in his writings[6] Swift stated quite clearly what he knew about the origin of his disease, the effects of which he first felt when he was nineteen years of age, that is to say, between November 30, 1686, and November 29, 1687, at which time he was a recent B.A. of Trinity College, studying for his degree of M.A. There is therefore no reason to doubt Swift's word about the year in which the disease, signified by attacks of giddiness and diarrhea at first, began. In his unfinished draft of a fragment of autobiography, headed "Family of Swift" and composed in 1727, when Swift was sixty, he wrote of himself: "For he happened before twenty years old, by a Surfeit of fruit to contract a giddyness and coldness of Stomach, that almost brought him to his Grave, and this disorder pursued him with Intermissions of two or three years to the end of his Life."[7] He continued, and the context makes it clear that he is referring to himself, aged nineteen, then temporarily located at Sir William Temple's estate of Sheen near Richmond, Surrey, where he was then visiting: "Upon this Occasion [in 1686-1687, when the first attack occurred] he returned to Ireld by advice of Physicians, who weakly imagined that his native air might be of some use to recover his Health. But growing worse, he soon went back to Sr Wm Temple." In a letter from this same year

[5] Wilson, "Swift's Personality," p. 42. Lord Orrery (*Remarks*, pp. 264-265) misunderstood the nature of one of Swift's attacks of giddiness caused by Ménière's disease which he witnessed in 1736, and was afterward led into writing, upon hearsay evidence, that by 1742 and after Swift's "rage encreased absolutely to a degree of madness ... [so that] he seemed appointed as the first proper inhabitant of his own hospital. ..." In this error Orrery was followed by Hawkesworth, Johnson, Scott, Thackeray, and others. Thus the legend was begun and perpetuated that Swift lived his last years and died an idiot and a madman.

[6] *Prose Writings*, V, 193. *Corresp.*, III, 232-233; IV, 455; V, 37.

[7] *Prose Writings*, V, 193 (T.C.D. MS I. 4. 7, pp. 15-16).

of 1727 addressed to a lady who was similarly afflicted, Swift also mentioned that he believed the attack of his first "Giddyness" at Sheen in 1686-1687 was caused by his "eating a hundred golden pippins at a time, at Richmond [i.e., Sheen]."[8] He then added, just as clearly, that his deafness first attacked him at Moor Park, Sir William Temple's new estate deeper into Surrey, "four years and a quarter" after 1686-1687, that is to say, in 1690-1691: "having made a fine seat about twenty miles farther in Surrey where I used to read and sleep, there I got my Deafness."

Jonathan Swift thus attributed his recurrent giddiness and diarrhea ("coldness of Stomach") to his eating too many small (and probably green) apples,[9] what our grandparents would have called *cholera morbus*. He associated the start of the disease, when he was nineteen years old, with Sir William Temple's estate at Sheen, famous for its fruit trees. By contrast, Swift associated his later and recurrent deafness and its attendant nausea with Moor Park in 1690 or 1691, when he was about four years older; that is to say, as beginning just before or after his return from wartime Ireland, where he had gone in June 1690 with the headquarters of Sir Robert Southwell, Secretary of State for Ireland, during King William III's whirlwind Irish military campaign of 1690.[10] Swift thus very clearly attributed his later deafness to his reading and sleeping out of doors in "a fine seat" at Moor Park, no doubt a reference specifically to the colds contracted[11] while reading, sleeping, and composing odes in the damp

[8]*Corresp.*, III, 232-233 (to Mrs. Howard, Twickenham, Aug. 19, 1727).

[9]*Corresp.*, IV, 455 (to Mrs. Pendarves, Dublin, Jan. 29, 1735/6): "I got a giddiness by raw [green] fruit when I was a lad in England, which I never could be wholly rid of...."

[10]*Corresp.*, I, 2 (Sir William Temple to Sir Robert Southwell, Moor Park, May 29, 1690). Swift was the bearer of this letter which he thus delivered to Southwell within a day or so of its being written. Within another day or two, on June 4, 1690, Southwell and his field headquarters left Kensington with William's entourage for Hoylake and embarkation to Ireland. Unless Swift traveled separately and clandestinely, which seems most unlikely, since travel was restricted and the ports guarded, he thus would have sailed with Southwell and the military expedition from Hoylake on June 11 and landed at Carrickfergus, Northern Ireland, on June 14, 1690. Had Swift been ill enough to require physicians at this time, Temple would have been morally obliged to mention the fact, which he does not, and Southwell, from his own observations, would have detected it, and Swift would not have crossed with the expedition. He returned to Moor Park on Christmas Eve, 1691.

[11]Dr. John Lyon added this marginal note to Hawkesworth's *Life* of Swift, when Hawkesworth referred to deafness and giddiness afflicting Swift before he was twenty: "& of violent Colds got, as he said, by reading in Sr Wm Temple's Gardens when he lived at Moor Park" (Forster No. 579, p. 120).

but romantic atmosphere of "Mother Ludwell's cave," still a part of that estate.¹² It seems to me that, with these facts before us, it would be a mistake to read Swift's rather compressed statement in his fragment of autobiography, as is sometimes done, to mean that Swift's English physicians had recommended his return to wartorn Ireland in 1690-1691 as a cure for the first attack of a disease that was almost fatal in 1686-1687.¹³

From the start Swift, like English doctors who first treated him, was convinced that his deafness and giddiness were two separate diseases. One English doctor who may early have advised him about his giddiness in 1686-1687 was "Mr. Kelsey." Another was Dr. Cockburn, who in 1710-1711 recommended oil drops for his ears to cure his deafness.¹⁴ A third was his close friend Dr. John Arbuthnot, the queen's physician, who sent him in Ireland prescriptions by post at a later time.¹⁵ In desperation Swift even tried out a "spice cap" of the famous Dr. Radcliffe when it was recommended by Lady Mountcashell in a note of 1733 still preserved among the Huntington manuscripts.¹⁶ As Swift and his English doctors reasoned it, since his giddiness and deafness began at different times more than four years apart, and since they occasionally attacked him separately¹⁷ as at the start,

¹²*Poems*, III, 1068-69; I, 51.

¹³On April 30, 1737, when he was almost seventy and in the midst of still another attack of Ménière's disease, Swift wrote from Dublin to an Irish friend, William Richardson, and in his letter he confused his age at the time that, as he thought, his attacks of giddiness caused by eating a surfeit of raw golden pippins began, with the colds at Moor Park more than four years later which, as he believed, had brought on his first deafness. Swift then wrote (*Corresp.*, V, 37): "In England, before I was twenty, I got a cold which gave me a deafness that I could never clear myself of." Among the doctors who advised the deathly sick Swift to return to his native air of Ireland in 1686-87 may have been Sir William Temple's personal physician, "Mr. Kelsey." See Homer E. Woodbridge, *Sir William Temple* (New York, 1940), p. 236.

¹⁴*Journal to Stella*, I, 77 (Oct. 31, 1710), and II, 564 (Oct. 9, 1712), where Swift wrote: "I have had my Giddiness 23 years by fits." He here appears to be referring to a second attack of giddiness which struck him again at Sheen in Oct. 1689, an attack which would then have confirmed that the first attack of 1686-87 was no isolated incident, that his giddiness would be, as it was, regularly recurrent, "by fits." In Nov. 1689 Swift removed from Sheen to Moor Park with Sir William Temple and his family (Woodbridge, *Sir William Temple*, p. 221).

¹⁵*Corresp.*, II, 303 (Dec. 11, 1718), and III, 413-414 (Nov. 5, 1730).

¹⁶HM 14360. See also Chap. I, above.

¹⁷*The Letters of Jonathan Swift to Charles Ford*, ed. D. Nichol Smith (Oxford, 1935), hereafter referred to as *Letters of Swift to Ford*, p. 160 (to Ford from Dublin, Nov. 20, 1733): "The Doctors here think that both these Aylments in me are united in their Causes, but they were not always so; for one has often left me when the other stayd."

they must have originated in different causes. The younger generation of Irish-trained doctors who attended Swift at Dublin, however,
were much more correct and modern in their diagnoses. We now
know that men like Dr. Richard Helsham, Dr. John Grattan, a "Dr.
Deally (Daley),"[18] Surgeon General John Nichols, and Dr. John
Whiteway were closer to the mark in treating Swift's giddiness and
deafness as if they were "united in their Causes."

As in many things else, however, Swift was always a little old-
fashioned in his hygienic ways; he continued to believe all his life
that his illness was really two separate diseases, in accordance with
his own empirical observations and upon the advice of the older
generation of English physicians who had first treated him. From the
time of his first nearly fatal attack of Ménière's disease at Sheen in
1686-1687 when he had returned dutifully to Ireland "by advice of
Physicians" and despite his frequent growls and grumbling, Swift
usually proved to be a good, obedient patient.[19] His pathetic eager-
ness to be cured and later, when he realized that a cure was impossible, his compliance with the orders of his doctors, his pitiful desire
to find relief, often of a temporary kind, at almost any cost, led him
into trying all kinds of prescribed cures, even to wearing Dr. Radcliffe's "spice cap," a remedy which he had earlier employed for an
amusing and satiric extended metaphor in *Mechanical Operation of
the Spirit*.[20] One of Swift's favorite treatments for attacks of deafness
was to stop his ears with cloves of garlic steeped in warm honey.[21] For
attacks of giddiness he reluctantly took draughts of brandy neat.[22]
Yet the oil drops, the steel taken inwardly, the spice cap, brandy,
cloves of garlic, and all the other prescriptions and remedies that

---

[18]Ibid., p. 147 and n. 3 (to Ford, Dublin, April 5, 1733). Swift here punned upon his
doctor's name as "Deally . . . daily." D. Nichol Smith believed he was Charles Daly,
M.D., like all Swift's Irish physicians, a product of Trinity College, Dublin.

[19]In his "Methods in Books about Swift," *Studies in Philology*, XXXV (Oct. 1938),
647, the late George Sherburn once shrewdly remarked of Swift that, "throughout his
life he was, seriously or humorously, a *grognard*," a grumbler or complainer. So he was
also about the many clysters, purges, vomits, and other nauseating medicines—"poi-
sons," as he called them—which he was required to take. But he took them, however
grudgingly.

[20]*A Discourse concerning the Mechanical Operation of the Spirit*, pp. 276-277 in *A
Tale of a Tub*, ed. A. C. Guthkelch and D. Nichol Smith, 2nd ed. (Oxford, 1958).

[21]*Corresp.*, II, 421 (to Knightley Chetwode, Dublin, March 13, 1721/2). See also
Letters from Swift to Ford, p. 100 (to Ford, Dublin, Jan. 19, 1723/4).

[22]*Journal to Stella*, I, 78, 103 (Nov. 1710). In Ireland Swift substituted Irish whiskey,
usquebaugh, for brandy. See *Corresp.*, VI, 87.

Swift tried never really gave him very much more than the most temporary relief. In his old age, especially after such a violent, long-lasting siege as that of September and October 1734, Swift tended increasingly to withdraw from society and to close himself up in his Dublin deanery, thus to wait out attacks with as much patience as he could muster.

Sometimes the attacks struck him without warning, with a devastating swiftness and at the most inopportune times. Therein lay his greatest fear and the cause of a lifelong anxiety. Occasionally the seizures would leave him as suddenly. To his great sorrow and intense personal mortification he was afflicted by an attack of Ménière's disease during the final months of his long-awaited (and last, as it turned out) visit to England in the summer of 1727.[23] The violence of the attack and its humiliating effects caused him to steal away from the London he loved and from his beloved English friends, Pope, Arbuthnot, and Gay, to whom he believed he had become a burden and an embarrassment in his sickness. By the time he had reached Holyhead, however, despite his hard riding over rough country along the way, his illness had left him as unexpectedly as it had arrived. Once more, in December of 1734 while he was visiting at Howth Castle near Dublin, Swift was literally struck down in public by the disease, much to his unutterable horror and private embarrassment.[24] Such "Fitts," as he called them,[25] especially those which visited him when he was in public or far from home, were a continual terror to Swift. After the lengthy and trying attack of 1734, for instance, Swift gave up sadly but forever a plan he had been nurturing for some time, to cross St. George's Channel once more in order to visit for a final time those of his English friends who were still alive. Thus it was that the attack of 1734 became a decisive one. The poem upon his deafness, composed at the height of his illness, summed up, characteristically both in Latin and in English, his feelings over the years about the unfortunate illness which had plagued him all his mature lifetime.

[23]See Chap. IV, above.

[24]*Corresp.*, IV, 276. See also "Account of Expences from Novbr 1st 1734-Novbr 1st 1735," p. 4 (R. I. A. MS 24. C. 31).

[25]Wilde, *Closing Years*, p. 10, and Thomas G. Wilson, "The Mental and Physical Health of Dean Swift," p. 177, have both noticed that Swift's careless use of the word "fits" to mean recurrent attacks led some earlier critics to assume that his disease was epilepsy, lunacy, or some form of madness.

II

A ROUGH MANUSCRIPT draft of this poem, *"On His Own* Deafness," is among the Swift manuscripts at the Huntington, which I came upon a decade or more ago, while examining some fragments of Anglo-Latin writings by Jonathan Swift. This version was then unknown to Sir Harold Williams in his first edition of Swift's poems of 1937[26] As printed by him and other editors of Swift, the poem is usually made up of four lines of Latin followed by eight of an English translation or paraphrase. The version in HM 14338 (p. 23), however, consists of four Latin and ten English lines and differs considerably from those published heretofore. Since it is written in the hand of Swift, it has therefore more authority than some of the many printed versions, discussed below, which were published in various London and Dublin periodicals soon after composition.

We know from his correspondence that another attack of Ménière's disease struck Swift about the end of the first week in September 1734.[27] Dr. John Lyon appended the following manuscript note to his copy of Hawkesworth's *Life* of Swift[28] concerning the date and circumstances of composition of the poem: "These Lines with ye rem:r of that small Copy of verses lay on his Table when his Servt brought up Dinner one day in Sepr 1734 which his Housekeeper Mrs Ridgway upon seeing them requested the Copy of, and he gave her the said Paper directly." Since Swift then gave Mrs. Ridgeway "the said Paper directly," the Huntington copy is more likely to be another, probably earlier, first draft of the poem, for Mrs. Ridgeway very soon after appears to have lent or sold her copy to a Dublin newspaper, as we shall see. It is, however, self-evident that both versions of the poem must have been composed some time in the last three weeks of September 1734, after the renewed onset of the disease, but before the end of that month.[29] Sir Harold Williams was

26But see *Poems*, II, 673.

27*Corresp.*, IV, 257 (to Mrs. Pendarves, Dublin, Oct. 7, 1734). See also IV, 261-262 (to Alexander Pope, Dublin, Nov. 1, 1734).

28Forster No. 579, p. 112.

29The poem, in all versions, assumes that the deafness and giddiness which is its subject is a present affliction, as was the case in Sept. 1734 when Dr. Lyon said that Swift gave Mrs. Ridgeway a copy that clearly was not the same as the Huntington version. The question then becomes one of whether the Huntington version was written earlier or later than that given Mrs. Ridgeway. As is discussed at greater length below, Swift altered the second and omitted the last two lines of the English portion of the Huntington version in order to remove what might have seemed a too private reference and another which might have been offensive to his friend Lady Acheson. These

of the opinion that the poem was "first printed in *The Gentleman's Magazine* for Nov. 1734," but, as the late Professor Sherburn long ago pointed out to me, the following verses also appeared in the *London Evening-Post* for November 9, 1734:

The following Poems in English and Latin, are said to be written by the Rev. Dr. Swift, D.S.P.D. which are procured from some of his Friends.

On his own Deafness.

Vertiginosus, inops, surdus, male gratus amicis;
Non campana sonans, tonitru non ab Jove missum;
Quod mage mirandum, saltem si credere fas est,
Vix clamosa meas mulier jam percutit Aures.

In English.

Deaf, giddy, helpless, left alone,
To all my Friends a Burthen grown:
No more I hear my Church's Bell
Than if it rang out for my Knell:
At Thunder now no more I start,
Than at the Rumbling of a Cart:
Nay, what's incredible, alack!
I hardly hear a Woman's Clack.

Apart from some few minor differences in punctuation and the interchange of "*Non*" for "*Vix*" in the fourth line of the Latin, this version is the same as those published in the *Gentleman's Magazine* and by George Faulkner in his Dublin edition of Swift's *Works* in 1746 (VIII, 466), from which Sir Harold Williams and other editors derive their modern texts.[30] All take "*Vertiginosus*" to be the first word of the poem, thereby introducing into the opening line a false quantity upon which William Bowyer, about 1740, commented in a Latin epigram printed by John Nichols in his *Literary Anecdotes of the Eighteenth Century*.[31] Nichols noted that "Mr. Bowyer was of

---

changes are in the direction of greater impersonality, and they are the kind that are apt to be made to the first draft of a poem rather than to a later draft. The Huntington version therefore seems to me to have been composed before the version that was given to Mrs. Ridgeway.

[30]*Poems*, II, 673.

[31]Vol. II (1812), p. 143.

opinion, that the false quantity rendered the line more expressive of the malady under which Swift laboured." But the fact is that the word is not what Swift wrote, as the Huntington manuscript assures us, and that Swift, at least, no matter how sick, was not the person who introduced a false quantity into the line in question. It is also a fact that the poem was first printed in two Dublin newspapers late in October 1734 and not until November in the various London periodicals, which merely copied the Dublin publications.

It is characteristic of Swift's unconcern for the fate of his writings, even of so personal and moving an autobiographical poem, that, upon her request, he immediately handed over the copy to Mrs. Ridgeway. It is equally characteristic that within a month of its composition Mrs. Ridgeway or someone at the deanery sold or gave to the two chief rival newspapers of that time at Dublin copies of the poem. Incorrect as these Dublin printings were, they were allowed by Swift to stand uncorrected. The English part of the bilingual poem appeared first in the *Dublin Evening Post* (Vol. III, No. 31), for Tuesday, October 22, to Saturday, October 26, 1734. The third word of the heading below should evidently be filled out to read "Doctor's":

> A Revd. D——r's Lamentation for the Loss
> of his Hearing.
> Deaf, Giddy, Helpless, left alone,
>   To all my Friends a burden grown;
>   No more I hear my Parish Bell,
>   Than if it rung for my own Knell:
>   At Thunder now no more I start,
>   Than at the rumbling of a Cart;
>   And what's incredible, alack;
>   No more I hear a Woman's Clack.

Not to be outdone, George Faulkner, who was then preparing to publish a Dublin edition of Swift's works that included a volume of verse, came out the next Tuesday with the following, fuller version of the poem in his rival paper the *Dublin Journal* (No. 895), for Saturday, October 26, to Tuesday, October 29, 1734:

The following Poems in English and Latin, are said to be written by the Rev. Dr. S. D.S.P.D. which we have procured from some of his Friends.

On Deafness.

Vertiginosus, inops, surdus, male gratus amicis:
  Non campana sonans, tonitru non ab Jove missum;
  Quod mage mirandum, saltem si credere fas est,
  Vix clamosa meas mulier jam percutit aures.

In English.

Deaf, giddy, helpless, left alone,
  To all my Friends a Burthen grown:
  No more I hear my Church's Bell
  Than if it rang out for my Knell:
  At Thunder now no more I start,
  Than at the Rumbling of a Cart:
  Nay, what's incredible, alack!
  I hardly hear a Woman's Clack.

On the same day, and in its next issue (No. 32), for Saturday, October 26, to Tuesday, October 29, 1734, the *Dublin Evening Post* also produced triumphantly *its* full version:

A Revd. D——r's Lamentation for the Loss
  of his Hearing.
Vertiginosus, inops, surdus, malè gratus amicis:
  Non Campagna sonans, tonitru non ab Jove *missum;*
  Quod magè mirandum, saltem si credere fas est,
  Vix *clamosa meas mulier jam percutit aures.*

Deaf, Giddy, Helpless, left alone,
  To all my Friends a Burden grown;
  No more I hear my Church's Bell,
  Than if it rang out for my Knell:
  At Thunder now no more I start,
  Than at the rumbling of a Cart;
  Nay, what's incredible, alack;
  I hardly hear a Woman's Clack.

It is apparent that the differences in the *Dublin Evening Post*'s first and second versions of the lines in English and in Faulkner's *Dublin Journal* publication, between them, compounded a number of errors and variations into the poem which were, unfortunately, copied by later printings. It is notable, however, that both newspapers agreed upon the first word of the Latin, "*Vertiginosus*," introducing into that line the false quantity for which Swift thereafter was blamed.

Fortunately, the Huntington manuscript allows some of these errors to be corrected. Swift began composition most economically by writing upon the cover of a letter addressed to himself. The bulk of the poem is written around the superscription, which appears to me to be addressed in the hand of Dr. Thomas Sheridan, Swift's fun-loving Dublin friend, with whom he exchanged Anglo-Latin *jeux d'esprit* about this same time. Swift had, in fact, earlier made some Anglo-Latin jottings upon this same cover, evidently to be sent off in a letter of reply to Sheridan. For instance, the canceled word "tulips," "two lips," written at the top of the page, is from Swift's "character" in Anglo-Angli "Of an Aged Woman," concluded on the facing page. Two lines at the bottom of the page, "Is hall hard lye tea chew/bett tarr man errs," "I shall hardly teach you better manners," were apparently intended for an Anglo-Angli letter to Sheridan. As the Latin and English poem composed on the same page with these Anglo-Latin *jeux d'esprit* testifies, Swift could be both playful and serious in both languages at once.

In HM 14338 (p. 23), the first lines of the Latin part of Swift's autobiographical poem appear in two different forms. Each, however, very clearly begins with the word "Verticosus," freeing the first line from the embarrassment of false quantity upon which William Bowyer commented. There are several corrections in the manuscript, and the whole has the appearance of being a tentative, possibly first draft of the poem, a later copy of which Mrs. Ridgeway begged successfully from Swift. It therefore may reflect Swift's first thoughts, and, since it differs considerably from those printed by Dublin and London periodicals as procured "from some of his Friends," it has also an authoritative claim to be considered reliable about what Swift first intended. Swift began by writing down the two opening lines of the Latin which convey a mood of self-pity. He deleted but then wrote again, above the first line, the final word, "amicis," and in the second line he then combined what later became the first half of the second line with the last half of the fourth:

> Verticosus, inops, surdus, male gratus amicis
> Non campana sonans nostros nunc arrigit aures

Then he began once more, this time canceling in the third line what appears to be "mulier nostros" and writing below it "matrone meas." It is noticeable in what follows that Swift composed the third line of the Latin last, but carried it in his head, since "Quod mage mirandum,

saltem si credere fas es" is out of proper order, although its true place
in the poem is clearly enough indicated by the order of the English
lines immediately following:

> Verticosus, inops, surdus, male gratus amicis
> Non campana sonans, tonitru non ab Jove missus
> Garrula non matrone meas nunc arrigit aures
>> Deaf, giddy, odious to my friends
>> Now all my Consolation ends
>> No more I hear my Church's bell
>> Than if it rang out for my Knell
>> At Thundr now, no more I start
>> Than at the rumbling of a Cart
> Quod mage mirandum, saltem si credere fas es
>> Nay though I know you would not credit—
>> Although a thousand times I said it,
>> A Scold whom you might hear a mile hence
>> No more could reach me than her silence

III

IN HIS PRIVATE SYSTEM of positive values Swift always, and understandably, associated wealth with health. In a letter of June 1, 1722,
addressed to the then fatally ill Vanessa, he remarked that "Riches are
nine parts in ten of all that is good in Life, and health is the tenth."[32]
In the summer and fall of 1734, Swift's own modest fortune, which
he was later to leave to found a hospital at Dublin, was, along with all
other land investments in Ireland, temporarily upon the decline, and
as a result, Swift was then involved in some costly lawsuits.[33] At the
same time, beginning about September 8 and lasting until about the
first of November, he was visited by the severe attack of Ménière's
disease, during which he wrote the poem on his deafness. As one consequence of this double misfortune, Swift had sadly to conclude that,
for reasons of health as well as of fortune, he would have to give up,
once and for all, his long-cherished plan to revisit England.[34]

Of these various emotions of sadness and depression, some are expressed only by the Huntington version of the poem. Although

[32]*Corresp.*, II, 427.

[33]*Corresp.*, IV, 248 (to Lord Oxford, Dublin, Aug. 30, 1734); IV, 263 (to Alexander
Pope, Dublin, Nov. 1, 1734).

[34]*Corresp.*, IV, 267, 268 (to Dr. Arbuthnot, Dublin, Nov. 1734); IV, 298 (to Mrs.
Pendarves, Dublin, Feb. 22, 1734/5).

Swift himself never gave the verses a title, editors entitled them so as
to emphasize his deafness, as was justified by the isolating quality of
his inability to hear. Variously expressed in the poem as a whole, deafness *and* giddiness ("Verticosus, . . . surdus . . .") came upon Swift
together in this particular attack. With them, presumably, came also
the nausea, vomiting, and diarrhea, earlier mentioned by Swift as the
usual depressing and humiliating accompaniments. The sense of self-
loathing, perhaps heightened by his recollections of the painful
events that had ended his final visit to his embarrassed English friends
in 1727, as well as his private fear that he might now become a financial burden ("inops") in addition, is probably better expressed by
the phrase ending the first line of the English translation in the Huntington manuscript, "odious to my friends," than the more pathetic
phrasing of the other versions, "helpless, left alone." "Odious" was
the very Swiftian word of contempt with which the King of Brob-
dignag, at the climax of Voyage II of *Gulliver's Travels*, had dismissed the pretensions of puny human beings, "little odious Ver-
min."[35] On the other side, the second line of the English, which appears only in the Huntington version, "Now all my Consolation
ends," was evidently too secretly poignant to be understood publicly
if it refers, as I believe it does, to the consolation and private solace
Swift had found in planning and anticipating a final visit to his English friends, a visit which, as he now knew full well, he would have to
forego forever. The tone and mood therefore, in any version and
both in the Latin and the English, at its opening, reveal those rare
and unusual emotions in Swift's poetry, self-pity and pathos, in a
poem frankly autobiographical.

It is characteristic of Swift that the ending of the poem, both in
the Huntington version and in the one printed by Faulkner, by
means of clever turns, reversed the serious, self-pitying tone of the
opening and mocked at itself, as though Swift were making good-
humored fun of himself. By means of an expression of mock-dismay
("alack!") and by the derogatorily onomatopoeic word, "Clack,"
with which Faulkner's version ends in a deliberate anticlimax, Swift
seems to imply that it is as well for him that he cannot hear "a
Woman's Clack"! In the Huntington version the same or a similar
effect is cleverly achieved (appropriately enough) by comic use of
feminine rhyme ending, doubled, where "A Scold" cannot be heard,

[35]*Prose Writings*, XI, 132.

and "a mile hence" chimes with "her silence." Thomas Sheridan, who may have been the "you" addressed in the Huntington version, answered line by line the Dean's poem,[36] and his rude boisterousness is more in reply to the mocking mood of the ending of Swift's two versions than to the serious and pathetic tone of his opening.

Someone unknown, writing about six months after the poem first appeared in the Dublin newspapers, gave a timely and appropriate political twist to the poem. The *Dublin Evening Post* (Vol. III, No. 88), for Saturday, May 10, to Tuesday, May 13, 1735, published the following:

> Epigram on Dean Swift's Deafness.
> What though the Dean hears not the Knell
> Of the next Church's Passing Bell;
> What though the Thunder from a Cloud,
> Or that from Female Tongue more loud,
> Alarm not! at the Drapier's Ear
> Clink but *Wood's* Halfpence, and he'll hear.

There was some justification for reading politics into Swift's poem, best expressed by the implications of the last half of the second line of the Latin, "tonitru non ab Jove missus." For here, it seems to me, Swift is poeticizing the Latin proverb, *"Procul ab Jove, procul ab fulmine,"* a warning which he elsewhere cast into Anglo-Latin rhyme for the benefit of that ardent Tory Sheridan at about this same time.[37] Unlike James Joyce, Swift displayed no obsessional fear about dogs or ordinary thunder and lightning, unless the dogs were bitches and the thunder and lightning of a political nature. One reason, for example, why Swift may have changed the ending of the Huntington version to the more generalized conclusion printed by Faulkner is that he had, in a poem of 1729, *The Journal of a Modern (Dublin) Lady*, employed precisely the same mocking, feminine rhyme about the scold, "Aura," who was, by 1734, commonly identified by the town with Swift's Dublin friend, Lady Anne Acheson:[38]

> *Aura*, whose Tongue you hear a Mile hence,
> Talks half a Day in Praise of Silence.

[36]See *Poems*, II, 673-674, *n.*
[37]Forster No. 530, p. 190:
> No rem edi certa in, in venis res is stans
> Mi ad vicis fore ver to beat adi stans
> No remedy certain, in vain is resistance
> My advice is forever to be at a distance
[38]*Poems*, II, 450.

IV

THE OVERALL EFFECT, then, of later versions of Swift's poem of 1734, when compared with what may be an earlier and more privately meaningful version in the Huntington manuscript, is that they have become more generalized, less particular, if no less moving. The self-consciously mocking and comical turn at the end intensifies the pathos and self-pitying tone of the opening, and the spiritually iso- lating effect of his recurring deafness, no matter how comically ex- pressed, the humiliating physical effects of the disease, touched upon in such expressions as "helpless," "odious to my friends," are real enough. And these, as we have come only recently to understand, as we have learned more about the illness from which Swift suffered, were effects of Ménière's disease, to which he was victim from his nineteenth year, when still a student at Trinity College.

In fact, it may have been at T.C.D., in the mixed Latin and English, the dog Latin and macaronics, of the Trinity *Triposes*, traditional mock-academic exercises composed annually there, that he first learned to conceal and reveal his feelings. Sometimes it is in Latin, or, as here, both in Latin and English, that Swift chooses to express his deepest and most carefully controlled emotions.[39] In this respect, even some of his apparently humorous and ingenious exercises in various Anglo-Latin dialects exchanged with his friend the learned Dr. Sheridan about 1734-1736 contain serious and revealing under- tones and echoes.[40] It is almost as if Jonathan Swift, like the young James Joyce, when he casts some of the conversation between Stephen Dedalus, his autobiographical hero, and Cranly, his best

[39]See, for instance, his Latin poem to his new friend, Sheridan, of 1717, "Ad Amicum Eruditum *Thomam Sheridan*" (*Poems*, I, 211-214); his anxiety-ridden poem of June 1723, composed within weeks of Vanessa's death and written upon the awe-inspiring sight of Carberry Rocks along the coast in Co. Cork, "*Carberiae Rupes in Comitatu Corgagensi apud* Hybernicos" (*Poems*, I, 315-319); and his tendency to fall into Latin when writing to Worrall, in Sept. 1727, when Swift was laboring under fears that "the greatest event that can ever happen to me," the death of Stella, was about to take place at the deanery in Dublin (*Corresp.*, III, 197, 235-236).

[40]See, for instance, the overtones of meaning in some of the Latin words and the echoes from the mood and wording of Swift's poem of 1734 that are also to be found in the Anglo-Latin jottings of about 1734-35 now bound up as Forster No. 530. "Heri sit de fendum no sole cum esto vi sit me, de sol a te, fors ac en," "Here I sit deaf and dumb no soul comes to visit me, desolate, forsaken" (p. 9), and "Formidinis in mi pate I can- thera bellat alpha quater offa miles Di stans," "For my din is in my pate I can't hear a bell at half a quarter of a mile's distance" (p. 191), are both written in the same mood of self-pity as the opening of the poem on his deafness. "Ab ova mi lens," "Above a mile hence" (p. 46), repeats the feminine rhyme of the penultimate line of the Huntington version.

friend, in dog Latin,[41] had to cast his deeper feelings into Latin or mock Latin before expressing them openly. The Huntington Library manuscript version of the poem on his deafness shows Swift's genuine feelings emerging first in Latin and evolving into English in the process of composition.

[41]See *A Portrait of the Artist As a Young Man*, Modern Library ed. (New York, 1928), pp. 227-234.

Chapter Seven

ANGLO-LATIN GAMES AND A
FRAGMENT OF
POLITE CONVERSATION

I

ALL HIS LIFE Jonathan Swift enjoyed punning, and he delighted especially to play games with the similar sound and sense of Latin and English. What began as a game in 1673 at Kilkenny School continued until the final creative period at the deanery in Dublin. The waggish dog (or bog) Latin of the schoolboy ended as the systematized Anglo-Latin *jeux d'esprit*, exchanged by Swift and Sheridan between 1730 and 1737. Hawkesworth, in his *Life* of Swift (1755), noticed that in the year 1673 Swift, aged six, was sent to school at Kilkenny. Dr. John Lyon, Swift's guardian and friend in his last years, added this manuscript note on "the School of *Kilkenny*":

as it is called. Being a large Building erected for that purpose, founded & endowed by ye Ormond Family. . . . And here he said, he first learned, soon after he entered ye School, those Words wch he termd *Latino-Anglicè, Mi Dux et amasti Cus*. This kind of writing was afterwards one of those whimsical Amusements that he sometimes entertained himself with, as he sunk in Years.[1]

Such learned foolery continued at Trinity College, Dublin, while Swift was there, in the Trinity *Triposes*. Because of its primarily verbal nature, few records of such ephemeral wit remain. One example, dated 1707, is an account in Swift's hand preserved in the Pierpont Morgan Library entitled "A Dialogue in the Castilian Language."[2] It shows Swift already become an experienced and facile

[1]Forster No. 579, p. 12. The Latin reads in English, "My Ducks ate a Mastiff, Coz."

[2]See Ball, *Corresp.*, I, 373-378 (Appendix II), where "A Dialogue" is regularized, dated, and discussed, and *Prose Writings*, IV, 257-259.

punster. The ampersand with which it concludes implies that the quibbles in Latin and English (with now and again a word in French or Greek) could and did go on endlessly between Pembroke, the pun-loving Lord Lieutenant, and the Anglo-Irish group around him. Letters in his correspondence and passages in the *Journal to Stella* make it clear that puns in Latin and English continued to pass between Swift and members of the "Castilian" crew from 1708 to 1713. Another page of manuscript in the Morgan Library records an April Fool joke for 1713. Below it Swift wrote a short account in English that punned upon all the terms from the trade of baker.[3] He concluded with a play upon *"Rot you low 'rum',"* rotulorum, a Latin word which Swift had used quite seriously not long before in composing the epitaph for the tomb of his late friend, the Earl of Berkeley.[4]

One of the first signs of Swift's reviving interest in the world after the death of Queen Anne and his own retirement to Ireland was the explosive outburst of wordplay that begins with "A Modest Defence of Punning," dated November 8, 1716, and in Swift's hand. The first two paragraphs especially of this Morgan Library manuscript make great play with Latin words and phrases. A letter dated March 28, 1717, to Archdeacon Walls, refers in a jesting way to an offensive habit of the Reverend Dillon Ashe and goes on to pun upon the Latin name of the gem *lapis lazuli* (*Corresp.*, II, 263). "Dilly" Ashe was one of the participants in the "Castilian Dialogue," and Swift mentioned him frequently in the *Journal to Stella* as a punning companion of the London days. "Dilly" had died in May 1716. It was thereabouts, or in 1717, that Swift met Thomas Sheridan, who was to become Swift's fellow jester and "Viceroy trifler" during the second part of his lifetime, much as "Dilly" Ashe had been in the first part.[5]

---

[3]Ball, *Corresp.*, II, 407 (Appendix II); *Prose Writings*, IV, 259-260.

[4]Ball, *Corresp.*, II, 237-238 (Appendix V). The phrase Swift used in the Latin epitaph was *custos rotulorum*, Keeper of the Rolls; it probably suggested to him this pun in a play upon terms from the baker's trade. He used the word again in some Latino-Anglicus jottings in Forster No. 530 (p. 63): "Ure a par sonas I here, Mari rotulorum," "You're a parson as I hear, Marry, rot you low 'rum!'" The cant word in Ireland for "a poor Country Clergyman" was "a Rum" as Swift used it in his poem of 1729, "The Grand Question debated."

[5]Sir Harold Williams makes out a good case for the first meeting of Swift and Sheridan in 1717 (*Poems*, I, 212). Ball (*Corresp.*, III, 19n) supports this date by referring to an entry in one of Swift's account books for 1717-18 (Forster No. 530), where Swift mentioned attending a Greek play at Sheridan's school in December 1717. Sheridan

Egged on by Swift and by the learned group around him at this time, Sheridan was soon at work systematizing the art of punning into a series of rules. The work, published in 1719, was playfully entitled *Ars Pun-ica, sive Flos Linguarum.* Embalmed therein, as illustrative of "Rule One," is Swift's most famous extemporaneous pun. Typically, it applies Vergil's *"Mantua, vae! miserae nimium vicina Cremonae!"* to the destruction of a Cremona violin caused by the careless frisk of a lady's mantua.

Such games continued, and by 1723 Swift had written to Sheridan the first of the many Anglo-Latin letters and trifles they were to exchange in the next fourteen years. By his wit and merry good humor Sheridan, like "Dilly" Ashe before him, had endeared himself to Stella, herself no mean wit. After her death Swift grew closer to Sheridan, the classical scholar and schoolmaster, than to any of his other Irish friends. By 1730 or 1731 they had so systematized their Anglo-Latin games that from then onward the last period in Swift's creative life became the years in which their Anglo-Latin games with language flourished most vigorously.

HM 14341 comes from this last period in Swift's life.[6] It consists of eight pages—one in English, the rest in Anglo-Latin—of a pocket notebook kept by Swift between 1734 and 1736. The single page in English contains entries intended for *Polite Conversation*; six (and possibly more) brief snatches of dialogue here recorded were incorporated when that work was published in 1738. Three pages of Latino-Anglicus prose make up as complete a manuscript as is possible for Swift's satire on doctors, "A Consultation of Four Physicians about a Lord that was Dying," first printed by Faulkner in 1746. The four remaining pages consist of fragmentary jottings in Latino-Anglicus, for the most part drafts of letters in that language to Dr. Sheridan. They include three satiric poems in the same dialect against the Honorable Richard Tighe, after 1725 the common enemy of Swift and Sheridan.

---

himself sent Swift a facetious parody letter on Christmas Day, 1734 (*Corresp.*, IV, 281), in which he said vaguely that Swift first met him "above sixteen years, and I believe a little more. . . . Two entries in Forster No. 530, possibly a draft in Latino-Anglicus of a reply to Sheridan's letter, say (when translated), "My happiness is I remember I met you at a friend o' mine" (p. 48, l. 7), and "I met you among a silly sort of Ashes" (p. 86, l. 1). It is possible that Swift is here referring to meeting Sheridan first at "Dilly" Ashe's sometime before the latter's death in 1716.

[6]I have arbitrarily lettered the leaves A-H and shall so refer to them throughout, adding line numbers where necessary.

It is unusual to find drafts of entries intended for the last major prose work to be published in Swift's lifetime cheek by jowl with "negligible" Anglo-Latin triflings in prose and verse. And yet, the composition of such *jeux d'esprit* went on side by side with the completing, after 1731, of *Polite Conversation*, which, when published, marked the end of Swift's creative efforts, even of "trifles." By 1734 or 1735, to write in one of the Anglo-Latin languages was almost second nature to Swift. In fact, upon several occasions, he jotted down in one or another of these dialects, snatches of overheard dialogue intended for *Polite Conversation*. Similar entries exist among the Latino-Anglicus jottings in Forster No. 530.[7] HM 14338 also contains an entry in Anglo-Angli, "Mower Saxon them ill," "More Sacks on the mill" (p. 12), that reappears as dramatized repartee in *Polite Conversation*:

> [Neverout, *as Miss is standing, pulls her suddenly on his Lap.*]
> *Nev.* Colonel, come sit down on my Lap; more
> Sacks on the Mill.[8]

The hundreds of pages of jottings in the three Anglo-Latin languages that are preserved in the Huntington and Forster collections are not much more than rough drafts that escaped burning, and the bulk of them may not even be dignified with the name of "trifles." If, however, they help to elucidate in some small way an aspect of Swift's major works, his methods of composition, or other biographic facts, they will have proved their use. Some justification for examining them may be found in what Swift once wrote to Harley in defining a literary genius, "Every Stroke of whose Pen," Swift

---

[7]All five entries in Latino-Anglicus from Forster No. 530, for example, reappear in the first dialogue of *Polite Conversation*; two of them also appear in the list in English in HM 14341, discussed in a later section of this essay.

Prose Writings, Vol. IV:	Forster No. 530:
(a) p. 145: "*Miss.* Well, well, To-morrow's a new Day…"	p. 158, l. 5: "Tomo rosa nudae."
(b) p. 145: "*Lady Answ.* . . . her dancing Days are over."	p. 37, l. 24: "Mi dans cinge des aro ver."
(c) p. 162: "*Nev.* Why, one that lives within a Mile of an Oak."	p. 13, ll. 22-23: "Mollis as imple tonas ani in tuenti miles o fano ac."
(d) p. 162: "*Col.* . . . like an Owl in an Ivy Bush."	p. 164, l. 11: "Justas ano lina nivibus."
(e) p. 174: "*Sir John.* My wife's well, Colonel; and at your Service in a civil Way."	p. 111, ll. 1-3: "Suis mi de armis tres, at ure cervice, Ime an, as far as ani fine vir tuus laedis civi litigo es."

[8]*Prose Writings*, IV, 149-150.

said, "is worth all the Paper blotted by Hundreds of others in the Compass of their Lives."[9]

II

QUIBBLES IN LATIN, or more especially in English, and sometimes in both languages, intrude not unsuccessfully into many of Swift's major works in prose and verse. In his hands the pun was eventually developed into a weapon of political and personal satire. His Anglo-Latin games with Sheridan, in which he amused himself and composed "trifles" for a small group of friends, were only the last and most extended exercises in that bilingual punning which Swift began at Kilkenny School. The Anglo-Latin word play, like *Polite Conversation*, depended upon catching the exact sounds of the spoken word.

Swift himself seems to have been of two minds about his *jeux d'esprit*. On November 1, 1734, he wrote somewhat shamefacedly to Pope: "God be thanked I have done with everything & of every kind that requires writing, except now & then a Letter, or, like a true old Man Scribbling trifles only fit for children or Schoolboys of the lowest Class at best, which three or four of us read & laugh at to-day, & burn to Morrow" (*Corresp.*, IV, 262). By September 25, 1735, when he wrote to Lord Orrery, to think and write in Anglo-Latin—especially in Latino-Anglicus, as his example shows—had indeed become almost second nature: "It is true indeed, I am gone so far in this Science that I can hardly write common English, I am so apt to mingle it with Latin. For instance instead of writing, *my Enemyes* I was going to spell it *mi en emis*" (*Corresp.*, IV, 396). In a reply to Sheridan of July 10, 1736, he spoke almost boastingly of his power to write in the Anglo-Latin languages: "I Received your two Letters. The first is mingled with *Latin* and *English*, one following t'other: Now I scorn that Way, and put both Languages in one" (*Corresp.*, IV, 517). "To put both Languages in one" is probably the best short definition of the aim of Swift's Anglo-Latin games with language.

The *jeux d'esprit* exchanged by Swift and Sheridan resembled somewhat the "Castilian" language of earlier days. Both these extended exercises in bilingual punning were based upon the similar sound or sense of Latin and English words when run together. "Cas-

---

[9]*Prose Writings*, IV, 19 (*A Proposal for Correcting, Improving, and Ascertaining the English Tongue*).

tilian," however, was more a spontaneous and sporadic punning up-on single words and phrases arising from conversation. The three Anglo-Latin languages were methodized into a system designed to exploit and exhaust all possibilities of resemblances of sound and sense in the ancient and modern languages. In keeping with Swift's age and poor health, the game, now more sedentary, less verbal, en-couraged extended composition in verse and prose in the three dia-lects. Groups and individuals were mocked satirically, in a way that was impossible in "Castilian."

The rules of the game demanded that each individual word be actual Latin or English, and that the whole when run together in combination would produce another sound or sense in English or Latin. It was necessary to remain true to the sound of the spoken word, especially in English, although a slight brogue, perhaps out of deference to Sheridan, was permitted. Fashionable pronunciations or mispronunciations, slang, cant, and jargon were tolerated, even parodies of the speech of particular individuals allowed. Some am-biguities persisted, but the lack of *h, w,* and *y* sounds in the Latin little hampered the players and only enlivened the game. Latin and Eng-lish were mingled so ingeniously that the combinations frequently became very witty, sometimes almost poetic.

Of the three different dialects or languages in this exhaustive game (literally hundreds of pages of jottings in the three varieties may be found in such manuscripts as HM 14338 and 14341, and in Forster Nos. 530 and 532), the first employed single English words in combination to produce another sense, which Swift called "our Anglo-Angli" (Forster No. 530, p. 18). Two prose "characters" in Anglo-Angli remain unpublished in HM 14338, as well as a letter to Sheridan which ought to be included in Swift's correspondence. Sheridan called it "Ann glow Ann Glee" (*Corresp.,* IV, 341). He wrote Swift eight letters in which he employed it in whole or in part; Swift used it in portions of four replies which have been published.[10] One of Swift's favorite games with this language was to make up long catalogs or families of words, all of which played upon the same initial or final syllable. An example that listed 160 words ending in "ling" is included in a letter to Sheridan of June 1735 (*Corresp.,* IV,

---

[10]*Corresp.,* IV, 246, 280, 299, 341, 346, 349, 354, 357, 391, 403, 501; V, 28, 188, 191, 346. A dialogue with Sheridan in this language is to be found in Forster No. 530, pp. 20-23. At the conclusion Swift refers to the mistaken reception of his ironic praise of the royal family in *On Poetry: A Rapsody* (1733). See also "Swift's Games with Lan-guage in Rylands English MS 659," *BJRL,* XXXVI (March 1954), 413-448.

346-348). The variation of cataloging similar sounds Swift called punningly "Familia de Lingua" in his headings in Forster No. 530.[11]

The second language used English words to be read off as Latin. Sheridan, with a pun upon the name of their Dublin enemy, "Dick" Tighe, called it "Angle owe Law Tigh no" (*Corresp.*, IV, 392). Swift told Lord Orrery that it was "English latinized" (*Corresp.*, IV, 396), and usually abbreviated the name as "Anglo-Lat." Sheridan's pun upon the name of Richard Tighe was no accident; "Dick" Tighe was often abused in prose and verse in all three languages. One letter in this language either to Sheridan or Lord Orrery was once published but has since been dropped out of Swift's correspondence.[12] The original remains in HM 14338.

The last of the three languages used Latin words to make English sense. To judge from the amount of it he wrote, it was Swift's favorite. Sometimes he called it *"Latino Anglicus"* (*Corresp.*, IV, 398) or "Latino-Anglica" (Rylands Eng. MS. 659, No. 17), and sometimes "Latino-Angle" (Forster No. 530, p. 79). Mrs. Whiteway incorrectly called it *"Latina-Anglia"* (*Corresp.*, IV, 445), and Dr. Lyon, in the quotation above, *"Latino-Anglicè."* Swift said it was "Latin Englyfyed" (*Corresp.*, IV, 396), and he abbreviated it as "Lat. Angl." An interesting prose account in Latino-Anglicus is to be found in Forster No. 530 (pp. 67-68); it is an ironic panegyric upon the royal family and resembles a similar passage in Swift's verses *On Poetry: A Rapsody* (1733). Seven pages of Latino-Anglicus are in the Huntington manuscript under discussion here, and they include a prose satire against doctors, several of the little satiric poems against "Dick" Tighe, as well as many random jottings.

In order to introduce the game, as well as to arrive at an approximate date for the manuscript, I should like now to examine briefly selected entries from the four pages of random jottings in Latino-Anglicus. With the same exacting ear that was at work during this period completing *Polite Conversation*, Swift noted precise diction; in words that were individually Latin he jotted down such expressions as "I fax" (p. A, l. 11), "Cursum" (p. A, l. 17), "Apera bellus" (p. B, l. 20), "A Cartago in" (p. B, l. 21), and "Relatum" (p. B, l. 21).

[11]For example, the table of contents of Forster No. 530 reads:
Latin Angl et Familia de Ling
et
Angl Angl
Bulls, Storyes, Polite &c.

[12]Hawkesworth, *Works*, ed. Deane Swift (1765), XVI, 422-423.

When translated as "I'facks," "Curse 'um," "A pair o'bellows," "A Cart a-goin'," and "Rail at 'um," it is apparent that Swift has caught the homely words and phrases, as well as the universal tendency to drop initial and final syllables, the slurring of careless everyday speech. Many other entries contain (when translated) such slangy words as "banter," "cuz," and "Teague" (p. A, l. 19), his word for an Irishman.[13]

Sometimes Sheridan seems to be speaking, and Swift manages to catch his slight brogue and even the tone of his voice. "Ritu," "Write you" or "Writ you" (p. A, l. 20), and "Syriam ures," "Sir I am yours" (p. A, l. 25), indicate that many of the jottings were intended to go off in Latino-Anglicus letters to Sheridan, in 1735 the new master of a school at Cavan, forty miles from Dublin.[14] He was addressed in one place as "Atomi. A Tom is Heri dando," "Ah, Tommy, ah Thomas Sheridan do" (p. B, ll. 4-5), and Swift noticed when "Tomis veri sic" (p. A, l. 21), as was the case in the fall of 1735, when Sheridan suffered an attack of asthma.

About 1735 and after, Swift often associated ideas of declining fortune with his increasingly poor health (*Corresp.* IV, 301, 333, 361). References to illness and death, to financial difficulties real or imagined, crop up in the Latino-Anglicus jottings, as well. His greatest fear was that he would become what he called in Anglo-Angli "as labb error," "a slabberer." The fear is reflected in such phrases as "Musti pro cur faculti," "Must I procure faculty" (p. H, l. 26), words that reappear in his "Consultation" and "I ferit mecum" (p. B, l. 13). "Iambicum a siccat. Siccandi," "I am become a sick cat. Sick and die" (p. C, l. 9), describes his state of health after November 1734, at which time he was racked by a terrible series of illnesses and depressed by financial worries. "Soporiferi" (p. A, l. 18) is a word that combines both fears in one; "so poor I fear I . . ." trails off, but the

---

[13]Swift writes to Francis Grant, March 23, 1733/4, "Thus I am a Teague" (*Corresp.*, IV, 229). Swift took the word from Thomas Shadwell's play, *The Lancashire Witches, and Teague o Divelli the Irish Priest* (1682), as an entry in Forster No. 530 (p. 61) makes clear: "A bimis ole, sed Tego Divelli; Prae macto mas." In his account book for 1709-10 (Forster No. 507) Swift noted that he gave at Clogher on Dec. 21, 1709, "Shaun o Teague 10d."

[14] Ball, *Corresp.*, V, 170 and n. 4. A little tale in English is written upside down, lightly canceled but still legible, in HM 14341 (p. B). It is headed "Storyes for Shern" and goes on: "A Poet sd to Wat Moyle, I'll take out all that's good in Plautus. Then he'll be even with you, he'll take out all that's good in you." Walter Moyle (1672-1721) was a versifying wit at Oxford, a friend of Dennis and Congreve, and translator of Lucian. Swift may have known him in his early days at London.

memory of the soporifics that doctors were urging upon Swift remains.[15] Still other entries refer to financial transactions, some with the improvident Sheridan. Thus Swift writes "Imas gladio une vera peni," "I'm as glad I owe you never a penny" (p. H, l. 8), and he mentions "Almi tuenti," "All my twenty" (p. A, l. 11), no doubt a reference to the £20 Sheridan was promising to repay in a letter of July 1735, but which Swift was still demanding as late as April 1736 (*Corresp.*, IV, 357, 479).

There are many references to daily life at the deanery: to eating, drinking, and cardplay. "Prae late Sternis notas positi vas ura binis," "Prelate Stearne is not as positive as your rabbin is" (p. H, l. 22), refers to Swift's predecessor in the deanery and his sometime friend. Another is about someone who was going to "Bi a gunto suit his enemi," "Buy a gun to shoot his enemy" (p. B, l. 17); it probably refers to Bettesworth's threats of violence in 1734 or "some [Legion] Club Enemies that would be glad to shoot me" whom Swift mentioned to Sheridan in a letter of May 15, 1736 (*Corresp.*, IV, 489). After such threats, the phrase "At hominis onus," "At home in his own house" (p. C, l. 9), is understandable. It illustrates, as well, the economy of Latino-Anglicus, since here three Latin words are made to do the work of six English.

Most of the jottings refer to a period between 1734 and 1736; many have to do with Sheridan, who went down to his new school at Cavan in early May 1735. The Anglo-Latin correspondence, pursued intensively over the years, now climaxed with the visit Swift paid Sheridan in November and December of that same year. The two friends continued "our learned correspondence," as Sheridan called it, writing "up and down stairs to one another" and in the process using up Swift's supply of paper (*Corresp.*, IV, 404, 433). Many of the representative entries discussed here point especially to events in 1735, and I conclude that it was about that year, or sometime between 1734 and 1736, that they were made.

III

THREE OTHER PAGES in the manuscript are a draft in Latino-Anglicus of the prose satire against doctors, at which Swift was at work in

[15]On Dec. 17, 1734, Swift wrote to the Rev. John Blachford that he was "taking Vomits and other Medicines prescribed for me by some Physicians who happen to be my Friends" (*Corresp.*, IV, 277). In Forster No. 530 he noticed that "Lauda num is ano pia te (or) is an opi at" (p. 102), and mentioned "Sumo pium" (p. 56).

December 1735 during his visit to Sheridan. On December 2, 1735, Mrs. Whiteway addressed a joint letter to the two punsters in the country. To Swift she wrote: "My son entreats you will finish your *Latina-Anglia* treatise; which he desires you will immediately send him a copy of."[16] The only work of Swift that could be called (however mistakenly) a treatise in *"Latina-Anglia"* would be his "Consultation of Four Physicians about a Lord that was Dying," first printed by Faulkner in 1746 (*Works*, VIII, 460-463). Recently Davis reprinted it as Appendix E in his edition of the *Prose Writings* (V, 271-272).

Mrs. Whiteway and her son by a previous marriage, Theophilus Harrison, were probably to be included among "those three or four of us" whom Swift said were permitted to enjoy the Anglo-Latin trifling. In spite of his poor health young Harrison was a medical student in 1735; once Swift referred to him jokingly from Cavan as "the Doctor" (*Corresp.*, IV, 427). It seems to me certain that the Latino-Anglicus treatise to which Mrs. Whiteway referred in her son's behalf was "A Consultation," a satire upon the prospective profession of Theophilus Harrison and one in which the young medical student would have a strong interest.

The piece, his longest prose composition in Latino-Anglicus, Swift was apparently never able to finish to his satisfaction. He worked over it, especially the opening and conclusion, made changes, and proposed additions. Swift's health or his faltering interest may not alone be the reasons why he never finished the treatise. Shortly after the mention of his concern for the work, Theophilus Harrison died suddenly in February 1735/6, and Swift was deeply moved. "I had set my heart very much upon that young man," he wrote to Mrs. Whiteway (*Corresp.*, IV, 460). It is possible that Swift put the piece aside after young Harrison's death and never returned to finish it.

Whatever the case, three stages of the work, some canceled, exist in Forster manuscript No. 530. They show the evolution of the treatise and give a hint of the additions contemplated in 1734 or 1735 for a conclusion. The three pages in this Huntington Library manuscript (E, F, G) furnish an almost complete version of "A Consulta-

[16]*Corresp.*, IV, 445. John Forster, Swift's biographer and the purchaser of a volume of Anglo-Latin jottings from the sale of Monck Mason's library in March 1858, believed that Mrs. Whiteway was referring to his purchase, what is now Forster No. 530. Opposite this allusion, in a copy of some uncataloged MSS in the Victoria and Albert Museum (F.44.E.4), he queried, "Is this my MS?"

tion," although it trails off and requires some small corrections at the end. These leaves are not likely to be the ones from which Faulkner printed in 1746, unless he took considerable liberties with his manuscript to give an air of finish to it. The Huntington version resembles Faulkner's but differs in many details and needs some additions. These I have borrowed from the 1746 edition and put into square brackets.

1   [A] Consult[ation]

(p. G)   En ter fore docto res o fis icto a sic mano qua lite.

        A Consultis de scribe dat his Pallas.

1st Dr. Is his Honor sic? Prae laetus felis puls. It do es

5 beat veris loto de.

2d Dr. No notis veri [hi], as qui cassi e ver [fel tu metri it. Inde edit is] as fastas an alarum, ora fire bellat nite.

3d Dr. Itis as hias

4th Dr. I findit beat veri loto [de.]

10   E veri doctor reti res[to a par lori na mel an coli post ure.]

(p. E)   1st Doctr. Itis a me agri mas i opi ne.

2d Doctr. No Docto rite quit fora quin si. Sorites para celsus. Prae anser me.

1st Doctr. No Doctor. I ne ver quo te aqua casu do.

15 2d Doctr. Sum arso:mi autor is no ne.

3d Dr. No quare lingat praesenti des ire. Mi pati entis sic offa colli casure as I sit here.

4th Dr. Itis Aether an Atro phi ora Colli casu sed. Ire membri re ad it in Doctor me ades esse.

20 3d Dr. Dr. Fer ne lis qui te offa di ferent noti o nas ire adit.

1st Dr. No notis ab ludi fluxit is plene.

2d Dr. I fit is a fluxit me re qui re ac lis ter.

3d Dr. I se his casis venere alas i disco ver edit in as hanc cor, an da poli pus in his no se; ago no rea me en sue.

25 1st Dr. Itis ad ange rus casas ani.

4th Dr. I mus tellure alitis ago uti humor in his belli.

1st Dr. It me bea pluri si, avo mitis veri pro per fora manat his age.

1st [2d] Dr. His dis ea sis a cataride clare.

(p. E) 30 3d Dr. Notis as tone in his quid ni es.

2d Doct. Prae hos his a poti cari? Ab lis ter me bene cessa risum decens, ime an a veri fudes. Itis as ure rem edi in manicas es. His pulsis veri loto de.

2d [3d] Dr. It isto late tot hinc offa rem edi fori here

35 his honoris de ad.

    2d Dr. Itis hi time.

    1st Dr. Nae, i fis Honor is de ad, laetus en [d]um apri esto

(p. F)   prae foris sole. Foris Honoris a Cato liquas i here.

    1st [2d] Dr. His time is cum. Api stolis alligat here,

40 bimi at en dans.

    [st Dr.] Alor dis sum times acu vetus hunc si findit.

    [3d Dr.] Mei ne vera tendo na nil ord.

        E veri docto reti resto a Roma bove stares.

    [2d Dr.] Nodo ut o fit. Here nat ure ope rates. Laetus

45 paco fit is hi time forus alto.

(p. G)   E veri doctor is as campe ringo fas fastas lac quis.

    [1st Dr.] Abigo ditis hi time, inde editis, forus alto

    fallas campe ringo fas fastas arato ut offa dari. Fori

    fera bea tinge veri minute. His Lac quis an das turdi,

50 as ausi, asto ut valet is re adi forus.

    [2d Dr.] Ab ast in a do in his Asso unda ab ast i

    na do [fori here ano is at adis stans.]

As with the rough drafts in the Forster Collection, the opening and especially the conclusion here were troubling Swift. In the Huntington manuscript the two parts are written out separately on the same page, the opening section canceled but still legible, the conclusion written clearly below, in a different ink and probably at another time. The ending here, as in Faulkner's version, seems to trail off and to be somewhat inconclusive. The doctors' fears about a beating appear not too well motivated dramatically, although a beating was certainly deserved, for negligence if for nothing else. The bulk of the piece, however, what corresponds to Faulkner's pages 461-462, is written closely in a fair hand on the other two pages.

The stages of progress of the work may be seen in the three separate versions in Forster No. 530. The first (p. 7) was a canceled rough draft of the opening and main sections of "A Consultation." It caught the weighty indecision of the four doctors (although no speakers were yet indicated), and it cataloged the incredibly numerous and conflicting diagnoses, all in Latino-Anglicus. The heading in English at this stage was merely "Disease."

A second and probably later entry in Forster No. 530 (p. 181) is a partially canceled rough draft of the conclusion. It is headed "For the Consult" and makes use of the words "fac ulti," much as they were used above by Swift in the Latino-Anglicus jottings from 1734 to 1736 in HM 14341. In the canceled portion some doctor is still mumbling that he thinks the illness a leprosy, and the rest are grumbling about the small fees they have received from the ill lord, who is now (quite understandably) dead. At this point the uncanceled portion shows the recriminations beginning and a quarrel started between two of the doctors:

> [2d Dr ?] I fis honor is de ad itis ure fauti de clare.
> Uva nil fac ulti.
> 1st Dr. Mi fac ulti isto cura nil ordo fani dis eas
> in nat ure.
> 2d Dr. No; Ure fac ulti isto prae scribe at a venture,
> ne ver consul ting at albi apri de in ure nat ure.

And Swift adds as comment or stage direction, "It mite pro voca sto icto herum at it."

Another, more conclusive, ending seems to have been contemplated by Swift for "A Consultation." It is found in Forster No. 530 (p. 205) and was first headed "Consult to finish," but this heading was canceled and another, "Consult enlarged," entered lower down on the page. This page of the Forster manuscript also contains a sentence in English destined for the "Letter from Captain Gulliver to his Cousin Sympson," which was prefixed to Faulkner's 1735 edition of *Gulliver's Travels*. Sir Harold Williams has called attention to the sentence and has dated it as about 1734 or 1735.[17] The Latino-Anglicus additions for "A Consultation" are probably of similar date and in all likelihood are closer to 1735 than 1734, since Mrs. Whiteway wrote to Swift in December 1735 to "finish" his Latino-Anglicus treatise, and he himself used the word "finish" in the canceled heading here.

The enlargements introduce a new squabble among the doctors about whether chocolate, tea, or coffee is suitable for the sick lord. They also serve to set the scene in London—adjacent to Hyde Park or Pall Mall—the same scene Swift adapted at about the same time for *Polite Conversation*. But most important of all, a dramatic motivation for the doctors' fears is introduced in a conclusive, almost topical way. The new note is murder, by means of a poisoned pear, or of a peer poisoned, and with this ominous suggestion the fragment ends:

---

[17] *Times Literary Supplement* (Jan. 10, 1929), p. 28, and *The Text of "Gulliver's Travels"* (Cambridge [Eng.], 1952), p. 49.

[1st Dr. ?] I ac olet is propp per as ab re ac
fasto His Honor.
2d Dr. Nono, te is pro per est. I fere sum de sine
is to per suus as far as hi de parcor pelle mel. Morderi
findit nec sto hi tres o nat ab aro sutis a fora juge.
[3d Dr.?] A dis hoc offis ab et ter orsum lene porrige.
[4th Dr. ?] Sum re porta peris piso ne dat his Pallas
bime ormi felo Fis is sciens.

If the "Consultation" could be spoken of as to be "enlarged" and
as something for Swift to "finish" in 1735, it stands to reason that the
work must have existed in an almost completed state in that year.
The manuscript version in the Huntington Library fits this description almost exactly, since it is complete except for a bit at the end.
And as the enlargements in Forster No. 530 (p. 205) suggest, the
conclusion was what Swift was at work upon in 1735 to make for a
more climactic and dramatically motivated ending.

One reason Swift may have left it unfinished, as suggested earlier,
was the death in February 1735/6 of Theophilus Harrison, for whom
the piece had especial interest. The Huntington Library version,
then, is as complete a manuscript as can be expected for "A Consultation," which was never finished; and the three pages were probably
written at various times between 1734 and 1735, with 1735 as the like-
liest date for the main part, short of the conclusion. This dating agrees
with that posited for the four pages of random entries in Latino-
Anglicus and gives strong reason to believe that the single page of
entries intended for *Polite Conversation* was also written between
1734 and 1736.

IV

IN POLITICAL SATIRE or personal invective Swift very often used the
pun, even in major works, to abuse the names—good or bad—of his
private and public enemies. He extended it to his Anglo-Latin satires,
and especially when writing Latino-Anglicus verse, to ridicule by
name his personal and political enemies. The names of Swift's enemies
often proved well-suited for such punning, and if they were not,
Swift soon made them so. One has only to remember the liberties
Swift took with the name of the Duchess of Somerset in *Gulliver's
Travels,* his endless puns in prose and verse upon the name of William
Wood during the Drapier controversy, or his attacks after 1733 upon
Sergeant Richard Bettesworth, which made that enraged enemy try

to change the very pronunciation of his surname. Again, Swift did not spare himself. He seems not to have objected to Vanessa's rebus upon both his names, except to dismiss the rebus as "a *Paraphrase* made on a *Punn*" in his answer (*Poems*, II, 716). He sometimes punned upon his own name as "Dr. *Shift*," for example, in a letter of November 15, 1735, from Cavan (*Corresp.*, IV, 427).

In attacking other people by name, however, Swift was confronted by a double problem. On one side he was in danger of perpetuating for posterity the names of his victims, an error about which he had warned Pope in vain. On the other side he was liable to legal action for slander and libel, or open to political retaliation by those Whig enemies in power whom he attacked by name. They could be satirized by printing the initial letters of their names followed by dashes or by pseudonyms like "Pistorides" and "Timothy" for Richard Tighe in such poems as "Mad Mullinix and Timothy" (1728) and "Traulus" (1730) (*Poems*, III, 772, 794).

But these methods never really satisfied Swift, although he was frequently forced to use them. By 1728 Swift and Sheridan had adopted the practice of calling Tighe safely and familiarly by his nickname of "Dick." There appeared in that year such verse attacks as "Dick, *A Maggot*," "Dick's *Variety*," and "*Tom Mullinex and Dick*" (*Poems*, III, 783-789). After 1731, when the Anglo-Latin games were methodized, Tighe began to be villainously attacked in these private prose and verse compositions under the Latin word for his name, "Dic." Meanwhile, he continued to be attacked publicly in English as "Dick." After 1734 Sergeant Richard Bettesworth was discovered to have, by sheer bad luck, the same Christian name as Tighe, and from that time he was also abused in Latin or English as "Dic" or "Dick."[18] A month before Tighe died in July 1736, Swift joined their two names and attacked them in his *Legion Club* as "the Puppy Pair of *Dicks*; . . . *Dick Fitz Baker*, *Dick* the Player" (*Poems*, III, 835). But it was in Latino-Anglicus, especially, that "Dick" Tighe until his death was most barbarously abused by both Swift and Sheridan.

Sandwiched in among the jottings from 1734 to 1736 discussed

[18]Several of such entries in Forster No. 530 are clearly concerned with "Booby" Bettesworth and not with Tighe. Such are the following: "Dic has ad agger at his Si de an de sines ito assa sinat me" (p. 10); "Dic has asper it veri pro per fora nacto rata comedi" (p. 125); "Dic is a boo bibi mi solas inverso in pro se" (p. 158). Others refer specifically to Tighe: "Dic is ab a cur sonas itis sed" (p. 83); "O fido es Dic beat his laedi?" (p. 101). In many other places the "Dic" abused could be either Tighe or Bettesworth.

above are three satiric poems in Latino-Anglicus in Swift's hand directed against "Dick" Tighe. These and other versions of them in Forster No. 530 are probably of similar date. That they are satires against Tighe seems to me to be confirmed by a short prose attack against his whole family among the jottings in the Huntington manuscript, p. C. It goes, "Heris mimis tristi. His Sonis adumbrat: his datoris a feri." The first words, "My mistress Tighe," are echoed in the second line of one of the poems as "Mimis tres," "My mistress." Tighe's ungentlemanly habit of beating his wife Swift had noticed in the *Journal to Stella*.[19] He had mentioned it again in 1728 in "Dick's Variety" (*Poems*, III, 788). One of the satiric poems in Latino-Anglicus refers to some new barbarism of Tighe, but the exact circumstances of this allusion can only be guessed at.

Two of the poems which appear together on the same leaf (p. H) in the Huntington manuscript were first printed together by Faulkner in his 1746 edition of Swift's works (VIII, 460). They have been reprinted many times, most recently by Sir Harold Williams in his edition of Swift's poems (III, 1039). Faulkner may have had this page before him as he worked, since there are only insignificant differences between his poems and the two in the Huntington manuscript. The first one Faulkner entitled "*A* Love Song," but the following, from the Huntington manuscript, is untitled:

> Apud in is almi des ire
> Mimis tres Ine ver re qui re
> Alo veri findit a gestis
> His mi seri ne ver at restis

The second poem is also untitled in the manuscript. Faulkner called it "*An* Epigram." Two other versions and half a dozen scattered references to it are in Forster No. 530.[20] One of these prose references seems to describe the poem as an enclosure sent along in a letter, possibly one in Latino-Anglicus to Sheridan: "Heris an at empto puta ringat his no se" (Forster No. 530, p. 197). The Huntington Library version goes:

> Dic heris agro at an da quarto fine ale
> fora ringat ure nos an da stringat ure tale.

Another version in the Forster manuscript (p. 35) omits the "Dic" and runs:

[19]I, 343, 360.
[20]Pp. 117, 132, 144, 148, 169, 197.

At ester is en dando poto fine ale
Fora ringat his no se an da stringat his tale.

Still another in Forster No. 530 (p. 205) is to be found on the same
page as the entries mentioned above for the conclusion of "A Consultation" and the trial sentence for the prefatory letter in the 1735
edition of *Gulliver*. This version, like the other entries on that page,
very likely comes from 1734 or 1735. It is longer than the others, has
been carefully revised in two places, and may well be the final version of this Latino-Anglicus poem against Tighe:

A Sui ne is abuti cum par ito Dic
A site offis fis it mite me cacat sic
Re diri no at es ter a quarto fine ale
Fora ringat his nos e an da stringat his tale.

The third little satiric poem against Tighe in the Huntington
manuscript (p. A) has never been printed so far as I can discover,
and it is without a title: [21]

In. mi. cum. pani. praedixit:
Claret: finis ne: ver: mixit.
Cantu tellus Dicas tori;
Cingat super Tori rori.
Aleto claret adit basis;
Tosta Laedi, fieri faces.

This I translate as:

In my company pray, Dick, sit.
Claret fine is, never mix it.
Can't you tell us, Dick, a story;
Sing at supper "Tory Rory."
Ale to claret added base is;
Toast a Lady, fiery faces.

Most of the political and personal allusions in the poem are now lost
to us. The last line Swift liked well enough to write out once more
at the bottom of the page on which he entered the poem; probably it
refers to some unmannerly action of Tighe, perhaps as the result of
mixing "ale to claret."

The notion that "Ale to claret added base is" was no new one to

[21]Echoes of this poem also appear in Forster No. 530, pp. 147, 176, 190. See also Forster No. 532, pp. 4, 8.

Swift. He had first used it to create a striking image in his *Letter of Advice to a Young Poet* (1721), a work the authenticity of which has recently been queried by Herbert Davis.[22] There Swift had solemnly warned the young poet to beware of religion, because "the smallest quantity of Religion, like a single drop of Malt-liquor in Claret, will muddy and discompose the brightest Poetical Genius."[23] The same idea is emphasized twice in this short Latino-Anglicus poem against Swift's enemy, and he used it once more to build an exchange in *Polite Conversation*, where the host and the hero of the piece say:

Ld. Sm. Tom Neverout, will you take a Glass of the *October?*
Nev. No, Faith, my Lord; I like your Wine, and I won't put Churl upon a Gentleman: Your Honour's Claret is good enough for me.[24]

As was noticed earlier, Swift sometimes recorded snatches of Dublin conversations intended for *Polite Conversation* in the various Anglo-Latin languages, as well as in English. It might also be that Swift was reminded to include there this favorite notion of his, by an uncouth public action of Tighe, the result of mixing ale and claret commemorated here in this Latino-Anglicus poem of 1734 or 1735.

V

AFTER THE DEATH of Queen Anne and his own retirement to Ireland, Swift maintained his concern for the arts of polite conversation and an uncorrupted language. But now his methods changed; the subtler devices of satire and irony took the place of earnest proposal and direct reform. From this changed viewpoint, *Polite Conversation*, when he returned to it in August 1731, had become no more than an ironically verbatim account of how low the art of conversation had fallen in Swift's own lifetime.

The work, as we have it, is cast in the form of three dialogues between five gentlemen and three ladies of quality. The scene is the London house of Lord Smart; the time is the morning, mid-afternoon, and evening of a Saturday. Frequent references—old-fashioned

---

[22]*Prose Writings*, IX, xxiv-xxvii.

[23]Ibid., 329.

[24]Ibid., IV, 186. The Dublin edition of 1738, which Davis follows, differs from the London edition followed by earlier editors in details of word order, punctuation, and use of italics for emphasis.

in the 1730's—to offstage happenings in Hyde Park, St. James's Park, or the Mall suggest that the period is closer to the reign of Queen Anne than to the time of the Georges. Such allusions are an argument for the early composition of at least some parts of the dialogues.

In general, the dialogues are made up of all the heterogeneous clichés, commonplaces, platitudes, and abuses to which Swift had long objected but which continued to furnish, in spite of him, the polite conversation of English society at almost any period in his lifetime. But now the parts are fitted together with a cleverly artistic economy that catches the exact curve of the thought and expression of that society. Swift's procedure here is to methodize the whole "into a short system," as he did in most of his other games with language.

Some of the raw material is contained in HM 14341 (p. D). There are, in all, twenty-one entries on the single page. They are written down in the form of question-and-answer dialogue, or as the direct retort of repartee, without indication as to speakers. They are in Swift's hand, are written rapidly and carelessly, and, because of the varying color of the ink and a bit of repetition, seem very likely to have been recorded at different times. Each sentence is entered in barest form; some even employ stenographic abbreviations like "yr." and "Ans." As they go down the page, they are increasingly written in so brief and cryptic a form as to become no more than private reminders.

POLITE.

(p. D) 1 Methinks a' Fire begins to smell well now.
          Sung very ill, They that would not come out of the
          fire to hear him, ought to be burnd.
          Come, do something for your Living.
        5 Is she handsome; Ans. She'll pass in a Croud
          Ay they that have much would have more.
          How are you. Heart whole and moneyless.
          To morrow's a new day. To morrow come never
          Well, you have lost a Collop (since you have been sick.)
       10 This table, or Chairs are no nothing, no Service.
          It's one a Clock. Ans. whats that among all us.
          I'm afraid that's too good news to be true
          He must rise early that would please every body
          I <have been sick.> Ans. You have lost a Collop.
       15 That's a note above Ela
          You may put it into yr Eye, and see never the worse.

Ay, that Rogue Nobody does all the mischief
Well, here's a Cup of thanks to you
I'll give you as good a thing (the same again)
20 He brought me a present. I gave him as good a
thing. (the same).—May you live 100 years.
Ans. pray don't stint me
Sings as a Man may say
I can't give my Opinion the first Glass
25 Friends in Leather Coats (Books)
At yr Service in a civil way.

Two late entries on the page are cryptic in their brevity. "Sings as a Man may say," in Swift's hurried hand, takes on new life, however, when it is padded out and put into the first dialogue as part of an exchange between Lord Sparkish and Lady Answerall:

Ld. Sp. Pray Madam, does not Miss sing very well?
Lady Answ. She sings, as one may say; my Lord.

(Prose Writings, IV, 137)

The briefly noted sentence, "At yr Service in a civil way," is made into a smart reply by Sir John Linger, the recently married "Derbyshire knight," in answer to a civil question by Colonel Atwit:

Col. And pray, Sir *John*, how does your Lady unknown?
Sir John. My Wife's well, Colonel; and at your Service in a civil Way. Ha, ha. [*He laughs.*]

(Prose Writings, IV, 174)

Another entry, "It's one a Clock. Ans. whats that among all us," is changed very little when it reappears in the first dialogue:

[*Lord* Sparkish *looking at his Watch.*]
Ld. Sp. 'Tis past twelve a Clock.
Lady Sm. Well, what is that among us all?

(Prose Writings, IV, 168)[25]

The last three manuscript entries involve Tom Neverout, the hero, and two of them are bickering exchanges with Miss Notable, whom Wagstaff called ironically "my Heroin." The sentences "To morrow's a new day. To morrow come never" become a pert reply by Miss Notable in the first dialogue to an offer of a present made her by Neverout:

[25]The London edition (p. 111) does not reverse the order of the last two words.

Nev. No, Miss, I'll send it you To-morrow.

Miss. Well, well, To-morrow's a new Day: But I suppose, you mean To-morrow come never.

(Prose Writings, IV, 144-145)

She bests him again in the second dialogue where "May you live 100 years. Ans. pray don't stint me" is expanded to become:

Nev. Come, all Quarrels laid aside: Here, Miss, may you live a thousand Years. [*He drinks to her.*]

Miss. Pray Sir, don't stint me.

(Prose Writings, IV, 183)

Tom Neverout finally has the last word when the sentence "You may put it into yr Eye, and see never the worse" is given him in reply to Lady Answerall's gossip about the rumored marriage of Ned Rattle to a lady of reputed wealth:

Nev. Faith, Madam, all he gets by her, he may put into his Eye, and see never the worse.

(Prose Writings, IV, 166)

Three other entries in HM 14341 echo, in a more general way, some of the repartee of the printed version of *Polite Conversation*. An exchange between Sir John Linger and his hostess goes:

Lady Sm. And, pray Sir *John*, what do you say to my Wine?

Sir John. I'll take another Glass first: Second Thoughts are best.

(Prose Writings, IV, 179)

The germ of this sparkling exchange is probably to be found in the sentence, "I can't give my Opinion the first Glass." Such is probably the case with a hoary chestnut that is still with us, "Is she handsome; Ans. She'll pass in a Croud."[26] Lord Sparkish remarks of a woman that "they say she is extreamly handsome." Neverout's brisk reply is, "She may pass Muster, and that's all" (IV, 145). There seems little to choose today between these two venerable commonplaces, but Swift's keen ear preferred the military expression, probably for its greater antiquity and frequency in his time. "He must rise early that would please every body" may be the source of Lady Answerall's remark about a woman gamester in the third dialogue:

[26]Writing to Stella and Dingley from London on Feb. 9, 1710/1, Swift used the expression: "How does Stella look, madam Dingley? Pretty well; a handsome young woman still. Will she pass in a crowd?" (*Journal*, I, 185).

Lady Ans. Upon my Word, they must rise early that would cheat her of her Money. Sharp's the Word with her: Diamonds cut Diamonds.

(Prose Writings, IV, 195)

The way in which Swift recorded these examples, writing upside down in the page of a pocket notebook, making hurried—even cryptic—entries, resembles the method by which Simon Wagstaff, Swift's mouthpiece, says that he took down examples of dialogue, fresh as he heard them used in actual conversations:

I always kept a large Table-Book in my Pocket; and as soon as I left the Company, I immediately entred the choicest Expressions that passed during the Visit; which, returning home, I transcribed in a fair Hand, but somewhat enlarged; and had made the greatest Part of my Collection in twelve Years, but not digested into any Method. . . .

(Prose Writings, IV, 100)

This page of the Huntington Library manuscript in Swift's hand looks very much like the entries that Wagstaff said he made in his table book, before they were transcribed, enlarged, and methodized. It may reasonably be concluded that Wagstaff's methods and Swift's were the same; that this page of manuscript represents portions of actual conversations which Swift overheard in Dublin drawing rooms and recorded in briefest form, hot as he heard them, later to be written out fair, and amplified.

Such a supposition is further reinforced when Wagstaff's remark about the number of entries he had managed to collect in recent years is compared with the actual number of those used from the Huntington Library manuscript. Wagstaff said that he began his collection early, and had worked on it sporadically over the years, in much the same way that Swift did. Wagstaff then went on, "For these last six or seven Years, I have not been able to add above nine valuable Sentences to enrich my Collection . . ." (IV, 101). There is some irony in what Wagstaff said, to be sure. But it is a striking coincidence that the period Wagstaff specified matches well with the time between 1731, when Swift told Gay he was at work once more on *Polite Conversation*, and July 1737, at which moment Swift sent off to Mrs. Barber one manuscript to be published in March 1738. If we believe that Wagstaff here was speaking for Swift, we should have to conclude that this single page of manuscript contained the bulk of such entries as Swift made between 1731 and 1737 for *Polite Conversation*. Six of the twenty-one examples recorded were clearly employed in the printed version, and three others furnished the general idea, if not the exact words, for further exchanges.[27]

It is admitted on all sides that *Polite Conversation* was begun sometime before 1731, but precisely when is a point of debate. By examining Swift's correspondence, however, it is possible to distinguish clearly two later periods, at least, in which Swift worked upon *Polite Conversation*. The first begins in August 1731 when Swift described to John Gay "a short System" he had in hand (*Corresp.*, III, 493). It ends with the letter of June 1732 to Pope, in which Swift said that it was "a thing in prose, begun above twenty-eight years ago, and almost finished" (*Corresp.*, IV, 31). Swift appears to have put by the piece untouched, probably because of his ill health, until November 1734 when he wrote again to Pope to say dejectedly that he was convinced that he would never finish it, although it wanted "nothing but Correction" (*Corresp.*, IV, 262). Sometime between November 1734 and July 1736, a second period of work began, and the piece was whipped into final shape, since Dr. William King of Oxford saw it in manuscript when he visited Dublin at the latter time (*Corresp.*, IV, 521, 540). Lord Orrery, who may have seen the work in manuscript as early as July 1735, carried one manuscript to Mrs. Barber in England in July 1737.[28] Swift himself saw another through Faulkner's Dublin press in early March 1738 when the English and Irish editions appeared (*Corresp.*, V, 94).

From these accounts I would deduce that *Polite Conversation* was most vigorously worked upon from August 1731 to June 1732, at which time the work was "almost finished." I would also conclude that in a second spell of work between November 1734 and July 1736 Swift made final additions and finished the correcting, so that by the latter date (or possibly earlier) chosen friends were able to see the work in manuscript. The page in HM 14341, which I date between 1734 and 1736, furnished several of the additions to *Polite Conversation*. The nature of these additions and the manner in which they were used seem to favor the time between 1734 and 1736 as the period in which Swift amplified and added them as finishing touches to *Polite Conversation*.

[27]The five entries in Latino-Anglicus mentioned in a footnote at the start do not contradict this conclusion, since two of them repeat sentences in the Huntington MS.

[28]*Corresp.*, IV, 369 (July 17, 1735). Here Swift alludes to *Polite Conversation* as if that work were known to Lord Orrery, who had arrived from England only two weeks before. See further *Corresp.*, V, 25, 60, 65.

The way in which the sentences used were distributed implies that the greater part of *Polite Conversation* was "methodized" and in some sort of final shape when these additions were made. Four of the entries from the Huntington manuscript were assigned to the lengthy and dramatic first dialogue. The second received two entries, the weak and very brief third dialogue none. It is apparent that Swift added to the first dialogue, in spite of its length and because of its already strong opening position, in a way that he could not hope to do in order to correct or perfect the third.

Something similar happened with the distribution among characters. All five men and three ladies received something from the Huntington manuscript additions, but only the chief characters received enough to increase dramatically their speaking parts and established characteristics. Two were given Miss Notable as pert replies to Tom Neverout; the additions increased the bickering tension that is kept up between these two as part of their dramatic characterization. Tom Neverout's smart-aleck humor was strengthened a bit more by the entry he received in repartee with Lady Answerall, who was further typed by her reply to Lord Sparkish. Lady Smart tartly pointed up the slow-wittedness of Lord Sparkish in the question-and-answer combination they exchanged, and Sir John Linger became a little more boorish with his reply to the civil question from Colonel Atwit. The three sentences that appear as greatly altered from the manuscript were assigned, one each to the three dialogues—to Sir John, Lady Answerall, and Tom Neverout. Such general effect as can be felt from the additions went to strengthen a little more the dramatic parts of the hero and heroine and such chief speakers as Lady Answerall and Sir John Linger, much as the distribution among dialogues strengthened structurally the opening of the piece. From this, I conclude that the main shape of the work and the relative dramatic importance of the characters were already well established, and that the additions from the Huntington Library manuscript, notations of actual Dublin conversations, were made to *Polite Conversation* between 1734 and 1736.

VI

ALL HIS LIFE Swift fought to reform polite conversation and to accord it a rightful place as an ameliorating force in a rude northern culture. He believed strongly that true social discourse from which women were not excluded was a powerful corrective of the corruptions he feared were destroying the English language. *Polite Conversation* was Swift's last and greatest effort to accomplish by means of satiric ridicule what he earlier had desired to achieve by reasonable argument and persuasive eloquence, to no avail.

The irony of time was even greater than Swift's developed art; the very perfection of his work has turned it against himself. *Polite Conversation* was designed to laugh out of use all the classical clichés. Instead, its artistry has preserved them forever, just as Pope perpetuated the names of the dunces he satirized. The precision with which Swift caught and fixed the banalities of his own society has made *Polite Conversation* a unique document in the history of English language and culture.[29] Another side of Swift's nature would appreciate this ironic situation. For his irrepressible wit, his lifelong tendency to expand, contract, or multiply meanings in games with language was surely as much a part of Swift's makeup and art as his desire for purity and permanence in language and manners. To find these two sides of Swift expressed together in one manuscript seems, in this view, most appropriate.

[29]*Polite Conversation* was twice produced on the Dublin stage within months of its first publication. Most recently it was presented in a streamlined version on the BBC's Third Programme, May 2, 1949, a broadcast repeated on Jan. 8, 1953.

Appendix

A BRIEF DESCRIPTION OF THE

SWIFT MANUSCRIPTS

AT THE HUNTINGTON LIBRARY

I

POETICAL MANUSCRIPTS BY SWIFT
OR CONTEMPORARY COPIES

ca. 1719

HM 14336. (a) A verse invitation to a wine-bottling from Thomas Sheridan to Swift (p. 1). 13 ll. rhymed upon "Dean" (pronounced "Dane") and a P.S. in 3 ll. rhymed with "Delany."

(b) A verse reply by Swift (pp. 2-3). 34 ll. rhymed upon "Wine" and dated (p. 2) "Decbr 15th." Followed by a list of 5 similar rhyme words, 3 of which are used in the closing lines. See *Poems*, III, 1016-18.

A. MS. 2 leaves (8⅞" x 7"). 4 pp. of writing. P. 3 consists of one line only which appears to read: "Society of Missasippi if y don't [?] come."

Addressed: by Sheridan (p. 4), "For/ The Revd Dean of St Patrick's."

Endorsed: twice by Swift (p. 4), "Sheridn & I."; "Same Rimes/ Sheridn & I."; once by Deane Swift, "Verses Shern."

Provenance: Theophilus Swift, James Smith "41," Frederick Locker-Lampson, W. K. Bixby.

Watermark: Heawood, Pl. 347, No. 2724.

1722

Acc. Nos. 143198-259, fols. 69-70. "Verses wrote on the great Storm/ which happen'd about Xmas 1722." A poem in 74 ll. Contemp. copy. 2 leaves (12⅛" x 7¼"). 3 pp. of writing. Bound in a vol. of Dublin broadsides. See *Poems*, I, 301-306. See also Wilde, *Closing Years*, pp. 179-181.

Not endorsed. The following annotation appears under the title: "Dr. H——/ Bp. of ——— and Dean Berkley were then/ on board the Yatch, and in great danger of/ being lost."

Provenance: George Smith, Esq., Sir William R. Wilde, Col. Francis Grant, Halsey Sale (1915).

1725

Acc. Nos. 352764-86. "On Wisdom's defeat,/ In a learned Debate." Contemp. copy. 1 leaf (7¾" x 6") written on the recto of the last flyleaf of a vol. of printed pamphlets. 1 p. of writing. 4 stanzas, 12 ll. of verse, signed at end: "Rose Common/ Shameless Woman." See *Poems*, III, 1117-18.

Dated: "22: Sept. 1725."

Not endorsed.

Provenance: J. Barry Brown (1962).

1728

HM 14340. "An/ Answer to the Ballyspellin Ballad." Contemp. copy. 2 leaves (7⅞" x 6¼"). 4 pp. of writing. A poem in 90 ll., 15 stanzas, in double cols. See B. M. Add. MSS. 4805. f. 181, for Swift's autograph version; *Poems*, II, 437-443; *Corresp.*, III, 302.

Endorsed: in contemp. hand (p. 4), " an answer/ to the Ballyspellin Ballad," and, lower down, in a later hand, "Swifts. printed."

Provenance: Theophilus Swift, James Smith "39," Frederick Locker-Lampson, W. K. Bixby.

1728

HM 14335. (a) "The five Ladies Answer to the Beau/ With the Wig and Wings at his head."

(b) "The Beau's reply to the five Ladyes answer."

A. MS. 4 leaves (7⅜" x 4½"). 4 pp. of writing. Pp. 1-2 contain "The five Ladies Answer," a poem in the hand of Dr. Sheridan of 7 stanzas, 28 ll. P. 3 contains Swift's "Reply," a poem of 4 stanzas, 16 ll. See *Poems*, II, 427-429.

Endorsed: twice by Swift (p. 4), "Sheridans answer to/ the Beau, and the/ Beau's reply," and "Sherdn/ 5 Ladyes answr to/ the Beau." A later hand also noted in pencil, "Swifts own. Read."

Provenance: Theophilus Swift, James Smith "30," Frederick Locker-Lampson, W. K. Bixby.

Watermark: Heawood, Pl. 347, No. 2723.

1729

Acc. Nos. 143198-259, fols. 64-65, 67. "The grand Question debated,/ Whether Hamilton's-Bawn shall be turn'd into a Malt-house or a Barrack." Contemp. copy. 3 leaves (12⅛" x 6¾"). 6 pp. of writing (fol. 64^{r-v} and pp. 65, 66, 67, 68 paginated by mistake). Bound into a vol. of Dublin broadsides. See *Poems*, III, 863-873, and Wilde, *Closing Years*, p. 165.

Not endorsed. Annotated "By Dean Swift" after heading.

Provenance: George Smith, Esq., Sir William R. Wilde, Col. Francis Grant, Halsey Sale (1915).

ca. 1732

Acc. Nos. 143198-259, fol. 69. "Advice to a Parson. An Epigram./ By *Dean* Swift." Contemp. copy. 1 leaf (12⅛″ x 7½″). 10 ll. of verse. Below it is another poem on Bishop Hort. Bound in a vol. of Dublin broadsides. See *Poems,* III, 808-809, and Wilde, *Closing Years,* pp. 167, 178.

Provenance: George Smith, Esq., Sir William R. Wilde, Col. Francis Grant, Halsey Sale (1915).

1732

HM 14339. "An Answer/ To a late Scandalous Poem, wherein/ the Author most audaciously presumes/ to compare a Cloud to a Woman/ By Dennis Nephelee, chief/ Cap of Howth."

A. MS. 6 leaves (5⅞″ x 3⅝″). 10 pp. of writing. An early draft of a poem in 180 ll. See *Poems,* II, 616-628.

Endorsed: by Swift on the cover (p. 1), "Answr to/ Clouds." Annotated there by him, "Qu[?] Shall it go./ Lin. 180," and again, "Mine here/ of no use."

Provenance: Theophilus Swift, James Smith "No. 1," Frederick Locker-Lampson, W. K. Bixby.

Watermark: Heawood, Pl. 75, No. 444.

ca. 1732

Acc. Nos. 143198-259, fol. 69. "An Epigram on Seeing a worthy Prelate/ go out of Church in the time of Divine Ser-/ vice to wait on his Grace the D. of Dorset/ on his coming to Town."

Contemp. copy. 1 leaf (12⅛″ x 7½″). 6 ll. of verse. Bound in a vol. of Dublin broadsides. Above it is another epigram, "Advice to a Parson." See *Poems,* III, 807-808, and Wilde, *Closing Years,* pp. 165, 178-179.

Provenance: George Smith, Esq., Sir W. R. Wilde, Col. Francis Grant, Halsey Sale (1915).

1733

Acc. Nos. 143198-259, fol. 80. "On the words Brother Protestants and fellow Christians./ which were used by the Presbiterians when they were endea/ vouring to get the Test taken off in the year 1733."

Contemp. copy. 1 leaf (12¼″ x 7⅜″). 2 pp. of writing. A poem in 64 ll. See *Poems,* III, 809-813.

Endorsed: under heading, "By Dean Swift."

Provenance: George Smith, Esq., Sir W. R. Wilde, Col. Francis Grant, Halsey Sale (1915).

1734

HM 14338. (a) A first draft of Swift's poem *"On His Own* Deafness" (1734).

(b) Anglo-Latin jottings for Dr. Sheridan, headed "Anglo Angl," "Angl Angl," "Angl Lat." P. 23 contains Swift's poem on his deafness, without heading. See *Poems*, II, 673, and Chaps. VI and VII above.

A. MSS. 15 leaves: 6 leaves (5⅞" x 3⅜"); 8 leaves (5½" x 3½"); 1 leaf (7⅛" x 4½"). 28 pp. of writing. Pp. 25 and 28 are blank. Numbered 1-15 and paged in pencil 1-30. The first two leaves and the last (pp. 29-30) are separate. The rest are conjugate.

Endorsed: P. 8 endorsed by Swift, "Angl. Angl/ to Dr Sh——n/ 1734." Pp. 22-23 were evidently once the cover of a letter addressed by Sheridan: "To the Revd. Dr. Swift/ Dean of St. Patrick's/ Dublin." P. 30 (reversed) was annotated by Swift: "Memorial <of> from My/ Lord <Hoath> Howth—/ July. 6th. 1734."

Provenance: Theophilus Swift, James Smith "9" (pp. 3-4), "10" (pp. 25-28), "11" (pp. 29-30), "13" (pp. 5-8), "36" (pp. 1-2), "37" (pp. 13-16), "40" (pp. 17-20), "48" (pp. 21-24), "49" (pp. 9-12), Frederick Locker-Lampson, W. K. Bixby.

Watermarks: Heawood, Pl. 75, No. 444. Fol. 15 (pp. 29-30) with chain lines only.

ca. 1734-35

HM 14345. "On Bishop Rundle."
Contemp. copy, in the hand of Deane Swift. 2 leaves (7⅛" x 4⅜"). 3 pp. of writing. See *Poems*, III, 819-821.

Endorsed: by Deane Swift (p. 4), "on Bp Rundle." Below, in another hand, is written, "not seen."

Provenance: Theophilus Swift, James Smith "14," Frederick Locker-Lampson, W. K. Bixby.

ca. 1735

Acc. No. 81494, Vol. II. Epistle to a Lady (1733) and 6 passages omitted from *On Poetry: A Rapsody* (1733). The omitted passages are not headed. The complete poem is headed, "A Letter to a Lady" (p. 3). See *Poems*, II, 628-659, and Chap. V above.

Contemp. copy. 8 leaves (8⅜" x 5¼"). 14 pp. of writing. Pp. 15-16 are blank. Bound into Vol. II of Faulkner's 1735 ed. of Swift's works between pp. 456 and 457. The 6 passages omitted from *On Poetry* (pp. 1-3) range in length from 2 to 36 ll. *Epistle to a Lady* in 280 ll. runs from p. 3 to p. 14.

Provenance: An unknown owner, Charles Tisdall, Gerrard family of Co. Meath (?), William Robinson Cat. 14 (1926), Lot No. 1121.

II

PROSE PIECES AND OTHER DOCUMENTS IN
THE HAND OF SWIFT

1712-13

HM 14380. Notes for Swift's *The History of the Four Last Years of the Queen* (1758).

A. MS. 1 leaf (6⅞" x 5½"). 1 p. of writing. Verso blank except for number.

Not endorsed.

Provenance: Theophilus Swift, James Smith "27," Frederick Locker-Lampson, W. K. Bixby.

Watermark: Heawood, Pl. 76, No. 442.

1713

HM 27943. "Prefermts/ of Ireland."

A. MS. 1 leaf (8¾" x 6¾") pasted to a larger sheet. 1 p. of writing. A list of ecclesiastical preferments and promotions in the Church of Ireland. These may be referred to in Swift's letter to Justice Nutley of Nov. 21, 1713. See *Corresp.*, I, 407.

Not endorsed. (Back pasted down.)

Provenance: Christie Sale of Dec. 18, 1964, Lot No. 85.

Not watermarked.

Note: This MS was purchased after the present volume was completed, as is noted in Chap. I, n. 2.

1723

HM 1599. "A Letter to a Young Lady upon Her Marriage" (1727). Begins "Madam" and is in the form of a familar letter to Mrs. Deborah Staunton Rochfort. There is neither cover nor postmark, however. Bound in russet leather cover stamped "SWIFT'S/ AUTOGRAPH MSS./ 1723."

A. MS. 9 leaves (9" x 7"). 18 pp. of writing. Twice paged, once as pp. 1-16, and later as pp. 1-[18], the correct numeration. See Wilde, *Closing Years*, p. 181, and *Prose Writings*, IX, 83-94. See also Chap. III above.

Endorsed: Signed "Jonath Swift" at end (p. 18) and there dated from "Deanry-house/ Febr. 11th 1722-3."

Provenance: Deborah Staunton Rochfort, John Rochfort, Esq., Rochfort family of Westmeath (?), Sir W. R. Wilde, Charles Sessler & Co. (1925).
Watermark: Heawood, Pl. 347, No. 2724.

1727

HM 14346. (a) "Proposal for Virtue."
(b) A draft of Swift's first will.
A. MS. 2 leaves (6¼" x 3⅞"). 3 pp. of writing. P. 3 is blank. "Proposal for Virtue" takes up pp. 1-2. See T. Scott, *Prose Works*, VII, 376, and Craik, *Life of Swift*, II, 166-167. The draft of Swift's will is written (reversed) on p. 4. See *Prose Writings*, XIII, 198, and Chap. IV above.
Not endorsed.
Provenance: Theophilus Swift, James Smith "25," Frederick Locker-Lampson, W. K. Bixby.
Watermark: Heawood, Pl. 519, No. 3914 (?).

1729

HM 14344. "Men famous for their Learning, Wit/ or great Employments or Quality of my/ Acquaintance, who are dead" (p. 1) and *"Men of* Distinction, and my Friends/ who are yet alive. Febr. 19th 1728–9." (p. 3).
A. MS. 2 leaves (5⅞" x 3¾"). 4 pp. of writing. The names of the 22 dead are listed down the left sides of pp. 1-2. A similar list of the 19 living covers p. 3. Opposite "Lord Bingley" in this second list Swift later wrote "dead."
Endorsed: by Swift (p. 4), "Amis Vivants/ et morts/ Febr. 19th <1728>/ 1728-9."
Provenance: Theophilus Swift, James Smith "51," Frederick Locker-Lampson, W. K. Bixby.
Watermark: Heawood, Pl. 23, No. 153 (?).

1730

Acc. No. 106600. "Leaven bread." A recipe for making bread.
A. MS. 2 leaves (5⅞" x 3½"). 3 pp. of writing. P. 3 is blank. Laid into the front of *A Tale of a Tub* (1704), with the bookplates of F. Locker-Lampson and E. Dwight Church, the previous owners. On p. 2 Swift noted: "March. 26th 1730/ I got this from Monsieur de Ponchart lately come from Paris."
Endorsed: by Swift (p. 4), "Mar: 26th 1730/ Monsr. Ponchart's receit, to make leaven Bread." Below is the signature in ink, "Frederick Locker."
Provenance: Frederick Locker-Lampson, E. Dwight Church.

ca. 1732-34

HM 14342. "A Dialogue in Hybernian Stile between A. and B."

A. MS. 1 leaf (7 3/16" x 5⅞") made into two by folding. Hence 2 pp. of writing; p. 2 and most of p. 1 being written down the right side only.

See *Prose Writings*, IV, 277-278.

Endorsed: by Swift (p. 2), "Hybernian Style."

Provenance: Theophilus Swift, James Smith "28," Frederick Locker-Lampson, W. K. Bixby.

Watermark: Heawood, Pl. 75, No. 444.

ca. 1732-34

HM 14343. "Irish Eloquence."

A. MS. 1 leaf (6⅛" x 3⅞"). 2 pp. of writing. See *Prose Writings*, IV, 278-279.

Not endorsed.

Provenance: Theophilus Swift, James Smith "26," Frederick Locker-Lampson, W. K. Bixby.

Watermark: Chain lines only.

ca. 1735

HM 14341. (a) Entries for *Polite Conversation* (1738). 1 p. (reversed).

(b) A portion of "A Consult of Four Physicians about a Lord that was dying." 4 pp. in Latino-Anglicus.

(c) Anglo-Latin jottings for Dr. Sheridan. 3 pp. in Latino-Anglicus.

A. MSS. 4 leaves (6¼" x 3⅞"). 8 pp. of writing. Unnumbered but arbitrarily designated by me as pp. A-H. Headed variously by Swift "Latin Angl," "A Consult, and/ Other Latin Angl" (p. E), and "Polite" (p. D).

Not endorsed. At the foot of p. B, however, Swift noted "Storyes for Sherin" and jotted down the outline of an exchange between Walter Moyle and a translating poet.

Provenance: Theophilus Swift, James Smith "33," "35," Frederick Locker-Lampson, W. K. Bixby.

Watermarks: Indecipherable or chain lines only.

1737

HM 14347. Directions to Mrs. Martha Whiteway in the event of Swift's death and a codicil to a will.

A. MS. 2 leaves (7⅛" x 5¾"). 4 pp. of writing. Dated, signed, and sealed with his Socrates seal by Swift, "April 22d 1737—Seven" (p. 2), with the signatures of the witnesses, "Ann Ridgway" and "Alexr Brouders [?]" (p. 2). P. 3 contains a list of 9 Dublin executors. See *Prose Writings*, XIII, 198-200.

Addressed: as a letter "To Mrs Martha Whiteway" (p. 4).

Endorsed: by Swift (p. 4), "Apr. 16/ 1737/ For Mrs Whiteway to read/ and keep, when finished—Codicill."

Provenance: Theophilus Swift, James Smith "3," Frederick Locker-Lampson, W. K. Bixby.

Watermark: Heawood, Pl. 212, No. 1549.

III

LETTERS TO AND FROM SWIFT AND HIS FRIENDS

1698

HM 24018.

A Forgery.

L. S. "J: Swift" to [——]. Moor Park, March 7, 1697-98.

1725

HM 24016. A. L. S. Swift to Edward Harley, 2nd Earl of Oxford. 2 leaves (9″ x 7 1/16″). 3 pp. of writing. P. 3 is blank. See *Corresp.*, III, 111-112.

Dated: "Dublin./ Octbr. 26th. 1725" (p. 2).

Not postmarked.

Not addressed. Cover missing?

Endorsed: by Harley (p. 4), "Dean Swift. Dublin/ Octr. 26. 1725./ Congrat."

Provenance: Croker Sale, Sotheby, Wilkinson (1858), Charles Sessler & Co. (1925).

Watermark: Heawood, Pl. 11, No. 73.

ca. 1730

HM 14330. A. L. S. to Swift from "Sacharisa." See Swift's *Works* (1824), I, 257-258 *n*. The authoress of this passionate love letter begs an early reply in George Faulkner's *Dublin Journal*, published from 1726. It may be a parody from someone like Dr. Sheridan as part of a practical joke upon Swift. Badly deteriorated from damp.

1 leaf (8⅞″ x 7⅛″). 2 pp. of writing.

Dated: "Thursday morn Four a Clock" (p. 1).

Not postmarked.

Not endorsed.

Provenance: Theophilus Swift, James Smith "21," Frederick Locker-Lampson, W. K. Bixby.

1732

HM 14381. A. L. S. Swift to Alderman John Barber of London.
2 leaves (7⅛″ x 5⅞″). 3 pp. of writing. P. 3 is blank. See *Corresp.,* IV, 57.

Dated: "Dublin. Aug. 10th/ 1732" (p. 2).

Not postmarked.

Addressed: "To Mr Alderman Barber" (p. 4).

Not endorsed.

Provenance: John Nichols, Charles Sessler & Co.(1925).

Watermark: Heawood, Pl. 74, No. 441.

1732

HM 14382. A. L. S. Swift to Alderman John Barber of London.
2 leaves (7 3/16″ x 5⅞″). 3 pp. of writing. P. 3 is blank. See *Corresp.,* IV, 92-93.

Dated: "Dublin. Decbr. 14th/ 1732" (p. 2).

Not postmarked.

Addressed: "To the Right Honorable/ John Barber Esqr, Lord/ Mayor of London" (p. 4).

Not endorsed.

Provenance: John Nichols, Charles Sessler & Co. (1925).

Watermark: Heawood, Pl. 75, No. 444.

1733

HM 14383. A. L. S. Swift to Alderman Barber of London.
2 leaves (8¾″ x 7¼″). 3 pp. of writing. P. 3 is blank. See *Corresp.,* IV, 175-176.

Undated.

Postmark: "18/IV" [July 18(?), 1733], franked, and stamped "Dublin."

Addressed: "To the Right Honorable,/ the Lord Mayor of London./ in London" (p. 4).

Not endorsed.

Provenance: John Nichols, Charles Sessler & Co. (1925).
Watermark: Heawood, Pl. 351, No. 2747.

1733

HM 14360. Lady Catherine Davys, Viscountess Mountcashell's recipe for a spice cap to cure deafness. Headed "Docter Ratliff's prescripction for a/ noisse in the head & deffness proseeding/ from a cold moyst humor in the/ head."
1 leaf (6¼" x 3⅞"). 2 pp. of writing. See Chap. I above.
Endorsed: by Swift (p. 2), "R. Novr. 8th. 1733/ Dr. Ratcliff's Receit for Deafness. Sent/ me by my Lady Montcashel."
Provenance: Theophilus Swift, James Smith "23," Frederick Locker-Lampson, W. K. Bixby.

1735

HM 22660. The first half only of A. L. from Swift of June 15-16, 1735, to Dr. Thomas Sheridan at Cavan. The second part of the letter is at the Victoria & Albert Museum, South Kensington (Forster No. 552). See *Corresp.,* IV, 349-352.
A. MS. 1 leaf (7" x 5⅞"), mutilated. 2 pp. of writing. Loops of letters still showing indicate top of leaf has been trimmed. The last words (p. 2) have also been torn away in the final sentence: "—16. Here has/ no body been hanged, marryed or dead that I hear of, ———."
Endorsed: lower left corner (p. 2), "Frederick Locker. 1872."
Provenance: "Mr. William Green's Library," Puttick's Sales Rooms, May 24, 1871 (Forster F. E. 4), Frederick Locker-Lampson, E. Dwight Church Sale, Lot No. 1130 (March 1916).
Watermark: Heawood, Pl. 75, No. 445.

1735

HM 14384. A. L. S. Swift to Alderman John Barber of London.
2 leaves (9" x 7¼"). 2 pp. of writing. Pp. 2-3 blank. See *Corresp.,* IV, 360-361.
Dated: "Dublin. July. 12th. 1735." (p. 1).
Not postmarked.
Addressed: To/ John Barber Esqre/ Alderman of London" (p. 4).
Not endorsed.
Provenance: John Nichols, Charles Sessler & Co. (1925).
Watermark: Heawood, Pl. 351, No. 2748.

1735

HM 14385. A. L. S. Swift to Alderman Barber of London.
2 leaves (7¼″ x 5⅞″). 4 pp. of writing. See *Corresp.*, IV, 380-381.

Dated: "Septbr. 3d. 1735" (p. 3).

Not postmarked.

Addressed: "To/ John Barber, Esqr/ Alderman of London" (p. 4).

Not endorsed.

Provenance: John Nichols, Charles Sessler & Co. (1925).

Watermark: Heawood, Pl. 75, No. 444.

1735

HM 14372. A. L. S. in an unknown hand (*not* Swift's), signed "J. S" (p.
1) to Deane Swift, then of Oxford.

1 leaf (10″ x 7¼″). 2 pp. of writing. See *Corresp.*, V, 260-261.

Dated: "Dublin 10 Oct: 1735" (p. 1).

Not postmarked. But franked and sealed. Stamp illegible: "——rris."

Addressed: "To/ Deane Swift Esqr/ St. Mary-Hall/ Oxon." (p. 2).

Endorsed: "A Paper ——/ of Humour" and "A Let——" (p. 2). The
cover is torn and much water-stained.

Provenance: Theophilus Swift, James Smith "52," Frederick Locker-
Lampson, W. K. Bixby.

1736

HM 14329. A. L. S. Dr. William King of St. Mary's Hall, Oxford, to Mrs.
Martha Whiteway of Dublin. 2 leaves (9″ x 7¼″). 1 p. of writing. Pp.
2-3 blank. See *Corresp.*, IV, 529-530.

Dated: "Edinburgh/ Sept. 14. 1736" (p. 1).

Not postmarked. Not stamped but franked.

Addressed: "To/ Mrs Whiteway/ at her house in Abbey street/ in/ Dub-
lin/ by London" (p. 4).

Endorsed: by Mrs. Whiteway, "Doctr King" (p. 4).

Provenance: Theophilus Swift, James Smith "20," Frederick Locker-
Lampson, W. K. Bixby.

1737

HM 24017. A. L. S. Swift to Alderman John Barber of London.

2 leaves (9″ x 7⅛″). 2 pp. of writing. Pp. 3-4 blank. See *Corresp.*, V, 18-
20.

Dated: "Dublin. Mar. 30/ 1737." (p. 2).

Not postmarked.

Not addressed: See P.S. (p. 2): "When I would write to you, I can not remember the Street you live in."

Not endorsed.

Provenance: Maggs Bros. Cat. No. 445 (1923), Lot No. 2909.

Watermark: Heawood, Pl. 351, No. 2747.

1737-38

HM 14386. A. L. S. Swift to Alderman John Barber of London.

2 leaves (7¼" x 6"). 4 pp. of writing. See *Corresp.,* V, 85-86.

Dated: "Dublin. Janr. 17th. 1737-8" (p. 3). But see also the P.S.: ". . . I wrote this Letter a week ago/ and thought it was sent till I found it this Morning, which is Jan [2]8th. 1737-8."

Postmark: 2/ FE, franked, and stamped "Dublin."

Addressed: "To/ John Barber, Esqr Alderman/ of London, at his House in/ Queen-Square [by?] Ormond-Street/ London."

Not endorsed.

Provenance: John Nichols, Charles Sessler & Co. (1925).

Watermark: Heawood, Pl. 75, No. 445.

1737-38

HM 14387. A. L. S. Swift to Alderman John Barber of London.

2 leaves (7¼" x 6"). 4 pp. of writing. See *Corresp.,* V, 95-97.

Dated: "Dublin. March 9th./ 1737-8" (p. 3).

Postmark: 20/ MR, franked, and stamped "Dublin."

Addressed: "To/ John Barber Esqr, Alderman/ of London, at his House in/ Queen-Square, by Ormonde-/ Street/ London."

Not endorsed.

Provenance: John Nichols, Charles Sessler & Co. (1925).

Watermark: Heawood, Pl. 74, No. 441.

1738

HM 14388. A. L. S. Swift to Alderman John Barber of London.

2 leaves (7¼" x 6"). 2 pp. of writing. Pp. 3-4 are blank. See *Corresp.,* V, 102-103.

Dated: "Dublin. March 31st/ 1738." (p. 2).

Not postmarked.

Not addressed.

Not endorsed.

Provenance: Charles Sessler & Co. (1925).

Watermark: Heawood, Pl. 75, No. 445.

1738-39

HM 14389. A. L. S. Swift to Alderman John Barber of London.
2 leaves (7¼″ x 6″). 2 pp. of writing. Pp. 3-4 are blank. See *Corresp.*, V, 137-138.

Dated: "Dublin/ Febr 16. 1738-9" (p. 2).

Not postmarked.

Not addressed.

Not endorsed.

Provenance: John Nichols, Charles Sessler & Co. (1925).

Watermark: Heawood, Pl. 74, No. 441.

1739

HM 14390. A. L. S. Swift to Alderman John Barber of London.
2 leaves (7¼″ x 6″). 3 pp. of writing. P. 3 is blank. See *Corresp.*, V, 146-147.

Dated: "Dublin. April/ 19th. 1739." (p. 2).

Postmark: 27/ AP, franked, stamp smeared, illegible.

Addressed: "To John Barber Esqr,/ Alderman of London, at His House in Queen-Square/ Ormonde-street/ London."

Not endorsed.

Provenance: John Nichols, Charles Sessler & Co. (1925).

Watermark: Heawood, Pl. 74, No. 441.

1739

HM 14349. A.L.S. Mrs. Martha Whiteway of Dublin to Alexander Pope.
2 leaves (9″ x 7¼″). 2 pp. of writing. Pp. 3-4 are blank except for endorsement. See *Corresp. of Pope*, ed. Sherburn (Oxford, 1956), IV, 184-185, where the letter is dated "*June or later.*"

Dated: "1739" in endorsement.

Not postmarked.

Not addressed.

Endorsed: by Deane Swift (p. 4), "Mrs Whiteway/ To Mr Pope/ 1739."

Provenance: Theophilus Swift, James Smith "12," Frederick Locker-Lampson, W. K. Bixby.

1740

HM 14351. A.L.S. Alderman John Barber of London to Mrs. Martha Whiteway of Dublin. 2 leaves (7⅝" x 6"). 1 p. of writing. Pp. 2-4 are blank except for endorsement. See *Corresp.,* V, 192.

Dated: "London,/ June 26. 1740." (p. 1).

Not postmarked.

Not addressed.

Endorsed: by Deane Swift (p. 4), "Alderman Barber."

Provenance: Theophilus Swift, James Smith "8," Frederick Locker-Lampson, W. K. Bixby.

1740

HM 14356. A.L.S. from Margaret Hamilton Boyle, Countess of Cork and Orrery, Caledon, Co. Limerick, to Mrs. Martha Whiteway of Dublin.

2 leaves (9¼" x 7¼"). 2 pp. of writing. Pp. 3-4 are blank. See *Corresp.,* V, 197-198.

Dated: "Caledon Decbr 24th. 1740" (p. 1).

Not postmarked.

Not addressed.

Not endorsed.

Provenance: Theophilus Swift, James Smith "17," Frederick Locker-Lampson, W. K. Bixby.

1740

HM 14373. Contemp. copy, unsigned, of a letter from Mrs. Martha Whiteway of Dublin to John Boyle, 5th Earl of Cork and Orrery.

4 leaves (8¾" x 7¼"). 3 pp. of writing. P. 4 is blank except for endorsement. See *Corresp. of Pope,* ed. Sherburn, IV, 320-322, and *Corresp.,* V, 198-200.

Dated: "De[c]r 30th 1740" (p. 3).

Not postmarked.

Not addressed.

Endorsed: by Deane Swift (?) (p. 4), "to Lord Orrery."

Provenance: Theophilus Swift, James Smith "6," Frederick Locker-Lampson, W. K. Bixby.

1740-41

HM 14355. A.L.S. from John Boyle, 5th Earl of Cork and Orrery, Caledon, Co. Limerick, to Mrs. Martha Whiteway of Dublin.

2 leaves (9¼″ x 7¼″). 3 pp. of writing. P. 4 is blank. The tops of the leaves have been torn off. See *Corresp. of Pope,* ed. Sherburn, IV, 325-326, and *Corresp.,* V, 200-202.

Dated: "[Jan?]y 2: 1740/41" (p. 1).

Not postmarked.

Not addressed.

Not endorsed.

Provenance: Theophilus Swift, James Smith "7," Frederick Locker-Lampson, W. K. Bixby.

1740-41

HM 14326. A.L.S. A joint letter from Alexander Pope and John, 5th Earl of Cork and Orrery, in London, to Swift at Dublin.

2 leaves (7¾″ x 6¼″). 4 pp. of writing. The first 1½ pp. are by Orrery and are signed by him (p. 2). Pope wrote the remainder and signed it "A. Pope" (p. 4). See *Corresp. of Pope,* ed. Sherburn, IV, 336-338, and *Corresp.,* V, 203-204.

Dated: "March 22d. 1740/1" from "Duke Street, Westmtr" (p. 1).

Not postmarked.

Not addressed.

Endorsed: by Deane Swift (p. 1), "Curious/ Pope."

Provenance: Theophilus Swift, James Smith "4," Frederick Locker-Lampson, W. K. Bixby.

1744

HM 14357. A.L.S. from Margaret Hamilton Boyle, Countess of Cork and Orrery, Marston, Somersetshire, to Mrs. Martha Whiteway of Dublin.

2 leaves (9¼″ x 7⅜″). 2 pp. of writing. Pp. 3-4 are blank. See *Corresp.,* V, 213.

Dated: "Marston March 26: 1744" (p. 1).

Not postmarked.

Not addressed.

Not endorsed.

Provenance: Theophilus Swift, James Smith "18," Frederick Locker-Lampson, W. K. Bixby.

1745

HM 14350. A.L.S. Mrs. Martha Whiteway of Dublin to one of Swift's executors.

2 leaves (9″ x 7⅜″). 2 pp. of writing. Pp. 3-4 are blank except for the endorsement. See *Corresp.,* V, 215-216.

Dated: "Octr 22nd 1745/ ten in the morning" (p. 2).

Not postmarked.

Not addressed.

Endorsed: by Deane Swift (p. 4), "Mrs Whiteway/ to some One of Dr Swift's Executors/ 1745."

Provenance: Theophilus Swift, James Smith "16," Frederick Locker-Lampson, W. K. Bixby.

IV

MANUSCRIPTS ENDORSED BY SWIFT OR

ONCE IN HIS POSSESSION

ca. 1709

HM 14366. (a) "Effigies Corporis & Animi Caroli XII,/ Sueciae Regis, a Polono Nobili descripta" (p. 1), a Latin "character" of King Charles XII of Sweden.

(b) "Supra stragem Regis Sueciae ad Pultavam" (p. 7). A poem in 10 ll. of Latin verse upon Charles XII's victory at Pultava.

A. MS in contemp. hand. 4 leaves (6⅞″ x 8⅝″). 6 pp. of writing. Pp. 6 and 8 are blank except for Swift's endorsement.

Endorsed: by Swift (p. 8), "Account of/ the K. of Sueden/ about An. 1709" and also "Mr Domville."

Provenance: Theophilus Swift, James Smith "57," Frederick Locker-Lampson, W. K. Bixby.

1717

HM 14368. "Musa Clonshogiana." A New Year's poem in 15 ll.

A. MS in the hand of George Rochfort, Belcamp, Co. Westmeath.

2 leaves (6″ x 7¼″). 2 pp. of writing. Folded as a letter. See *Poems,* III, 965-966.

Dated: "Bellcampe Janry. 1st. 1717." (p. 1).

Postmark: 4/ IA, franked, sealed but not stamped.

Addressed: "For the Revd. Dr. Swift Dean/ of St. Patrick's at Lara Corr/ near/ Trim" (p. 4).

Endorsed: by Swift (p. 4), "G Rochforts/ Verses" and again "Ge. Rochfots Verses."

Provenance: Theophilus Swift, James Smith "46," Frederick Locker-Lampson, W. K. Bixby.

1722

HM 14328. "Stella to the Dean on his Birthday/ November 30 1722." A poem in 58 ll.

A. MS in contemp. hand *not* Esther Johnson's, restored, but still badly damaged along left margin from damp. 2 leaves (8⅞″ x 6⅞″). 3 pp. of writing. P. 4 is blank. See *Poems,* II, 737-738.

Not endorsed.

Provenance: Theophilus Swift, James Smith "5," Frederick Locker-Lampson, W. K. Bixby.

1723-24

HM 14369. "To the Dean of St Patricks." A New Year's poem in 68 ll.

A. MS in the hand of Thomas Sheridan. 2 leaves (6¼″ x 3⅞″). 3 pp. of writing. See *Poems,* III, 1039-41.

Endorsed: by Sheridan (p. 4), "A new Year's-Gift/ for the Dean/ of/ St Patricks given/ him at Quilcah/ 1723/4."

Provenance: Theophilus Swift, James Smith "43," Frederick Locker-Lampson, W. K. Bixby.

1724

HM 14370. "Punch to the Ladies his Petition."

Contemp. copy. A poem in 108 ll. 2 leaves (9⅛″ x 7⅛″). 4 pp. of writing. See *Poems,* III, 1108-09, and Acc. No.143201 for a printed Dublin broadside annotated, "Written upon Secretary Hopkin's refusing/ to let Stretch act without a large Sum/ of Money." Stretch was a Dublin puppet-master.

Endorsed: in the same contemp. hand (p. 4), "Punch's Petition to/ the Ladies." Several ll. in pencil are now illegible.

Provenance: Theophilus Swift, James Smith "55," Frederick Locker-Lampson, W. K. Bixby.

ca. 1727

HM 14359. "A Paraphrase on the Seven/ Penitential Psalms, by the/ Reverend Mr R——d D——l, D. of A/ Or Strephon to Belinda." A poem in 60 ll. on the *Psalms* of the Rev. Richard Daniel, Dean of Armagh.

A. MS in a contemp. hand.
1½ leaves (12⅛″ x 8″, and 6⅛″ x 7¾″). 3 pp. of writing. The margin of the smaller leaf is badly damaged by damp. Unpublished.

Endorsed: in contemp. hand (p. 4), "Strepho[n] —— Belinda."

Provenance: Theophilus Swift, James Smith "53," Frederick Locker-Lampson, W. K. Bixby.

1733

HM 14354. "To Mr Pope." A poem in 8 ll. on Pope's epitaph on Gay.

A. MS in the hand of John Boyle, 5th Earl of Cork and Orrery.
2 leaves (8⅞″ x 7⅛″). 1 p. of writing. Pp. 2-4 are blank except for Swift's endorsement. See *Gent. Mag.* (1733), III, 319, and Pope, *Works* (1872), VIII, 373*n.*

Endorsed: by Swift (p. 4), "Orrery's/ [overwritten by what looks like 'Edward ooo'?] on Mr/ Pope Epitaph on Gay."

Provenance: Theophilus Swift, James Smith "42," Frederick Locker-Lampson, W. K. Bixby.

1733

HM 14363. "—— / Of the Furniture belonging to —— Room/ In T:C.D./ In Imitation of Dr Swifts Ma[nn]er/ Written in ye Year 1725." A poem in 38 ll. by William Dunkin.

A. MS in the hand of Dunkin, badly damaged by damp.
2 leaves (7¼″ x 5¾″). 2 pp. of writing. Pp. 3-4 are blank except for Swift's endorsement. Unpublished.

Endorsed: by Swift (p. 4), "Octbr. 30th 1733./ By Mr D——n."

Provenance: Theophilus Swift, James Smith "2," Frederick Locker-Lampson, W. K. Bixby.

1734

HM 14374. "The/ Faithfull Few/ An ODE/ Inscribed to all/ Lovers of their Country ... 1734." A poem of 12 stanzas, 138 ll.

A. MS in a contemp. hand. Water-stained and deteriorated from damp.
4 leaves (9 1/16″ x 6⅝″). 7 pp. of writing. P. 2 is blank. Unpublished?

Endorsed: by Swift (p. 1), "Scotch [?] ——."

Provenance: Theophilus Swift, James Smith "56," Frederick Locker-Lampson, W. K. Bixby.

ca. 1735

HM 14361. "A Farewell to the Audience, Written by Masr Dawncy."

A. MS. An epilogue for a school play (possibly Sheridan's school at Cavan) in 36 ll. of verse. 1 leaf (12¼″ x 7¾″). 2 pp. of writing. Unpublished. The speaker's name may also read "Danncy."

Not endorsed.

Provenance: Theophilus Swift, James Smith (repaired, number covered), Frederick Locker-Lampson, W. K. Bixby.

1735

HM 14378. (a) "On seeing some Verses of Lord Lansdowne's subscribed John Hind" (p. 1).

(b) "On hearing some Verses read of Mr. Cibber's at/ Bath."

(c) "Epitaph on Mr. R. who dyed by leaving off Wine and drinking Water" (p. 3). 3 epigrams of 4, 6, and 11 ll., respectively.

A. MS. 2 leaves (6¾″ x 3⅞″). 2 pp. of writing. P. 2 is blank. Unpublished?

Endorsed: by Swift (p. 4), "Verses/ every one good/ but the last best./ R Jun-1735."

Provenance: Theophilus Swift, James Smith "34," Frederick Locker-Lampson, W. K. Bixby.

ca. 1735?

HM 14375. "From W: T: to C: W: the Second Part to ye same tune." A poem in 12 stanzas, 72 ll.

A. MS. 2 leaves (7⅛″ x 4⅜″). 4 pp. of writing. Unpublished?

Not endorsed.

Provenance: Theophilus Swift, James Smith "50," Frederick Locker-Lampson, W. K. Bixby.

ca. 1735?

HM 14376. "In Vain Dr. Chloe you Suggest. . . ." A song in 5 stanzas, 30 ll. of verse. The first 6 ll. are in pencil.

A. MS in an unidentified hand, possibly that of James Inman.

1 leaf (11¾″ x 7″). 1 p. of writing. P. 2 is blank except for the endorsement. Unpublished?

Endorsed: by Deane Swift (p. 2), "Verses" and "Inmans."

Provenance: Theophilus Swift, James Smith "29," Frederick Locker-Lampson, W. K. Bixby.

ca. 1735

HM 14377. "Not half so Charming seem'd the Queen of Love. . . ." A song in 7 stanzas, 28 ll. of verse.

A. MS in an unidentified hand.
1 leaf (9¼" x 5¾"). 2 pp. of writing. Unpublished?

Not endorsed.

Provenance: Theophilus Swift, James Smith "47," Frederick Locker-Lampson, W. K. Bixby.

ca. 1735

HM 14362. "Peg Rat Cliff the Hostess's Invitation to Dean Swift./ Written with a design to be spoken by her, on his arriving at Glassnevin./ Doctor Delany having Complimented him with a House there." A poem in 24 ll.

A. MS. 1 leaf (12½" x 7¼"). 1 p. of writing. P. 2 is blank but pasted down. MS is water-stained and badly damaged by damp. See *Poems,* III, 1049-50.

Not endorsed.

Provenance: Theophilus Swift, James Smith (number covered, pasted down by repair), Frederick Locker-Lampson, W. K. Bixby.

1736

HM 14364. "A full and true Vindication of Sir Thom. P——/ from the many scandalous Libels lately written/ against him, with the Resolutions of the House/ By a Member of House of Commons." A poem in 166 ll.

A. MS in the hand of Rev. William Dunkin, M.A.
4 leaves (7½" x 6"). 7 pp. of writing stitched together as a pamphlet. P. 8 is blank except for Swift's endorsement. See *Poems,* III, 831*n.*

Endorsed: by Swift (p. 8), "Vindication of/ Sir T. P—— Sent me/ by an unknown hand/ May 25th 1736./ By Dunkin I am sure."

Provenance: Theophilus Swift, James Smith "59," Frederick Locker-Lampson, W. K. Bixby.

1739

HM 14379. "Sr *** [Speech?] upon the ——— / To the Tune of the Abbot of Canterbury/ This was Printed at London by Jacob Lock 1739/ Sir *** Speech &c, &c." A poem in 10 stanzas, 40 ll.

A. MS in an unidentified hand. The MS is badly deteriorated and water-stained at top and along the crease.

2 leaves (7⅝″ x 6″). 3 pp. of writing. P. 4 is blank except for the endorsement. A note at the end (p. 3) reads: "x Mem This Ballad was printed upon/ one Sheet of Paper Price 6d."

Endorsed: in an unidentified hand (p. 4), "——berts/ —— Speech/ a Ballad."

Provenance: Theophilus Swift, James Smith "51," Frederick Locker-Lampson, W. K. Bixby.

V

OTHER MANUSCRIPTS RELATING TO DEANE SWIFT

AND THE THEOPHILUS SWIFT PAPERS

ca. 1736

HM 14352. "An Elegiac poem on —— Death of ye Rt Honbl/ Mary Ponsonby the Countess of Drogheda." An elegy in 120 ll.

A. MS in an unidentified hand.

4 leaves (7¼″ x 5¾″). 5 pp. of writing; the pp. stitched together. Pp. 6-7 are blank. See Moore Booker, *The True Gratification of the Sensual Appetites . . . With an Elegiac Poem . . . Not Till Now Published* (Dublin, 1756).

Endorsed: by Deane Swift (p. 8), "By Mr Booker."

Provenance: Theophilus Swift, James Smith "54," Frederick Locker-Lampson, W. K. Bixby

ca. 1736

HM 14353. "A Tale." A poem in 90 ll.

A. MS in an unidentified hand. 2 leaves (9″ x 7⅛″). 3 pp. of writing. P. 4 is blank except for endorsement. Unpublished?

Endorsed: by Deane Swift (p. 4), "Verses/ by Mr Booker/ <Various Hands>."

Provenance: Theophilus Swift, James Smith "32," Frederick Locker-Lampson, W. K. Bixby.

ca. 1745

HM 14367. "The Latin Inscription & Trans ——/ were wrote upon Lady Rochfor—— ——/ Bird." Below is written: "x Lucy Countess of Rochford." A Latin epitaph in 11 ll., with two additional epitaphs in English of 8 ll. and 14 ll.

A. MS. 2 leaves (7¼" x 4½"). 3 pp. of writing. Badly deteriorated at top and water-stained.

Endorsed: by an unknown hand (p. 4), "Inscription/ on Lady Rochford's/ Bird/ in Eng. & Latin."

Provenance: Theophilus Swift, James Smith "44," Frederick Locker-Lampson, W. K. Bixby.

ca. 1755

HM 14365. A.N.S. from (———) Garbet to Mr. and Mrs. [Deane?] Swift. 1 leaf (7¾" x 6¼"). 1 p. of writing. Referring to the return of MS to "Miss Swift."

Dated: "Saturday noon" (p. 1).

Not addressed.

Endorsed: in red crayon (p. 2), "Seen."

Provenance: Theophilus Swift, James Smith "15," Frederick Locker-Lampson, W. K. Bixby.

ca. 1761

HM 14371. "English Blunders." A list of 8 "Irish bulls"; one (p. 2) is copied from "Gloucester Journal Octr 20 1761."

A. MS in the hand of Deane Swift.
1 leaf (8¼" x 6½"). 2 half pp. of writing, the right-hand column only being used. See Swift's *Works* (1824), VII, 158.

Not endorsed.

Provenance: Theophilus Swift, James Smith "38," Frederick Locker-Lampson, W. K. Bixby.

1766

FAC 456. Photostat of A.L.S. from Deane Swift, Esq., of Worcester, to someone unknown at London.

Dated: "Worcester/ May 8th 1766."

Provenance: The gift of Herbert Davis of Oxford.

1786

HM 14358. John Calder's annotations to Swift's *Character of Thomas, Earl of Wharton* (1710) for John Nichols' new ed. of the *Tatler* (1786).

A. MS in an unidentified hand.

2 leaves (12¾" x 8"). 3 pp. of writing. P. 4 is blank. See also *Gent. Mag.*
(1786), LVI, Pt. II, 693-694, 739-743.

Not endorsed.

Provenance: Theophilus Swift, James Smith "22," Frederick Locker-
Lampson, W. K. Bixby.

ca. 1812

HM 14348. "Extracted from the Registry of his Majesty's/ Court of
Prerogative in Ireland." An early 19th-century copy of the last will and
testament of Esther Vanhomrigh (Vanessa), the original of which is
destroyed.

A. MS in the hand of the Dublin Registrar.
2 leaves (11½" x 7¼"). 3 pp. of writing, attested to be a true copy by
"John Hawkins D Reg." (p. 3). P. 4 is blank except for endorsement. See
Swift's *Works* (1824), XIX, 379-382.

Dated: "this 1st day of May in/ the Year of our Lord 1723," signed and
sealed by "E: Vanhomrigh" and 3 witnesses (p. 3). Proved and probated
"the 6th of June 1723" (p. 3).

Endorsed: by Matthew Weld Hartstonge, Molesworth Street, Dublin,
Scott's assistant in gathering Irish material for his eds. of 1814 and 1824
(p. 4), "Copy,/ of the Will/ of/ Esther Vanhomrigh/From/ The Registry of/ The Prerogative Court/ in Ireland."

Provenance: M. W. Hartstonge, Sir Walter Scott, James Smith, Frederick
Locker-Lampson, W. K. Bixby.

1820

HM 14337. A.N. from James Smith, Esq., then of London, to Sir Walter
Scott, accompanying a packet containing the Theophilus Swift papers.
1 leaf (4" x 6¼"). 1 p. of writing. P. 2 is blank. See Chap. I above.

Dated: "5th. April 1820/ Wed:" (p. 1).

Not postmarked.

Not endorsed.

Provenance: James Smith, Frederick Locker-Lampson, W. K. Bixby.

1820

HM 14331. A.L.S. Sir Walter Scott at London to James Smith, Esq., then
of London and Bideford, Devon, acknowledging arrival of packet containing the Theophilus Swift papers.

2 leaves (8¾" x 7¼"). 1 p. of writing. Pp. 2-4 are blank except for the address. See Chap. I above.

Dated: "Wedy. 5 April/ 96 Piccadilly" (p. 1).

Not postmarked. Sealed with Scott's Egyptian seal.

Addressed: "James Smith Esq" (p. 4).

Not endorsed.

Provenance: James Smith, Frederick Locker-Lampson, W. K. Bixby.

1824

HM 14333. (a) A.N.S. in the hand of James Smith, Esq., of London and Bideford, Devon, concerning the conditions under which he loaned Scott the Theophilus Swift papers.

2 leaves (8" x 6⅜"). 3 pp. of writing. P. 3 is blank. See Chap. I above. Included are copies of the advertisement for the forthcoming 2nd ed. of Scott's *Works* of Swift from *Redgauntlet*, Vol. III, and Scott's acknowledgment from the Preface of the 1824 ed.

(b) Copies of Scott's acknowledgments in his 1824 ed. of his indebtedness to James Smith for the use of the Theophilus Swift papers, in the hand of Frederick Locker-Lampson.

Dated: (a) is dated "Bideford 2d. Septbr. 1824" (p. 4).

Provenance: James Smith, Frederick Locker-Lampson, W. K. Bixby.

1824

HM 14332. A.L.S. Sir Walter Scott from Abbotsford, Scotland, to James Smith, Esq., of Bideford, Devon.

2 leaves (9¾" x 7¾"). 1 p. of writing. Pp. 2-3 are blank. See Chap. I above.

Dated: "Abbotsford Melrose/ 13 September–" (p. 1).

Not postmarked.

Stamped: "MELROSE/ 377—B."

Addressed: "James Smith Esquire/ No. 3 New Buildings/ Biddeford/ Devon."

Provenance: James Smith, Frederick Locker-Lampson, W. K. Bixby.

1825

HM 14334. A.L.S. Sir Walter Scott, Edinburgh, to James Smith, Esq., of Bideford, Devon.

2 leaves (9⅞″ x 8″). 1 p. of writing. Pp. 2-3 are blank. Scott writes that he is returning the Theophilus Swift papers with thanks and has included a copy of Esther Vanhomrigh's will (HM 14348). See Chap. I above.

Dated: "Edin. 8 feby 1825" (p. 1).

Addressed: "James Smith Esq/ Bideford/ Devon."

Postmarked: "Feb. W 8 A 1825," stamped, sealed and franked.

Not endorsed.

Provenance: James Smith, Frederick Locker-Lampson, W. K. Bixby.

1881

HM 14327. A.L.S. Sir Henry Craik of London to Frederick Locker-Lampson of Rowfant, Sussex. A request, upon the advice of "Mr. Murray," to consult the Swift MSS then in Locker-Lampson's library.

2 leaves (6⅞″ x 4½″). 2 pp. of writing. Pp. 3-4 are blank. The 1st ed. of Craik's *Life* of Swift came out in 1882.

Dated: "Hill Side,/ Notting Hill Square. W./ 8. June 81" (p. 1).

No envelope.

Not endorsed.

Provenance: Frederick Locker-Lampson, W. K. Bixby.

Index